I AM GOD'S CREATURE

Martin Luther and a Theology of the Body

R. T. Fouts

Theologia Crucis Publications

Cover designed by Rebecacovers

Cover Artwork: *Adam and Eve*, Lucas Cranach (1526), Public Domain

R.T. Fouts
Visit my website at www.RTFouts.com

Printed in the United States of America

First Printing: Dec 2017
Theologia Crucis Publications
Holden, Missouri

For Ashley

עֶצֶם מֵעֲצָמַי וּבָשָׂר מִבְּשָׂרִי

TABLE OF CONTENTS

I AM GOD'S CREATURE i
ACKNOWLEDGEMENTS viii
ABBREVIATIONS ix
CHAPTER 1: INTRODUCTION 1

- The Thesis 4
- The Current Status of the Question 4
- The Issue in the Context of Current Scholarship 29
- The Methodological Procedure to Be Employed 53
  - Primary Source Material 55
  - Theological Method and Structure 61
- The Outcome(s) Anticipated 64

CHAPTER 2: AN EXEGETICAL STUDY 66

- The Body in the Old Testament 66
  - Genesis 1-2: Origins and Order 70
  - Genesis 3: The Body and Sin 79
  - The Flood and God's Covenant with Noah 82
  - Body, Soul and Spirit 84
  - Circumcision and the Abrahamic Covenant 88
- The Body in the New Testament 91
  - The Resurrected Body 94
  - According to the Flesh...According to the Spirit 96
  - A Temple of the Holy Spirit 99
  - The Body of the Christian and the Body of Christ 100
- Conclusion 100

CHAPTER 3: THE BODY IN THE BEGINNING 101

- John Paul II's Return to "The Beginning" 102
  - The Meaning of Original Solitude 105
  - The Meaning of Original Unity 108
  - The Meaning of Original Nakedness 111
  - The Spousal/Nuptial Meaning of the Body 112

best
meat ①

Would be
more
relevant
to discuss
actual.
slavery

②

③

economics, social orders,
biological determinism etc.
too thin, too Messianic

This sections but ok one–new.

ACKNOWLEDGEMENTS

"God chose what is foolish in the world to shame the wise; God chose what is weak in the world to shame the strong." (1 Cor. 1: 27, ESV).

That this now appears in print is testimony to the fact that the Apostle spoke truthfully. God, indeed, has chosen foolish and broken vessels nearly exclusively to accomplish his purposes in this world. In many respects, this work has been completed in spite of myself.

This book is an adaptation of my doctoral dissertation, the seeds of which were sown and began to germinate during my time at Concordia Seminary—thus I must acknowledge many of my teachers and colleagues there whose support and instruction were influential in both my development as a theologian and whose insights contributed to this dissertation. Robert Kolb's mentorship and guidance—along with a rare combination of humility and *gravitas*—has inspired me both as a theologian and as a disciple of Jesus Christ. His work and influence is largely responsible for charting my course toward the topic at hand. Charles Arand's direction and insight invaluably contributed to my initial exploration of this topic and the construction of my thesis. Jeff Thormadson's friendship and support—along with his admirable commitment to our Lord's mission to "make disciples of all nations"—has been both a source of encouragement, in spite of my many setbacks, and a constant reminder that the work I have undertaken is ultimately in service to God's kingdom and mission.

Several who have pastored me in recent years, including George Borghardt III, Joel Kurz, Dan Wilburn, Garrett Lahey, and others have been an unwavering source of support and spiritual guidance as I've navigated many spiritual trials and tribulations in route to the completion of this work.

I should also thank my dissertation supervisor Robert Grossman whose guidance rendered this work more than an insight of historical intrigue but encouraged me to ground it all in Scripture thereby rendering these conclusions more solidly sound and relevant to the discipline of theology as a whole. His Reformed confession has helped me traverse the "gap" from my Lutheran confessional heritage to the present broader Lutheran-and-Reformed audience this book now seeks to engage. *but you cannot attribute the Westminster Confession to Luther (p.12)*

I should also thank my parents, who not only saw to it that I was raised and catechized in the Christian faith, but also paid the lion's share of my tuition. Their love and support is a true blessing.

Finally, I reserve my most heartfelt thanks to my dearest wife Ashley and my sons Elijah and Ezra. It was their support—and their sacrifices—that ultimately made the completion of this book possible.

ABBREVIATIONS

BDAG   Walter Bauer, F.W. Danker, W.F. Arndt & F.W. Gingrich. *A Greek-English Lexicon of the New Testament and Other Early Christian Literature, 3rd ed.* Revised and edited by F. W. Danker. Chicago: The University of Chicago Press, 2000.

BDB   Francis Brown, S. R. Driver & Charles A Briggs. *The New Brown-Driver-Briggs-Gesenius Hebrew-English Lexicon.* Peabody, MA: Hendrickson Publishers, 1979.

LW   *Luther's Works. American Edition.* 55 vols. Edited by Jaroslav Pelikan and Helmut Lehmann. Philidelphia and St. Louis: Fortress Press and Concordia, 1955—.

NIB   Katharine Doob Sakenfeld, ed. *The New Interpreter's Dictionary of the Bible (NIB),* 5 vols. Nashville: Abingdon Press, 2009.

TOB   John Paul II. *Man and Woman He Created Them: A Theology of the Body.* Translated by Michael Waldstein. Boston: Pauline Books and Media, 2006.

TDNT   G. Kittel and G. Friedrich, eds., *Theological Dictionary of the New Testament,* 10 vols. Grand Rapids, MI: Wm. B. Eerdmans Publishing Co., 1984.

TWOT   R. Laird Harris, Gleason L. Archer, Jr. & Bruce K. Waltke. *Theological Wordbook of the Old Testament.* 2 vols. Chicago: Moody Press, 1980.

WA   *D. Martin Luthers Werke: Kritische Gestamtausgabe. Schriften. 64 vols.* Weimar: Böhlau, 1883—.

WABr   D. Martin Luthers Werke: Kritische Gesamtausgabe. Briefweschel. 18 vols. Weimar: Böhlau, 1930-1985.

WATr   D. Martin Luthers Werke: Kritische Gesamtausgabe. Tischreden. 6 vols. Weimar: Böhlau, 1930-1985.

CHAPTER 1:
INTRODUCTION

"I hold and believe that I am God's creature...that
he has given me and constantly sustains my body,
soul, and life..."[1]

[handwritten: all of this is given in Genesis as the mud inbreathed with God's breath. There is nothing if God does not constantly constitute and perpetuate]

MARTIN LUTHER, THROUGH THESE WORDS of *The Large Catechism*, exhorts the Christian to consider what it means to be a human creature. Luther's theology of the human body could be said to begin with an affirmation of man's identity as God's creature. The body is not only created by God, having its origins in the genius of God's design, but is still cared for by God throughout the earthly life of each human being. As God's creature, it is clear that God values the entirety of man: body, soul and life.

[handwritten: but you are already splitting; stick w/]

[handwritten: then leave it entire; part of Hebrew 'mudling' — dirt + God's breath creature]

One cannot deny, much less despise, his somatic identity as an embodied creature if he is to cherish what God himself values. To affirm that God has created the body, and still takes care of it, is to affirm that the body is important to God's ongoing work as creator caring for his creation. God's care for the human body extends beyond the Creedal first article as well. The second article affirms that the Son of God, while begotten not created, assumes a creaturely body and dwells among God's creatures. The Son's

[handwritten: human being → body/mind/breath is a gift.]

[handwritten: embodied creation — far cry from "takes flesh" incarnates — Jesus!]

---

[1] Robert Kolb, Timothy J. Wengert, and Charles P. Arand, eds. *The Book of Concord: The Confessions of the Evangelical Lutheran Church* (Minneapolis: Fortress, 2000), 432. *[handwritten: which document?]*

[handwritten: God creates the human creature as a mudling inbreathed by God. In time, God sustains us as human beings, not as a somatic identity. This seems to complexify what is scripturally simple.]

[handwritten: eck! sounds Docetic]

1

wow — this guy confuses the Son and son in a way that is extremely gendering and unhelpful in trinitarian discourse

death is a bodily death. His resurrection is a bodily resurrection. Not only does God value the body to the extent that as creator he cares for the bodily life of man, but he cares for the body in such a way that he sent his only son to redeem human kind in the flesh. The third article, finally, affirms the bodily resurrection of all human creatures as the consummative hope of Christian faith. The human body is a major player throughout the entire creedal narrative. In each instance, however, it is neither merely the body nor the soul alone that emerges front and center. It is, rather, the totality of the person: the total human being, body and soul, created. It was the total Christ, body and soul, who suffered and rose from the tomb.[2] And it is the total Christian, body and soul, who will be raised in the end. It could be said that the biblical and creedal narrative is preeminently concerned with the embodied creature from the beginning, through the redemption of man after the fall, to the final restoration of creation itself.

It is simpler to state: There is no human being in time without a body. Only God "is" without a body.

These narratives are primarily focused on God...

The body is, quite literally, inescapable. Every human interaction, be it with the creation or other creatures, happens in the locus of one's body. Many of the political, social, and economic issues and challenges facing contemporary American society are intimately linked to how one considers the body. Questions regarding human sexuality, from homosexuality to how one considers the nature and permanence of marriage, are deeply vested in one's relationship to his or her body. Contemporary debates regarding human life, from abortion matters to end-of-life concerns, are fundamentally concerned with the body's intrinsic value. It is this author's hope that this book may lead to further exploration on these issues. Perhaps more fundamental, though, for these purposes is the general value of the body and the basis for how as God's creatures we ought to understand our responsibility to care for it without succumbing to the temptation to make of the body more than is scripturally warranted.

This expression implies that a creature exists outside the body. So — pre-birth?

makes exclusions of each other

no, historically these issues are funded theologically on the question of when God's life in the creature [soul-breath] begins.

Only Jesus is such a creature.

Theologies of the body are particularly unique in that the theologian who considers it is always both the subject and object of his reflections. Those who attempt to theoretically deny or diminish the bodily existence of

i.e. made flesh

---

[2] "This office [of mediator] the Lord Jesus did most willingly undertake; which that He might discharge, He was made under the law, and did perfectly fulfil it; endured most grievous torments *immediately in His soul, and most painful sufferings in His body*; was crucified, and died, was buried, and remained under the power of death, yet saw no corruption." *The Westminster Confession of Faith*, 8.4. Emphasis added.

not just as a zygote, but as a soul

God can resurrect whomever God chooses, but not limited to "Christians." even Christians are only "becoming" Christians throughout their daily dying and rising

The language for his subject is so imprecise!

man soon find themselves in an ironic position of having to deny the very thing that makes such denials possible. One cannot jump outside of his body in order to deny it. No one has ever denied the bodily dimension of human personhood who did not, himself, have a body. No matter if one embraces or wishes to escape one's bodily existence, the fact remains that all human creatures have a body and reflecting upon its importance is both unavoidable and universally relevant. This fact, along with the recognition that the body "looms large" through each major article in the Christian creedal narrative while simultaneously engaging many of the issues relevant to contemporary *(being a topic of engagement in)* society, makes the human body prime fodder for theological examination.

Various forms of dualism, attempting to define, separate and prioritize the various faculties of the human creature, have emerged both alongside and within the Christian tradition throughout history. Some have advocated an "escape" from the body through mystical experience or contemplation. Others have imagined that true humanity can only be experienced after death, as disembodied souls in the company of God. Still others, not seeking to escape the body, nonetheless have denigrated the body as little more than a "vessel" for the thinking man. *You have already done it yourself*

While many dualisms have plagued western thought for centuries, and have emerged in a variety of ways, what they all have in common is the basic premise that the body is a hindrance to a fuller expression of humanity. On the opposite end of the spectrum many materialists—most recently evoking the insights of neuroscience on the mind/body connection—have sought to eliminate the concept of the soul entirely by insisting that man's identity resides exclusively in his physical body.

Christianity, however, offers another alternative that embraces the body without, at the same time, making it the sum and substance of man's existence. For Christians the body is not something to despise, escape or reject, or for that matter, worship. For Christianity, the fullest expression of human identity is "experienced" in the body. Why is a Christian understanding of embodied life, in the flesh, important for understanding our entire lives as creatures of God? Answering this question is the purpose of this book.

Human self-understanding is a reflexive capacity of the human body which grounds human being in time.

Unpack that glittering claim!

R. T. Fouts

the human being as a bodily creature — (flesh, mind, spirit - conscience)

The Thesis

This is faulty already

Luther's theology bequeaths to subsequent generations of Christians a holistic understanding of ~~the body that holds body and soul~~ together *which is held* in relationship to God, neighbor, and the creation in which we reside. In doing so, it can overcome *Luther?* various manifestations of Western dualism, on the one hand, and materialism on the other. Rather than seeing bodily life *in time* on the earth as something to be denied or suppressed, Luther's embracing of life in creation, particularly in the light of his paradigmatic distinction between the "two kinds of righteousness," provides a theological paradigm, consistent with Scripture, through which contemporary questions regarding the nature and care of the human body can be adequately addressed.

split this into its claims

The Current Status of the Question

why so awkward

Week after week in their services Christians confess within the Creed the "resurrection of the body." In spite of this, however, many Christians still remain confused regarding the ultimate hope of man's redeemed identity in Christ. Many popularly imagine an eternity as disembodied souls in heaven as their consummative hope. Seeking to shed their several pounds of flesh in ascension toward a disembodied eternity, many wonder what relevance the body has here and now. Is it relevant at all, or is the body merely an "earth suit" that the soul temporarily adorns? Further, what care if any should one give to *her or his* their body during this earthly life? If one's own body is not valued from the perspective of one's Christian faith, then why should one care for his neighbor's bodily needs? Is serving the body merely a means toward the end of ministering to the soul in a grand bait-and-switch missiological scheme? Or, rather, is serving the body actually part and parcel of loving one's neighbor? Even more, might one understand acts of service directed toward bodily needs as a proleptic participation in God's ultimate restoration and consummation of creation? Needless to say, in spite of the clear Biblical witness affirmed in the Creed each week, many Christians remain confused about the place of the body in their own daily life and salvation. If the age-old maxim, *lex orandi–lex credendi*, held true one would think that the Creedal affirmation of the body and all its relevant implications would be widely accepted and understood amongst Christian laymen and theologians alike. For such a deep-seated Christian truth reflected nearly unanimously in Christian liturgy through the ages to be so

finally a lovely idea

4

drastically ignored or even denied in common thought can only be explained by an equally deep-seated competing tradition. The fact is that this "competing tradition" has, in various manifestations, taken root in Christian thought from the earliest days of the church.

Early Christians were faced with an incredible challenge. In spite of the centrality of mankind's bodily existence to the Christian message, the early church stepped into a world that embraced philosophies making such a "fleshly" faith difficult to swallow. The Hebraic concept affirming a unity of body-person stood in stark contrast to the Greek Platonic dualisms that maintained antagonistic division between body and soul, the material and immaterial universe.[3] The term "Gnosticism," derived from gnosis the Greek word for knowledge, encompassed a variety of dualistic movements that became problematic in the first few centuries of Christianity. For Gnostics, the fundamental problem of man was not sin *per se*, but materiality. Philosophy was revered above all disciplines because it allowed man to ponder and participate in higher, immaterial reality. As such, "knowledge, and it alone, was redemptive."[4] Through philosophical knowledge, coupled with a rejection of the material world, Gnostics hoped to ascend to the divine.

While Christianity certainly had its impact on the world of thought in the first few centuries, Christians did not emerge from these tensions entirely untouched by Gnostic influence. Peter Brown describes in detail how Valentinus, a Christian spiritualist in second century Rome, utilized the Gnostic tensions between matter and spirit to embrace a salvation narrative more akin to Greek ideas than the Biblical account. In the myth, as told by Valentinus, Sophia, or the divine Wisdom (who once resided in an entirely spiritual existence), failed in an attempt to attain God's divine knowledge. Out of rebellion, being separated from God, Sophia created the material world as "an abortive attempt to imitate an infinitely distant, invisible, and ever-elusive model. The world created by Sophia spoke only of the chasm that separated what was from what would be."[5] While Valentinus did not

---

[3] An excellent in-depth contrasting of the Greek and Hebrew views of man can be found in George Eldon Ladd, *The Pattern of New Testament Truth* (Grand Rapids, MI: Eerdmans, 1958), 13-40.

[4] Mary Timothy Prokes, *Toward a Theology of the Body* (Grand Rapids, MI: Eerdmans, 1996), 8.

[5] Peter Brown, *The Body and Society: Men, Women, and Sexual Renunciation in Early Christianity* (New York: Columbia University Press, 1988), 108.

[handwritten margin note top right: how show?]

[handwritten margin note left: would need to see Valentius' own words...]

discount Christ entirely, Jesus' mission was not so much a/redemption of the created world, but an entrance into the fallen physical/world only to put Sophia's rebellion to an end and ultimately rectify Sophia's mistake. The eschatalogical hope of Christians was not a bodily resurrection but a hope that "parts of the universe, the human body among them, would eventually be cast off as abortive and misconceived creations."[6] While Valentinus' Hellenized narrative of Christian salvation was refuted, vestiges of its disparaging influence on physical existence, particularly regarding the human body, continued to reemerge in Christian thought for centuries. Manichaeism, also an ancient gnostic heresy, gained some traction in Christian communities between the third and seventh centuries. Other Neoplatonic influences, beyond Gnosticism, made their way into Christian thought. It is no mistake that Christological controversies, regarding the relationship between the divine and human natures of Christ, emerged at the same time that the church struggled with gnostic conceptions of man.[7] Docetists, who taught that the historical and physical body of Christ was a mere phantasm, were also a product of the Neoplatonic attitudes about the material world.

The struggle between Neoplatonists of late antiquity and those who intended to maintain the Scriptural unity of the total human person, both body and soul, continued into the medieval period. Thomas Aquinas taught that the soul is the form of the body. While it could be argued that Thomas' complex metaphysical anthropology explicitly rejected Platonic dualism in favor of Aristotle's affirmation of body–soul unity,[8] it is the principle of

---

[handwritten note: and so the body is the substance.]

[6] Ibid., 109.

[7] This is not the place to rehearse that history, but figures such as Irenaeus of Lyons stood up for the goodness of mankind's embodiment arguing that since Jesus Christ himself assumed human flesh, the human body along with the soul constituted the whole nature of redeemed humanity: "God will bestow salvation upon the whole nature of man, consisting of body and soul in close union, since the Word took it upon him, and adorned it with the gifts of the Holy Spirit, of whom our bodies are, and are termed, the temples." Irenaeus, "Against Heresies," in *Ante-Nicene Fathers*, ed. Alexander Roberts, (Peabody, Mass: Hendrickson Publishers, 1994), 1:531.

[handwritten margin note: body as Temple - as image of ?]

[8] Cooper argues that Thomas' hylomorphic theory of human nature actually became a corrective for both materialism and Platonic dualism, affirming that all of the created world is substantially real and good. Cooper's argument is that Thomas' concern to affirm the "soul" and the "form" of the body is not a disparagement of the body, *per se*, but is asserted precisely in order to affirm the uniqueness of the human body as matter that is distinct and exalted more highly than other "bodies" such as the bodies of rocks,

"intellect" according to Aquinas that determines the identity of the human creature and the intellect belonged principally to the soul. Thomas believed that the body, while the inseparable locus of the intellect of man, diminishes the intellectual capacity of the soul.[9] In spite of Aquinas' rejection of platonic dualism, though, dualistic misappropriations of his hylomorphic theory were advanced by the scholastics of the pre-Reformation period who, while maintaining the unity of body and soul, nonetheless divided man into higher faculties more proper to the soul (intellect and will) and into lower faculties associated more closely with the body (passions and emotions).[10]

While the influence of Gnosticism upon Christian thought during the formative years of Christian theology often shoulders much of the blame for the disparagement of the body through the centuries, it is the thinking of Descartes, and other seminal thinkers of modernity, who more directly bear responsibility for dualistic tendencies that emerged during modernity. René Descartes' famous dictum, "I think, therefore I am" (*cogito ergo sum*), left the "thinking" component of man the sole aspect of human identity that could be trusted. For Descartes, sense perceptions left anything in the physical universe generally, and the bodily senses specifically, incapable of offering certain knowledge. Accordingly, Descartes asserts that "we are essentially mind, even though we also have bodies, and that matter is essentially extension."[11] That is to say, from our perspective, matter is

---

trees, or other forms of matter both animate or inanimate. See Adam G. Cooper, *Life in the Flesh: An Anti-Gnostic Spiritual Philosophy* (Oxford: Oxford University Press, 2008), 85-107.

[9] Prokes, *Toward a Theology of the Body,* 15-16.

[10] See Heiko A. Oberman, *The Harvest of Medieval Theology* (Grand Rapids: Baker Academic, 2000), 57-67; also Charles P. Arand, "Two Kinds of Righteousness as a Framework for Law and Gospel in the Apology," *Lutheran Quarterly* 15 (2001): 422.

[11] Diogenes Allen, *Philosophy for Understanding Theology* (Atlanta: John Knox Press, 1985), 176-177. Descartes explains the difference between body and mind thus, "...the human body, insofar as it differs from other bodies, is composed of merely a certain configuration of members, together with other accidents of the same sort. But the human mind is not likewise composed of any accidents, but is a pure substance. For even if all accidents were changed, so that is understand different things, wills different things, senses different things, and so on, the mind itself does not on that score become something different. On the other hand, the human body does become something different, merely as a result of the fact that a change in the shape of some of its parts has taken place. It follows from these considerations that a body can very easily perish, whereas the mind by its nature is immortal." René Descartes, "Meditations on First Philosophy," in *Classics of Western Philosophy,* ed. Steven M. Cahn (Indianapolis: Hackett Publishing, 2002), 458.

always viewed as an object, *i.e.* it is viewed from without, from its surface. Mind is known always as subject, *i.e.* it is viewed from within, from its center. Descartes was not the first to engage these themes,[12] but he was the first to turn these themes toward mechanical physics setting the groundwork for the industrial and technological revolutions.[13] When Cartesian thought invaded the English universities its chief influence was to deal the death blow to Aristotelianism, setting the groundwork for Francis Bacon and others who furthered empirical scientific methodology. That said, theological movements have also swum along similar currents. "Surprisingly, Calvinistic Puritanism seems to have contributed an important motivation to the advance of scientific technology because its millenarianism suggested the coming of a 'new age' in which humanity would gain remarkable control over nature."[14] As such, there is an eschatalogical dimension to any theology of creation, including theologies of the body, which will also impact how one considers creaturely life here and now.

As industrial and technological advancements exponentially increased over the last couple centuries, the philosophical bases underlying this change have become entrenched in the psyche of modern man. It is not necessary for these purposes to engage the complex philosophical foundations, and history, of the industrial and technological revolutions. That said, it can be said without much argument that these movements have

---

[12] In Epicurean philosophy matter, too, was no more than an extension of substance, substance having numerable parts. All its other attributes or qualities can be reduced to the arrangement of such parts. The difference between ancient Epicurean thought and Descartes, however, is that "Descartes hesitated to go all the way and reduce matter to unalterable particles moving in a void by some purposeless, inherent force. He retained the Aristotelian notion that the world is a material *plenum*, and then attempted to account for all the phenomena of physics in terms of *vortices* or self-perpetuating currents set up by the Creator in this fluid cosmic mass." Benedict Ashley, *Theologies of the Body: Humanist and Christian* (Braintree, MA: The Pope John XXIII Medical-Moral Research and Education Center, 1985), 209.

[13] "What was most original about Descartes was not his revival of these traditional philosophical themes, but the way in which he applied them to the development of mechanical physics. Paradoxically, what was to make his thought so vastly influential was not its grounding in self-verifying innate ideas nor in self-affirming consciousness, but rather that these assumptions seemed to receive a practical confirmation by their fruitfulness in the advance of science." Ibid., 208-209.

[14] Ibid., 211.

[handwritten top margin, left:] It is the rise of non-thinking and the increasing poverty that supports the spiral down, not techne per se.

[handwritten top margin, right:] Obesity and health issues among rich/powerful folk are ancient — see Proverbs

had a vast impact on the life of people in the world today. Fewer American jobs require physical labor than in decades past. Emerging technologies have further fostered sedentary living, prioritizing convenience over "hard work," leaving most people seemingly more dependent upon man's own inventions than creation itself.[15] If it is true that God designed the human body to be active and working, as the Genesis narrative seems to indicate,[16] then living in patterns that, while not necessarily sinful, do not reflect the creature–creation relationship of interdependence surely is not without spiritual consequence. *[handwritten:] personal, social, economic — too vague*

Consider, for example, questions of health and wellness. The rising obesity crisis in America has been well documented.[17] Some projections, in fact, predict that over 50 percent of Americans will be considered obese by 2030 if current rates continue.[18] For children, and even many adults, video games and television have too frequently replaced what outdoor sports and play were for previous generations. Technology has not only impacted personal life, but communal life as well, allowing people to interact through technological media without ever having to move from place to place. In a sense, technology has separated us both from the world and from other people, allowing us to have a semblance of "connection" to either but to do so without fully engaging the five senses. All of this has further fostered both

[handwritten:] so you think it is dis-embodied contact...

---

[15] "The great motive and the great 'selling point' of industrialism has been 'less work.' Our national goal, indeed, has been less work, and we have succeeded. Most people who work are now working less or with less effort (and skill) than they once did, and increasing numbers are not working at all." Wendell Berry, *The Art of the Commonplace* (Berkley: Counterpoint, 2002), 48. *[handwritten:] Not true of intellectual workers...*

[16] See Genesis 2:15.

[17] According to the U.S. Department of Health and Human Services the prevalence of obesity among Americans increased steadily during the last decades of the 20th century and has continued to increase to the rate of 35.7% of Americans being considered obese in 2009-2010. Particularly concerning is the increase of obesity rates among men. In 1999-2000 27.5% of men were obese, and by 2009-2010 the prevalence had increased to 35.5%. Women saw a more moderate increase from 33.4% to 35.8% during the same time span. Ogden CL, Carrol MD, Kit BK, Flegal KM. 2012. "Prevalence of obesity in the United States, 2009-2010." *NHCS data brief*, no 82 (January). http://www.cdc.gov/nchs/data/databriefs/db82.pdf (accessed March 1, 2012).

[18] Michael J. O'Grady and James C. Capretta. "Assessing the Economics of Obesity and Obesity Intervention," Robert Wood Johnson Foundation, http://www.rwjf.org/content/rwjf/en/research-publications/find-rwjf-research/2012/03/assessing-the-economics-of-obesity-and-obesity-interventions.html (accessed September 23, 2012).

9

sedentary living and the isolation and elevation of the individual apart from the community.[19]

Even the American diet tends to prioritize convenience and taste over nutritional value. At the same time, pop-culture icons tend to embody a physical image that, due to the aforementioned factors and others, more and more Americans find difficult to attain.[20] As such, in addition to suffering from the physical ailments that can accompany obesity and sedentary lifestyles, many Americans suffer a plethora of psychological effects as they struggle with the tension between the lifestyle their culture encourages and the ideal image of beauty their culture simultaneously upholds.[21]

There is no shortage of solutions to the problem. Fitness centers continue to thrive in spite of a lethargic American economy. Day time infomercials offer innumerable fitness programs, gadgets, and fads that are individually catered to almost every demographic category. Fitness and weight-loss oriented magazines and books populate the shelves at

---

[19] Perhaps even more fundamentally problematic, though, than the sedentary lifestyle such trends have encouraged is the very fact that all of this has created an artificial medium of existence whereby many human beings live much of their lives with no sense of "connection" to the God-given world around them. Relationships can be fostered across social media with little personal investment into another human being, and such relationships can just as easily be severed with the click of a few buttons. The Edenic call of man to "work the ground" for his own sustenance has been replaced by supermarkets, drive-thru restaurants, and home delivery. If it is true that man's essential earthly identity is Biblically conceived of in relationship of his own body to the ground, the world around him, and his neighbor, one cannot help but be concerned that the present situation would usher in an identity crisis of epic proportions.

[20] It would appear to be something of a paradox of culture that one would be caught between the trend to both disparage the body, while idolizing the body at the same time. This author believes that some of this derives from Cartesian origins of human self-awareness that sees the body as an "extension" of self. This philosophy will be discussed in more detail later. While the body is disparaged, because it is thought not to be the truest form of human identity, the body is still an "extension" of the true self. Being that the "body" is the only means by which we can engage the world, and society, the body becomes inescapably reflective of one's identity. While one might look at a cup and immediately associate it with the sort of beverage it would typically carry (*i.e.* a coffee cup), while all they see is the cup they nonetheless associate the "container" with its contents. Thus, many see their body as a "project" of sorts to undertake, mold, and fashion in a way that reflects who they believe themselves to be on the "inside." Thus, at the same time the body is disparaged, but also reflective of human identity.

[21] Richard Louv, *Last Child in the Woods: Saving Our Children from Nature-Deficit Disorder* (Chapel Hill, NC: Algonquin Books, 2008). Here, Richard Louv has persuasively argued that a major contributing factor to childhood obesity, hyperactivity, attention deficit disorders, depression, and other relatively "new" problems has been an increasing trend whereby children become absorbed with in-door entertainment and technology and have progressively "lost" their connection to the natural world. This, Louv terms a "nature deficit" disorder.

bookstores and supermarkets. Even weight-loss themed television shows soar in the ratings. In spite of an increasingly abundant number of solutions, however, the obesity rates continue to rise or stay the same, year after year. The culture of fast-food and convenience and the exercise culture of the perfect physical physique compete for the loyalties of men and women. No matter which side of the battle claims one's loyalties in today's world, the spiritual implications abound, and the spiritual problem in either case is remarkably similar. *and what is that? state it*

The church would be remiss to simply ignore the spiritual impact the above situation has on the lives of Christians and potential converts. The motivation for weight-loss and physical fitness in American culture is not always salutary, often emerging from values inconsistent with a Christian worldview. The idolatry of pop-culture "beauty," prideful and egotistical pursuits of the perfectly crafted physique, and attempts to avoid death by imaginary pursuits of prolonged life through scientific progress, all come in to play in many Americans' pursuits to [care for *or despise "*] their bodies. Ray Kurzweil, and others, have predicted an age when technology will literally transcend biology, allowing the human consciousness to finally escape frail flesh and be "transferred" to technological media.[22] The movement to which Kurzewil belongs is known as posthumanism. It is gaining in popularity in both philosophy and literature, and posits that the human being is in nowise *already have* unique amongst the animals, and that man's next stage in evolution will *in bionic* occur as biology and technology merge, eventually replacing the frailty of *devices* flesh with variously technologically enhanced bodies.[23] Technology and

---

[22] Inventor and scientist Ray Kurzweil has predicted that an age will come in the near future, which he terms the "singularity," where death will no longer be a reality. "What, then, is the Singularity? It's a future period during which the pace of technological change will be so rapid, its impact so deep, that human life will be irreversibly transformed. Although neither utopian nor dystopian, this epoch will transform the concepts that we rely on to give meaning to our lives, from our business models to the cycle of human life, including death itself." Ray Kurzweil, *The Singularity is Near: When Humans Transcend Biology* (New York: Penguin Group, 2005), 2. *A more recent Clockwork Orange...*

[23] While this book does not engage posthumanism at length, it is an emerging view that undermines the priority of the human being as God's viceregent in creation, and results in reduction of the human body to a sort of imperfect lump of flesh, frail by definition, that must be transcended by human ingenuity and technology. The spiritual implications of a posthumanist worldview are profound, and responding to this philosophy will undoubtedly be necessary in coming years. In addition to Kurzweil, other volumes that might serve as a "primer" to posthumanism include Pramod K. Nayar, *Posthumanism.* (Malden, MA: Polity Press, 2014) and Stefan Herbrechter, *Posthumanism: A Critical Analysis.* (New York: Bloomsbury,

scientific progress are not sinful in their own right, but the advancements of man have often blurred our perception of the utter dependence of man upon both the creator and the creation.[24] False hopes for a "better day" brought about through scientific and technological achievement are envisioned in spite of the fact that today's reality already exceeds the expectations of years gone by, without living up to the utopian hopes once placed upon them.[25]

On the one hand, many underlying problems contemporary culture faces regarding the body are unique to today's world; on the other hand, they are literally as old as dirt. As pervasive as the problem is in society today to neglect the body, so also is an obsessive pursuit of physical health that sees the body as a project to be undertaken, or even worshipped. While these problems may seem like polar opposites, they are symptomatic of the same underlying sin. Whether one neglects the body, or turns it into an idol, it is the same sinful tendency of man to take what God intends as gift and presume we have the right to decide for ourselves its value or lack thereof. Seeing the body as a project to perfect has become an opportunity to revel in the original sin to be "like God" as we strive to form the body in our own image—whatever that ideal image might be. Neglecting the body, in turn, is an act of thanklessness.

2013).

[24] "We do not rule, we are ruled. The thing, the world, rules man. Man is a prisoner, a slave of the world, and his rule is illusion. Technology is the power with which the earth grips man and subdues him. And because we rule no more, we lose the ground, and then the earth is no longer *our* earth, and then we become strangers on earth. We do not rule because we do not know the world as God's creation, and because we do not receive our dominion as God-given, but grasp it for ourselves." Dietrich Bonhoeffer, *Creation and Fall* (New York: Touchstone, 1997), 42-43.

[25] One of the primary texts used by Alcoholics Anonymous articulates this very conundrum in recognizing the need to "humbly" ask God to "remove our shortcomings." Many have found themselves trapped in addiction relying on the pride of man's achievements: "With great intelligence, men of science have been forcing nature to disclose her secrets. The immense resources now being harnessed promise such a quantity of material blessings that many have come to believe that a man-made millennium lies just ahead. Poverty will disappear, and there will be such abundance that everybody can have all the security and personal satisfactions he desires. The theory seems to be that once everybody's primary instincts are satisfied, there won't be much left to quarrel about. The world will then turn happy and be free to concentrate on culture and character. Solely by their own intelligence and labor, men will have shaped their own destiny." Alcoholics Anonymous World Services, Inc., *Twelve Steps and Twelve Traditions* (New York: Alcoholics Anonymous World Services, Inc., 1981), 70-71.

The existential and psychological angst experienced, particularly by many of America's young people, as they try to live within the tension of the "ideal" body exemplified by pop-culture idols and the culture's competing ideals of convenience, poor nutrition, and sedentary lifestyle, cannot be ignored. In American culture, the human body is one's own to do with whatever one pleases, so long as it makes him happy and does not harm others. This focus on "happiness" is codified by the recognition that "...the decisions we make about the body are almost always grounded in therapeutic reasons—what makes us feel fulfilled or complete or happy—rather than through determining whether there are any objective standards that should guide our decision-making."[26]

While the relativism of pop-postmodern America may rule the day when it comes to individual decisions regarding the body, American Christians have often found themselves ill-equipped with very little in their theological arsenal to rely upon when addressing these matters. Vestiges of various philosophically-molded anthropological paradigms have too frequently hindered the ability of Christian theologians to address these matters seriously. If the philosophical remains of Gnosticism and Neoplatonism informed the theologians of Luther's day, Cartesian dualism has further exacerbated the problem in the modern era.[27] Even while contemporary philosophers, on account of modern scientific advancements, would mostly consider Descartes' dualism obsolete, in practice his separation of "mind" from body remains pervasive in numerous contemporary disciplines ranging from the medical sciences to biblical interpretation.[28]

---

[26] Matthew L. Anderson, *Earthen Vessels: Why our Bodies Matter to our Faith* (Minneapolis: Bethany House, 2011), 24.

[27] "A dualistic society dominated by mind involves a number of dangers, of which the degradation and destruction of the material world is only the most obvious." Berry, *The Art of the Commonplace,* 57.

[28] "A second obstacle is the ease with which our contemporaries have read a Cartesian interest in 'the mind' back into the Bible. This is an example of the problem of ethnocentrism – the erroneous assumption that all people everywhere think, believe, and act as we do – in biblical interpretation. For René Descartes the physician and philosopher, we may recall, to understand a human phenomenon we must ascertain whether to attribute it to the soul or body for these are characterized by an essential, a real distinction. Given the importance of the horizons of our own taken-for-granted assumptions in acts of reading and interpretation, and given the pervasive influence of the Cartesian idea of a disembodied mind even today, it is no surprise that many readers of the Bible have found body-soul dualism in its pages. We

At the same time, while philosophical perspectives on the body/soul distinction or lack thereof have undoubtedly been influential, there is also an enduring tradition of folklore, literature, fiction and movies that engage popular notions of body and soul that differ from the Biblical witness.

If a separation of body and soul is prevalent in the Western philosophical tradition, folklorists of various Western traditions have separated body and soul even more radically. Several stories emerge in older Teutonic lore wherein an individual under threat of peril stores his or her soul, or a part of it, in another object so that the person may remain unharmed even if his or her body should be destroyed.[29] This notion of an "external soul" distinct from an "internal soul," renders the body as little more than a corporeal vessel that can potentially be exchanged for nearly any other physical "container." This folkloric theme has also recurred in contemporary fiction. For example, in J.K. Rowling's *Harry Potter* series the villain Voldemort can only be vanquished if the boy-protagonist and his friends manage to destroy every "horcrux" into which the evil warlock magically managed to enchant a sliver of his soul. While such tales remain fantastical, they nonetheless reinforce the notion that the body is merely a "container" not dissimilar from any other inanimate object. Add to this various tales in folklore, fiction and film involving ghosts, heaven and hell, or Faustian legends whereby the "soul" becomes a bargaining chip that can be "sold" to the devil for some sort of worldly benefit. It is wholly likely that popular beliefs in American culture regarding the relationship of body and soul are influenced as much, or more, by these tales as they are by the Western philosophical tradition. With so many other competing influences the Biblical account of the body, soul and the human creature is often neglected, ignored or forgotten.

---

can illustrate the problem with reference to Western medicine, where the Cartesian mind-body split is pervasive. Only with slight hyperbole can Trinh Xuan Thuan remark, 'To this day, the brain and mind are regarded as two distinct entities in Western medicine. When we have a headache, we consult a neurologist; when we are depressed, we are told to see a psychiatrist.'" Joel B. Green, *Body, Soul, and Human Life (Studies in Theological Interpretation)*. Kindle edition. (Grand Rapids, MI: Baker Publishing Group, 2008), 48.

[29] James George Frazer. *The Golden Bough: A Study in Magic and Religion.* (Bartleby.com, 2000), 166.

due to feminism

Despite the dualistic anthropological models of the modern era, a reemphasis on the creaturely dignity of the human body in recent years has been encouraging. In the light of a resurgence in First Article theology among Lutheran and Reformed theologians, and its impact on the lives of God's people, caring for the body from the perspective of Christian theology ought to be more fully explored and addressed. Biblical theologians have also examined, during the course of the last century, how the body relates to human personhood in a way that has tended to militate against Hellenistic dualism and has affirmed, in varying degrees, a greater unity in the human person's constitution. Beginning with Bultmann's assertion that, "man does not *have* a *soma*; he *is soma*,"[30] a chorus of agreement has emerged amongst both Old Testament and New Testament exegetes.[31] While Bultmann, arguably, overstated the issue the insight has proven influential in the long-term. The Church today no longer feels burdened by the old philosophical shackles that once constrained her anthropology by dualistic categories. There has never been a better time to shake off that philosophical baggage and explore a dynamic view of the human creature that values the body enough to consider it worthy of care, discipline, and respect. The therapeutic impetus for dealing with bodily matters in culture can, and should, be refined for Christians in terms of the body's inherent God-given value in creation, redemption, and in the forward-looking hope of the bodily resurrection. *(! sociology feeds theology! help!)*

YES so stop talking about "embodied"!

During the last decade Luther scholarship has seen a number of contributions pertaining to somatology in general. Lutheran and Reformed exegetes and systematicians alike have made great contributions to the recovery of the human body with respect to its role in soteriology, particularly regarding the resurrection of the flesh.[32] Much of this work has

---

[30] Rudolf Bultmann, *Theology of the New Testament*, 2 vols (New York: Charles Scribner's Sons, 1951-55) 1:194. *and the old — hebrew nephesh*

[31] For example, Robert A. Di Vito, "Old Testament anthropology and the construction of personal identity." *The Catholic Biblical Quarterly* 61, no. 2 (1999): 217-238. Hans Schwarz, *The Human Being: A Theological Anthropolgy.* (Grand Rapids: William B. Eerdmans Publishing Co., 2013), 5-13.R. Reed Lessing has said the same with respect to the soul:" Human beings live as souls; they do not 'have' souls." R. Reed Lessing, "The Good Life: Health, Fitness, and Bodily Welfare" in *The American Mind Meets the Mind of Christ* ed. Robert Kolb (Saint Louis: Concordia Seminary Press, 2010), 35.

[32] See Jeffrey Gibbs, "Five Things You Should Not Say at Funerals," in *Concordia Journal* 29, no.

been attributed to a reaffirmation of some of Luther's key theological distinctions. In recent years, there has been a resurgence of First Article theology within the context of Luther's "Two Kinds of Righteousness" that does much to recapture a theology of Christian living that is both profound and relevant to the common layman. While scholastic theology had understood the human being primarily in terms of categories such as body, soul and spirit, Luther's anthropology was primarily articulated in terms of the human creature's relationships. That is to say, the human creature can only be rightly understood in terms of man's relationship to God (*coram Deo*) and man's relationship to his neighbor and the rest of creation (*coram mundo*).[33] This is termed "two kinds of righteousness" because to be righteous, for Luther, is "to be the human creature God envisioned when He created us."[34] In other words, man is essentially a relational creature. While Luther did not reject the categories of body, soul, and spirit, sometimes engaging a dichotomous (body and soul) and at other time a trichotomous (body, soul and spirit) division of man, within his schema of the "two kinds of righteousness" it is always the total man (*totus homo*) who participates in relationship to creator and creation. It is never the soul alone that stands in relationship to God, nor is it the body alone that engages a relationship with neighbor. Both relationships involve the entirety of man. Man lives, passively, within a relationship with his creator and simultaneously he lives, actively, in relationship to other creatures.[35] While these two relationships are distinct, they are not separated. Righteousness before God (*coram Deo*) frees the human creature from his efforts to earn God's favor through good

4 (2003): 363-66.

[33] Robert Kolb and Charles Arand, *The Genius of Luther's Theology: A Wittenberg Way of Thinking for the Contemporary Church* (Grand Rapids, MI: Baker Academic, 2008), 23ff.

[34] Ibid., 26.

[35] Luther sometimes referred to the "two kinds of righteousness" as passive righteousness and active righteousness. These terms are prone to some confusion. By "passive" righteousness Luther does not exclude the activity of faith. Rather, he is emphasizing how this relationship is established and the terms whereby it remains ongoing. Man is a passive actor in the genesis of his relationship before God, receiving this identity wholly as an undeserved gift. The relationship occurs through God's activity alone and man receives the gift. Man's relationships in the world, however, involve willful action and activity. Thus, righteousness before the world is based on human action, and man is righteousness in the world on account of such activity.

works. Precisely because the relationship of man before God is given to man passively, man is able to direct his good works along the horizontal plane in love of neighbor through gratitude on account of Christ. Conversely, when man's works are considered within the veil of his earthly calling, man is able to recognize that they properly serve creation in such a way that also serves the Creator.[36] Simply because good works do not merit favor before God does not mean that man's activity in creation lacks value. It is precisely because man can only fully embrace his humanity when both of these relationships are maintained that activity toward creation is dignified in the redeemed human creature. To be "fully human" means to embrace human identity in terms of both relationships. Understanding these dual relationships as an essential component of human identity dignifies first article concerns as valid theological endeavors. While not much work on the subject has touched on Luther's understanding of the human body itself, a lot of what has been done regarding the First Article, and "active righteousness," has focused on one's horizontal relationship with fellow creatures, and creation in general. Charles Arand and Joel Biermann have articulated this relationship accordingly:

> "...righteousness in the world with our fellow creatures (*coram mundo*) depends on our carrying out our God-entrusted tasks—tasks spelled out with sufficient specificity in the Law both revealed and written on human hearts—within our walks of life for the good of creation. God has created human beings as male and female to complement and complete one another. Together the first man and woman formed human community, and together they were given responsibility for tending God's creation. To guide them in their task, God hardwired His Law into the creation itself."[37]

How does Luther's concept of righteousness *coram mundo*, also apply, however, to the internal relationship man has with his own flesh and bone?

---

[36] Ibid., 31.

[37] Charles Arand and Joel Biermann, "Why the Two Kinds of Righteousness?" *Concordia Journal* 33, no. 2 (2007): 119.

by whom,?

In other words, <u>what is man's created responsibility to himself?</u> It will be the intention of this book to show that Luther's theology of the human creature, particularly regarding the creaturely body, provides an answer to this question. Because the "two kinds of righteousness" *theory* essentially refutes dualistic conceptions of man, upholding the totality of man in both spheres, it will be treated extensively in terms of Luther's overall theology of the body and man's responsibility to care for it. As such, Luther has a considerable amount to say about the "active righteousness" of man with respect to his own flesh.

The Commission on Theology and Church Relations (CTCR) of the Lutheran Church - Missouri Synod released a report in 2010 entitled "Together with All Creatures: Caring for God's Living Earth." The report affirmed that "We best care for God's earth when we embrace our creatureliness."[38] Much of the history of man's understanding of himself with respect to creation in general parallels much of the history of man's understanding of the body.[39] The CTCR points out that, from Francis Bacon through Descartes, visions to improve the human estate through scientific knowledge and technological innovation led to a view of man that conceived of the human being much like a machine.[40] Rehearsing various postures that man has taken, at different times and places, in relationship to creation, the report turns to Martin Luther's theology of human creatureliness as a balanced, Biblical alternative. The CTCR report turns to the Small Catechism where Luther makes the statement that God has "made me together with all creatures" as foundational for providing an "ecological identity."[41] Luther's theology of the human creature affirms both the common creatureliness we

---

[38] "Together with All Creatures: Caring for God's Living Earth," A Report of the Commission on Theology and Church Relations of the Lutheran Church–Missouri Synod (Saint Louis: April, 2010), 2.

[39] Ibid., 10ff.

explicate

[40] "Positively, the rise of the scientific and technological revolution gave people unprecedented control over nature and the ability to improve human health and the standard of living as never before. Negatively, it led to a materialistic, atomistic, and reductionistic view of the world. Nature came to be seen primarily as a stockpile of raw materials waiting for humans to use for their benefit." Ibid., 15.

[41] Ibid., 30.

[handwritten margin notes: do your word studies / all creatures breath his / from God and goes back to God...]

have with other creatures,[42] as well as the distinctive and unique sort of creatureliness that bears a special dignity and sets the human creature apart from other creatures.[43] In one sense, the human body can be understood as a body created like any other created body. The human body owes its origins to God's design and creating activity. The human body stands unique, however, in that the body was not created ex nihilo, but from the dust of the ground. *[handwritten: in one account]* The link between the body, and the body's origins in the matter of creation itself, affirms a dependent relationship of man upon the creation. On the other hand, the human body was vivified by the breath of God. This *[handwritten: NO]* sets man apart, unique from other creatures. Thus man is both dependent upon the creation, and has dominion over it. The relationship between man and the creation is a relationship that reciprocates in mutual dependence. From this dependent relationship, the CTCR is able to conclude that, "human health and wholeness is thus found within the bond we have to the earth."[44] *[handwritten: This is secondary to the bond we have to the Word who spoke all creation into being. Do not argue a lesser ontology.]* "Together with All Creatures" offers a great insight into a theology of the body by affirming the creatureliness of the body as a component of human *[handwritten: splits]* identity. The body, as a part of the created order, is not something to be suppressed or denied any more than the human being in entirety can suppress or deny its dependence upon creation as a whole. Embracing life in creation is to embrace life in the flesh. This book engages this theme more fully, beginning likewise with Luther's theology of the human creature, and exploring how this theme is developed across other themes in Luther's theology. Whereas the CTCR has affirmed the mutually dependent link between creation and the human creature for the sake of ecological concerns, this book affirms the same for the sake of the body's own wellbeing. These themes play into Luther's "two kinds of righteousness," discussed earlier, quite well. While Luther never uses the term, a "creaturely righteousness" of sorts will emerge as Luther's affirmation of the creatureliness of man intersects with his understanding of man's righteousness, relationships and responsibility *coram mundo*. *[handwritten: his thesis]*

---

[42] Ibid., 30-38.

[43] Ibid., 39-46.

[44] Ibid., 58.

19

Adam G. Cooper, of the Lutheran Church of Australia, in his book *Life in the Flesh* dedicates an entire chapter to Luther's theology of the flesh, beginning his evaluation with a rather poignant observation: "There are few more potent antidotes to gnosticizing spirituality than the writings of Martin Luther (1483-1546)."[45] While Life in the Flesh does much to contribute toward an appropriation of a theology of the body for contemporary issues, the chapter dedicated to Luther's theology of "flesh" only engages two central themes within Luther's theology. After rehearsing how Luther studies have often neglected, or mistaken him as a sort of "Manichean figure scarred by a deeply pessimistic vision of human nature,"[46] Cooper addresses Luther's theology of the body through his Christology. The first theme that Cooper addresses is Christ's flesh as God's self-localization. "Luther was particularly captivated by the prominent Old Testament theme of God's self-localization in such places as the ark, the tabernacle, and the Temple in Jerusalem."[47] Consistently, Luther affirms that God's primary way of dealing with man is through the creaturely senses God gave him in the beginning. That is to say, God frequently employs physical means to communicate spiritual realities. The Old Testament pattern of God's self-localization (also frequently known as the "Immanuel Principle") is carried on in the New Testament.[48] The Incarnation of Christ is the pivotal and paradigmatic example that unlocks the "key" to understanding how God had worked with man all along, and how God would continue to do so sacramentally until the Parousia. Cooper argues, accordingly, that Luther's basic question was not Roland Bainton's celebrated, "How can I get a gracious God?" so much as, "Where can I find the real God?"[49] Accordingly, Cooper turns to the second theme he identifies in Luther's theology of the flesh: his theology of the

---

[45] Cooper, *Life in the Flesh*, 108.

[46] Ibid.

[47] Ibid., 112.

[48] See O. Palmer Robertson, *The Christ of the Covenants* (Phillipsburg, NJ: Presbyterian and Reformed Publishing, Co., 1980), 46.

[49] Cooper, *Life in the Flesh*, 114.

Lord's Supper.[50] Again, it is the theme of God's desire to meet man through the senses that Cooper identifies as central to Luther's thought:

— but the meal without the Canon is just a meal...

> Luther's special contribution, however, lies in the fact that he recognized in this dynamic a pervasive biblical motif, a kind of hermeneutical key that unlocks the whole salvific vista of God's revelatory dealings with human beings. That the realities communicated by 'the embodied word' may not be accessible in their full opacity to the testimony of the senses in no way calls into question the fact of their objective presence and objective efficacy. Just as true faith is not scandalized by Christ's humanity, neither is it blinded by the humility of the physical means of the Spirit.[51]

Cooper

Cooper rightly identifies the "earthy" nature of Luther's theology. He is quite correct in recognizing Luther's starting point in Old Testament theology. Recognizing God's normative means to deal with man through physical means allows Luther to link God's self-revelation in the Old Testament to the Incarnation, and ultimately the Lord's Supper. There is a physical dimension to Luther's theology that locates his touchpoint with man in physical elements that, in turn, encounters man through the senses of his own body. This point stands independently of Luther's doctrine of the real presence—Luther's primary concern was to demonstrate the intimacy by which God deals with man, in ways natural to man's total existence, including the bodily senses. Covenant theologians, for example, who do not subscribe to Luther's doctrine of the real presence nonetheless affirm how covenant signs, including the elements in the Lord's Supper, reflect God's concern to engage the senses for the sake of providing assurance to man's conscience.[52] While Cooper, later in his book, engages themes of the body on

but always with/word

be careful. Luther would not argue for things seen & heard apart from the word.

---

[50] Ibid., 118.

[51] Ibid., 120.

[52] The Belgic Confession of Faith, for example, states "We believe that our good God, mindful of our crudeness and weakness, has ordained sacraments for us to seal his promises in us, to pledge his good will and grace toward us, and also to nourish and sustain our faith. *He has added these to the Word of the gospel to represent better to our external senses both what he enables us to understand by his Word and*

a practical level, such as human sexuality and bodily death, he never really links Luther's theology of physical means to man's identity as an embodied creature. While man h̶a̶s̶ a body, and God meets man in physical means precisely because man is essentially both body and soul, Cooper's argument has more to do with Luther's understanding of God's reason for engaging man through physical means (because man has a body) than it has to do with the body itself. *which is God-given so . . .*

Carl and Lavonne Braaten also engage the theme of "locatedness" in Luther's theology in their book The Living Temple.[53] Also consistent with Cooper's project, the Braatens argue against dualistic anthropologies that would prioritize the soul or spirit over the body.[54] By rejecting dualism, and affirming the body-soul unity of the human person the Braatens are able to articulate a theological approach to holistic health.

> The body itself is a spiritual fact. The essence of a person lies not in himself but in being open to the Spirit who shares with us the embodied wholeness of God in Jesus the Christ–our Savior and Healer. Theology must move down the scale and engage in dialogue with those who try to heal at the base of somatic existence. We should not ask doctors to become more spiritual, rather for theologians to become more somatic in their perspective, thus overcoming the heresy of angelism in their own heritage. Angels don't have bodies. A holistic approach to health calls for theology to take more seriously the

Yes, they do – see Isaiah + Hebrews fixed.

---

what he does inwardly in our hearts, confirming in us the salvation he imparts to us. For they are visible signs and seals of something internal and invisible, by means of which God works in us through the power of the Holy Spirit. So they are not empty and hollow signs to fool and deceive us, for their truth is Jesus Christ, without whom they would be nothing." Belgic Confession, Art. 33, *Ecumenical Creeds and Reformed Confessions* (Grand Rapids: CRC Publications 1988), 111. Emphasis added.

[53] "For Luther a God without flesh was good for nothing, for as such he could only be the object of naked speculations." Carl E. and Lavonne Braaten, *The Living Temple: A Practical Theology of the Body and the Foods of the Earth* (New York: Harper & Row, 1976), 7.

[54] "We must still work for the liberation of the human *soma* from its schizoid condition in traditional-mind theology, where mind and spirit are pitted against body and nature. A person does not have a body; he is his bodily being from crotch to crown. A person is also spirit, but *aLWays embodied* spirit. He is also a piece of nature, a lump of the earth, from dust unto dust, as Genesis 3:19 puts it." Ibid., 6.

life of the Spirit in the body. Bad habits, bad food, bad air, bad water, overeating, overdrinking, oversleeping, overworking– all these are threats to the incarnation of the Spirit in human life.[55]

In many respects, releasing this book in the mid-1970s, *after Rachel Carson in 1963* the Braatens were ahead of their time. They had begun to see the impact of living in a culture that saw the relationship of the human being to the creation in an antagonistic way as taking a toll both upon the health of the human creature, and the creation. Theologies of the body were not in vogue yet in the 1970s, *Nelson's Embodiment was not...* but they prophetically addressed a matter that would become a prominent theological topic in the decades to come. Similarly, the Braatens find the technological revolution which, at the time, had not even conceived of the potential it would reach by the 2010s, a contributing factor to the problem. The rapid development of technology has given people a false sense that life *– but the problem was turning from God* is improving.[56] If that were true in the 1970s, it is certainly true today. The Living Temple is an engaging work that challenges the church in America to reevaluate its approach to somatic issues. That said, while Luther is a conversation partner at times in order to bolster their argument, the Braatens are not arguing for Luther's theology of the body *per se*, but a Lutheran perspective on the issue. This book will engage this work when appropriate, placing many of the Braatens' arguments within a more robust theological framework in Luther's thought.

Garth Ludwig's *Order Restored* examines the concepts of health and healing from a Biblical perspective. Ludwig, prior to his untimely death in 1998, devoted much of his life's work toward "bridging the gap" between theology and the medical sciences. He writes from the perspective of a Lutheran pastor, professor, anthropologist and theologian. In Order *Italics* Restored he begins with an affirmation of what he calls a doctrine of

---

[55] Ibid., 26.

[56] "While the standard of living has been increasing, the quality of life has been going down. Gradual decay has been taking place, not only in our cities but in our bodies. The growth of technology has given us a false trust that things are getting better and better. To be sure, technology has given us new techniques in sanitation, antiseptics and surgery. But the degenerative diseases have been quietly galloping to epidemic proportions." Ibid., 32.

"wholism," defined as "a total [view of the] person, an individual with social, mental, emotional, and spiritual needs as well as obvious physical needs."[57] Ludwig's intent is to present a biblical perspective of health, with an anthropological approach to the biblical narratives. What did it mean to be "sick" in the biblical age, in an age far different than our own? Conversely, what did it mean to be healthy? How, then, do we appropriate the biblical values of "health" into an age that has far advanced beyond biblical times in terms of medical knowledge about the body? Ludwig suggests that disease should not be thought of as "dis-ease," or a mere lack of comfort, but is really disorder at the core of human identity.[58] The Old and New Testaments provide an answer to pervasive disease that goes beyond easing temporal discomfort and restores order to the human condition. Ludwig suggests that the biblical picture of health, in both the old and new testaments, is expressed by the single word, shalom. The words "wholeness" or "peace," best reflect the meaning of Shalom in English translation. Shalom, "refers to the unity of all things under the rule of God."[59] Health, then, is defined as "the wholeness of God's creative love at work in our lives. It is the expression of what God created us to be— functionally, mentally, emotionally, socially and spiritually."[60] Biblical health is about bringing order to the totality of human personhood.

Ludwig suggests that interpretations which focus on Jesus' healing ministry, for example, as though he were curing diseases miss the point. Jesus isn't merely a healer of disease; his acts of healing were about restoring wholeness in the lives of people whose lives have fallen into the disorder of a fallen world. Eschatology affirms the ultimate end of the Biblical model of health—all order will be wholly restored. This does not mean, though, that health is of no concern until the end of times. The Kingdom of God, no less, continues to break through into the daily lives of people bringing about restoration, wholeness, and healing. The medical sciences, among other

---

[57] Garth D. Ludwig, *Order Restored: A Biblical Interpretation of Health Medicine and Healing* (St. Louis: Concordia Publishing House, 1999), 13.

[58] Ibid., 22.

[59] Ibid. 118.

[60] Ibid.

vocational disciplines, are gifts given man by God that reveal the restorative character of God's redemptive plan. Healing and health involves a present participation in the future of God's redemptive work and man's ultimate hope. When put into proper perspective, health is not something that is pursued merely to "fend off disease" and to postpone death, but it is a profound and faithful expression of the present reality of God's promise to finally restore perfect order to creation.[61]

Thomas Hafer, embracing a dual career as both Lutheran pastor and physical therapist, has offered some unique insights into the subject as well. In his book Faith & Fitness: Diet and Exercise for a Better World, Hafer has explored the relationship between faith and fitness as a response "to God's call to be good stewards of our own health, our neighbors' heath, and the health of our planet."[62] Hafer explores biblical notions, such as fasting, in terms of understanding the communal connection of our own bodies to the bodies of our neighbors. While in the American world our bodies are often well-fed, fasting allows us to fulfill the Christian's calling in the church to bear the burdens our fellow human creatures who are starving.[63] Hafer's work, though, only scratches the surface in terms of his theological foundation for bodily wellbeing. He affirms the value of the body, and the importance of caring for it, but moves quickly from his theological basis into practical application. His theological basis is not wrong, but it is incomplete and could be further developed.

R. Reed Lessing has explored the questions of bodily health and fitness from the perspective of biblical theology. Lessing identifies two tendencies with regard to the body in American culture: to reject the body and to strive

---

[61] See also N.T. Wright, *Surprised by Hope* (New York: HarperCollins, 2008), 154. Wright suggests that the colloquial expression that says someone who is ill is a "shadow of their former self," ought to better be expressed in terms of man, in any present time of affliction, being a shadow of his "future self." Like Ludwig, Wright affirms a picture of eschatalogical man that upholds a Biblical picture of perfect health.

[62] Tom P. Hafer, *Faith & Fitness: Diet and Exercise for a Better World* (Minneapolis, MN: Augsburg Fortress, 2007), 11.

[63] For example, "Like most people of affluent societies, we have the luxury of never being malnourished. Yet, like most people of affluent societies, we have the pain of weight problems or poor health as a result of inappropriate diet and lack of exercise. Typically, when we speak of our personal wellness, we don't think in terms of Christian compassion and love." Ibid., 15.

to perfect the body. The tendency to reject the importance of the body has its roots, Lessing argues, in ancient Gnosticism but has been embraced in contemporary American culture through the New Age Movement. "New Age spirituality abandons the 'evil' world and seeks answers from the 'god within' by means of 'mystical experiences.'"[64] Lessing finds a Christian answer to the problem of rejecting the body in Holy Baptism where the entire person, body included, is cleansed and restored.[65] Lessing's Lutheran confession, particularly relevant to baptism, is evident in this interpretation. That said, the same conclusions can be drawn by embracing that which Baptism signifies—namely, regeneration. *— reduces baptism!*

Perhaps more popular than rejecting the body in American culture, Lessing argues, is to perfect the body at all costs. The tendency, through such *a "we 'create" our new "self*"* obsessive pursuits, is the "worship of what is created rather than the Creator."[66] Steroids, obsessive exercise, and various forms of cosmetic surgery are all on the rise. Modern medicine is often turned to "as an insurance policy that gives people a sense that they will not have to come to terms with the reality of their own death."[67] Lessing appeals to 1 Corinthians 6:20 as a corrective–those who seek to perfect their bodies are called upon to honor God with their bodies, not to honor themselves.[68]

Contrasted against either of these misguided perceptions of the body in the American mind, is the mind of Christ which, Lessing argues, empowers another approach–to respect the body and bodily life. The question of good stewardship of the body has suffered largely "due to our neglect of the doctrine of creation."[69] Lessing suggests that the answer is in *and the meaning of sacramental elements the sacrament addresses us as bodies*

---

[64] Lessing, "The Good Life: Health, Fitness, and Bodily Welfare," 32.

[65] "In Holy Baptism the Triune God not only cleanses our conscience (1 Pt 3:21), but also our *bodies*. In fact, our 'bodies are washed with pure water' (Hebrews 10:22). In baptism both body and soul become a new creation (2 Cor. 5:17) and even though outwardly the body wastes away, the baptized accept their bodies knowing that at the Second Advent of Christ they will receive glorified bodies (Phil 3:21)." Ibid.

[66] Ibid.

[67] Ibid., 33.

[68] Ibid.

[69] Ibid., 34.

recapturing the Old Testament roots of the Christian faith, and argues from the perspective of Old Testament biblical theology. Contrasted against Platonic antagonism between body and soul, Hebraic thought unites "soul" and "spirit" in reference to the entire person. "Human beings live as souls, they do not 'have' souls."[70] In other words, the Old Testament "views people as animated bodies rather than incarnated souls."[71] Because Old Testament biblical theologies over the last hundred years, or longer, have largely started with Yahweh's call to Abram in Genesis, marginalizing Yahweh's relationship to his creation, the ramifications of the Hebraic concept of "soul" and "spirit" has often been overlooked. Hegelian dualism separating the spiritual from the material is partially to blame, along with theories from Von Rad and others who dismissed the "pre-patriarchal history" in Genesis 1–11 as having origins in a different "sphere of culture and religion."[72] Lessing argues that one must speak of Yahweh in terms of "creation" rather than merely in terms of "history" in order to be faithful to the biblical text; "we must understand Yahweh's redemptive acts in history as his way to restore his creatures and bring about his new creation, which ultimately is in Christ."[73] Like Cooper, Lessing also sees in Luther's sacramental theology an emphasis on the unity between creation and redemption via the flesh of Christ, and the bodily presence of Christ in the Lord's Supper.[74] While Lessing's Lutheran perspective on Baptismal regeneration and the true presence of Christ's body and blood compliments the point well, one who does not embrace a Lutheran view of the Sacraments can still embrace the overall argument. The fact that the Lord uses corporeal signifiers to encounter embodied creatures in a way that appeals to the senses, thus communicating that which is signified to the entire person, is an insight that can be embraced by Lutheran and Reformed alike.

---

[70] Ibid., 35.

[71] Ibid., 39. *correct — nephesh*

[72] Von Rad, quoted in Lessing, 36. *so did you check Von Rad's argument not just quote the quote!*

[73] Lessing, 38.

[74] Ibid.

Charles L. Cortright, of the Wisconsin Evangelical Lutheran Synod (WELS), has written a dissertation entitled, *Poor Maggot Sack That I Am: The Human Body in the Theology of Martin Luther.*[75] Completed in 2011, it represents the most complete attempt to date to try and understand what Luther actually wrote about the body. That said, the title is somewhat misleading. While Cortright demonstrates that in many respects Luther's comments on the body are not far removed from his medieval predecessors, it is hard to discern from Cortright how Luther actually viewed the body within his larger theological corpus. Thus, while Cortright identifies a number of insights on the body from Luther, he never really presents a comprehensive theology of the body that takes into account Luther's paradigmatic way of thinking. A part of the problem with Cortright's analysis is that his survey of the medieval period prior to Luther is incomplete. He addresses nominalism briefly, but never considers such prominent and influential figures on Luther's early theological development such as Gabrial Biel. Accordingly, Cortright concludes, "...with respect to his foundational understandings about the body, Luther was no innovator. His understanding of the human person was 'traditional' in that he defined the person as body and soul and understood their relationship in late medieval terms: the soul provided the 'whatness' of the self in combination with the material of the body, as it did Aquinas."[76] If Cortright, however, had evaluated scholasticism more thoroughly he would have found the previously discussed distinction between the higher and lower faculties in man as taught by Biel and others. Accordingly, while Luther often speaks of body and soul in a traditional manner, the various "faculties" of man into "higher" and "lower" parts, is starkly contrasted by Luther's relational and paradigmatic view of man according to the two kinds of righteousness. By focusing almost entirely on the body/soul distinction in his comparison of Luther to his medieval predecessors, Cortright misses some fundamental aspects of Luther's understanding of the human creature that bear significance on fundamental questions regarding the body. That said, however, Cortright does provide a

---

[75] Charles L. Cortright "Poor Maggot Sack That I Am: The Human Body in the Theology of Martin Luther" (PhD diss., Marquette University, 2011).

[76] Ibid, 242.

28

very helpful discussion regarding Luther's evolving views of human sexuality by contrasting his earlier writings prior to marriage and those later after he was married. According to Cortright, Luther's position is ultimately that sex is good, but it is always accompanied by sin even within the marriage bed.[77] His work on Luther's own body, his conception of disease and death, is also very helpful. His insights here will be taken into consideration.

it is a gift given to the human being

The call for Christians to take responsibility for their own well-being is certainly in the forefront of popular discussion, but as of yet these concerns have not been fully explored in terms of the greater framework of Luther's theology. While some, such as the CTCR, Cooper, Lessing, and others have thematically examined bodily concerns in Luther's theology, the place of these themes in his larger theological framework hasn't been sufficiently addressed. This author intends to "bridge the gap" between popular concerns in the matter of personal wellness, and the larger corpus of Luther's theology. More importantly, it is hoped that these insights, derived from Luther, can be translated into contemporary application that may aid Christians of all stripes to have a better grasp on what it means to live righteously as "embodied" creatures. *no, as bodily selves*

his goal

The Issue in the Context of Current Scholarship
Pope John Paul II

Somatology has been a popular theme in contemporary theology, largely following the impetus of Pope John Paul II's seminal works on the bodily dimension of human personhood.[78] John Paul II rightly set the stage for his works in the context of a Christian worldview that has been infected with Cartesian dualism, modern rationalism, and super-spiritualism[79] all representing disembodied anthropologies in the modern world. *A Theology of the Body* consists of 133 distinct lectures delivered between September 5, 1979

---

[77] Ibid., 151-178. *— really, is that the best you can do JPII?*

[78] John Paul II, *Man and Woman He Created Them: A Theology of the Body* (Boston: Pauline Books & Media, 2006). [Hereafter, *TOB*.]

[79] This term, not entirely unique to John Paul II, seems to encompass some tendencies within mysticism as well as enthusiasm.

and November 28, 1984. Pope John Paul II viewed his work largely as a follow up to Paul VI's encyclical letter *Humanae Vitae*.[80] A controversial encyclical in the west, *Humanae Vitae* was written in 1968 largely to address the emergence of oral contraceptives. As such, Paul VI explored a number of themes dealing with the identity of man and woman in creation. While John Paul II doesn't dwell on the matter of contraception, *per se*, in his *Theology of the Body*, the sexual component of humanity is a central theme. Human embodiment is essentially sexual embodiment. *— is this reductive or is that what it says?*

The pope's work did much to emphasize the theological, not merely the biological, character of the human body in contemporary Christian thought. John Paul II leads his reader to understand who the human creature is according to God's original plan and how and why mankind fell from His plan. His prevailing theme concerns how the death and resurrection of Jesus Christ can effectively transform our understanding and experience of sexual embodiment as redeemed creatures. *as we discern if...*

According to John Paul II, "Through the fact that the Word of God became flesh, the body entered theology...through the main door."[81] While the majority of the pope's initial discussion revolves around the Genesis account of the creation of man, he insists that this becomes the starting point of a theology of the body primarily because Christ has himself appealed to the "beginning" in his dialogue with the Pharisees about marriage.[82] For several lectures the pope engages the text of Genesis exploring the meaning of original solitude, original unity and original nakedness without shame. The fruit of this analysis is the concept of a "spousal meaning of the body," which has been called the central concept of his Theology of the Body. *spousal meaning of Body (wow — reductionist —*

---

[80] Paul VI. 1968. *Humanae Vitae*. http://www.vatican.va/holy_father/paul_vi/encyclicals/documents/hf_p-vi_enc_25071968_humanae-vitae_en.html (accessed July 11, 2017).

[81] *TOB*, 221.

[82] "And Pharisees came up to him and tested him by asking, 'Is it lawful to divorce one's wife for any cause?' He answered, 'Have you not read that he who created them from the beginning made them male and female, and said, "Therefore a man shall leave his father and his mother and hold fast to his wife, and the two shall become one flesh"? So they are no longer two but one flesh. What therefore God has joined together, let not man separate.' They said to him, 'Why then did Moses command one to give a certificate of divorce and to send her away'" He said to them, 'Because of your hardness of heart Moses allowed you to divorce your wives, but from the beginning it was not so.'" (Matthew 19:3-8 ESV)

[In offspring]

"It is not good that man (male) should be alone."[83] These words account for the "original solitude" of man, the first point of departure for John Paul II's reflection on the "beginning." From the beginning, man is aware that there is both continuity and discontinuity between himself and the rest of the created order. He has a body, but he was in a very particular way created from the "dust of the ground." While he, like other animals, has a body he alone is able to cultivate the earth and subdue it. "The structure of this body is such that it permits him to be the author of genuinely human activity. In this activity, the body expresses the person."[84] The solitude of man quickly becomes part of the meaning of the original unity of man when woman is created. Nonetheless, man has a body before it is ever properly termed "male." "Man falls into that 'torpor" in order to wake up as 'male' and 'female.' In this way, the circle of the human person's solitude is broken, because the first 'man' awakes from his sleep as 'male and female.'"[85] It is not that original man was neuter, per se, but unaware of any definite sexual identity. Sexuality only emerges when original solitude gives way to original unity in the differentiation of the sexes. Masculinity and femininity are seen as "two reciprocally completing ways of 'being a body' and at the same time of being a human...femininity in some way finds itself before masculinity, while masculinity confirms itself through femininity."[86] Because "it is not good" for man to remain in a state of solitude alone, man can really only grasp the full meaning of being "human" in conjugal spousal unity.[87] This is an act of self-gift, male and female reciprocally giving of oneself to the other, that becomes a sort of revelatory experience allowing both male and female to comprehend their bodies completely through unity.[88] This leads into John Paul II's discussion of original nakedness. It is through their

Marginal handwritten notes: "community is the primary goal —", "fit helpmate", "not fit", "reprod mate...", "not really true", "ok —", "eisegesis", "fudge factor", "how to apply to children — they see it long before they are pubescent", "fudge —", "maintains the "male" primacy", "so why celibacy?", "self-gift — self-giving is Christ's act once for all..."

---

[83] Genesis 2:18

[84] TOB, 154.

[85] Ibid., 159-160.

[86] Ibid., 166.

[87] For a Lutheran appraisal of this theme see The Commission on Theology and Church Relations of the Lutheran Church–Missouri Synod (CTCR), *The Creator's Tapestry: Scriptural Perspectives on Man-Woman Relationships in Marriage and the Church* (Saint Louis: December, 2009)

[88] TOB, 169.

31

Would read JPII
documents to see if they
are as reduced as he
represents them to be...

original nakedness
was sheer diversity
not lust-bitten

nakedness in a "reciprocal experience of the body," that man experiences femininity and woman experiences masculinity, which ties the body together in original unity. In such original nakedness they felt no shame.

From all of the above, John Paul II affirms that the body is best essentially understood as spousal. The spousal attribute of the body is defined as "the power to express love: precisely that love in which the human person becomes a gift and—through this gift—fulfills the very meaning of his being and existence."[89] Original happiness, then, is rooted in spousal love. This relationship of mutual gift between man and woman reflects, also, the relationship between man and God. "If creation is a gift given to man, as we have already said, then its fullness and deepest dimension is determined by grace, that is, by participation in the inner life of God himself, in his holiness."[90]

so community is not created by love — that is triune but bio-attraction...

or is it in Adam's song of joy: This at last mirrors me

All of the aforementioned constitutes a summary of the first chapter of a Theology of the Body. The second and third chapters, like the first, begin with a word from Christ. If the first chapter is an appeal, from the words of Christ, to the "beginning," the second chapter can be called an appeal to the "human heart," and the third to the "resurrection." The categories addressed above from John Paul II will be further elaborated upon in chapter two.

Credi: I, II, III articles structure Bubba!

John Paul II begins the second chapter from Jesus' words regarding adultery in the Sermon on the Mount. "You have heard that it was said, 'You shall not commit adultery.' But I say to you that everyone who looks at a woman with lustful intent has already committed adultery with her in his heart." (Matthew 5:27-28 ESV) Before elaborating further on these words, however, John Paul II returns to the pages of Genesis to observe the origin of sexual concupiscence and the formation of "the man of concupiscence."[91] The fall of man corrupted the unitive meaning of the body, and the spousal connection has been lost. After taking the forbidden fruit, original nakedness in innocence turns quickly to shame in their naked bodies. While their nakedness had been a gift given and received between man and woman, once

---

[89] Ibid., 186.

[90] Ibid., 191.

[91] Ibid., 234.

This quote seems dropped in — what does the document do itself — does it close off spousal love by plopping in God's grace. Then is grace/love in human community just secondary derivative?

Makes a mess of Trinitarian (Augustine's) love metaphor — and literalizes △ intimacy

CONFUSES CATEGORY

— deforms the communal connection —
also resurrection —↗ male, ↗ female, no fun
or
Gentile

sin enters into the world, man and woman become aware of their bodies
apart from their spousal connection, thus covering them in shame. As the
"spousal" unity of the body had been defined "in the beginning" by
reciprocal self-gift from each partner to the other, the passions of the flesh *(interesting psychology but*
have turned man's desire toward the self, leading to shame within the
human heart. The pope examines all sorts of adulterous actions "of the *does not root properly*
heart," that do not necessarily involve the visible participation of the rest of
the body as, no less, corruptions of man's humanity. The problem of *as* *^ spousal^*
pornography, for example, is no insignificant matter.

> What is at issue is an extremely important and fundamental
> sphere of values to which man cannot remain indifferent
> because of the dignity of humanity, because of the personal
> character and eloquence of the human body. Through works of
> art and the activity of audiovisual media, this whole content
> and these values can be formed and deepened, but they can
> also be deformed and destroyed in man's heart."[92]

— this approach is problematic. It would be imperative for Jesus to have married

Ultimately, when another human being becomes an object to satisfy
one's own sexual urges (even within the context of marriage), rather than
the completion of his or her own humanity, man is left in a solitude far worse
than that which he experienced even in the beginning. Original solitude,
while the only thing declared "not good" prior to the fall, nonetheless, was
shameless before God. Man is left, after the fall, in a solitude of shame; a
never-ending quest to try to satisfy within himself what could only be
rightly satisfied in a God-given spousal union. *Unmarried folk are permanently incomplete ...!*

"In the resurrection they will not marry." (Matthew 22:30) These
words are foundational for John Paul II's third chapter, Christ's appeal to the
resurrection. The pope takes up the question of the resurrection and the final
fulfillment of the spousal meaning of the body in the vision of God, first in
the teaching of Jesus and then in the teaching of Paul. Virginity is to be

---

[92] Ibid., 373.

[handwritten margin note at top: but the spousal union created order was "good" in God's — so the "fall" did not destroy that — this makes God correcting God's original design of humanity...]

praised precisely because it is an anticipatory sign of the resurrection.[93] The resurrection of the body is relevant here and now, it "helps man, above all, to discover the whole good in which he achieves the victory over sin and over concupiscence."[94] It could be argued that the third chapter, on the resurrection, is John Paul II's theological defense of the Roman Catholic position on celibacy in the priesthood. If the body is essentially "spousal," the question of celibacy raises problems. This is resolved in two ways. First, the "spousal" meaning of the body is not neglected through celibacy because the priest is still giving of himself freely in reciprocal relationship with the Kingdom of God expressed in the church. Second, the priest stands as a sign of the age to come, when man will neither be married nor given in marriage.

[handwritten margin note: dis-embody / Yet given we are Christ our bridegroom repeatedly in Bible"]

The three chapters described above make up "part one" of John Paul II's Theology of the Body and fully articulate his foundation. "Part two," turns to the meaning of the Sacrament of Marriage in the Roman Catholic Church and explores Paul's teaching on marriage and the church in Ephesians 5:31-32. The principle discussion in "part two" is the distinction between the grace of the sacrament and the sacramental sign that signifies and realizes this grace. He writes, "Given that the sacrament is the sign by means of which the saving reality of grace and the covenant is expressed and realized, we must now consider it under the aspect of sign, while the preceding reflections were devoted to the reality of grace and the covenant."[95]

Initially, it seems that John Paul II's theology of the human body would have very little connection to Luther's understanding of the human creature. Perhaps, being that this book introduces Luther into the dialogue on the body that John Paul II initiated, it would be better to say that it initially seems like Luther's theology of the human creature wouldn't have a direct import into these discussions. There is, however, one particularly significant element where the pope's work and Luther's theology intersect. Both Pope John Paul II and Martin Luther understand the human creature essentially through relational categories. In either case, this relationship is a material one.

[handwritten margin note: Luther precedes JPII"]

[handwritten note at bottom: So Pope JPII follows ML's understanding of relational categories for human beings. It is only after Luther's precedent is given its historic place that we speak of JPII]

---

[93] Ibid., 446.

[94] Ibid., 462.

[95] Ibid., 532.

and this is why JPII argument flounders. It centers on human sex, not on what God is doing

Whereas the pope builds this foundation through the spousal relationship, which similarly reflects the relationship between man and God, Luther articulates his relational anthropology through "two kinds of righteousness" intended to distinguish, but not separate, the dual relationships of man before God, and before the world. Both Luther and John Paul II, through relational anthropologies, offer a corrective to the dualistic conceptions of man that had dominated the anthropological thought in their own time. When confronted with differing dualistic anthropologies of their day, the post-Aquinas scholastic dualism for Luther and Caretesian and Hegelian dualism in the modern era for John Paul II, both theologians found an answer by understanding the human creature primarily in relational terms. In both cases, Luther and John Paul II advanced a relational concept of the human creature that was able to maintain to dignity of the total man (*totus homo*). Accordingly, noting this point of contact, a further conversation across the centuries between Luther and John Paul II will be engaged.

but ML is coherent and JPII is not... no, Pope's flounders

as God's creature

John Paul II's relational view of the body, defined through spousal unity, is a very specific way of construing the relational essence of the human creature. Luther's distinction between the "two kinds of righteousness," on the other hand, is far broader. Either approach has merit. The application of John Paul II's theology, predictably, focuses on bodily matters largely dealing with human sexuality–contraception, adultery, pornography, divorce and remarriage, gender roles, etc. While, having effectively refuted dualism, he does occasionally address other matters of concern for the body, this is not his primary emphasis. Luther's emphasis on the human creature in relationship to the creator and creation, via the "two kinds of righteousness," may not as readily address any single issue for practical application regarding the body in this life, but it does set a groundwork that allows theologians to engage virtually any bodily matter in daily life that affects God's people. While placing Martin Luther into conversation with any pope certainly results in an "odd couple" of sorts, this author is not so concerned with John Paul II's status as a pope as with his theological contribution to the topic. In this respect, the coupling is not so "odd" at all.

does not work

really?

we do not get to see this in your presentation

there you go

they share a spousal love, a sexual ennuendo

Benedict Ashley

orphaned heading, editors!

35

Shortly after John Paul II completed his lectures on the theology of the body, another Roman Catholic theologian, Benedict Ashley, published *Theologies of the Body: Humanist and Christian.* One would think that Ashley would build upon the thought of John Paul II in his work, but he admits in his preface to the second printing of this book that he was little acquainted with the original thoughts of Pope John Paul II when he wrote it.[96] This is likely due to the fact that, writing only a year after John Paul II completed his lectures, they had yet to be published in English.

Ashley's method is, as the title suggests, an evaluation of two different theoretical approaches to the body: the Christian one (to which, Ashley admits, he is committed) and the Humanist one in which he was born and has been in contact with throughout his life.

Ashley begins outlining what science has revealed about the human body in dynamic relationship to nature. He then proceeds to examine the various "theologies" which Humanism, since about 1700, has devised to interpret these scientific findings. Ashley, then, evaluates the ethical implication of these insights. These Humanist "theologies" are then compared to various Christian theologies of the body developed both before and after the rise of modern science. Ashley proceeds to, then, construct a philosophical approach to the scientific facts regarding the body and, finally, proposes a Christian theology of the body that he believes to be congruent with his philosophical interpretation of scientific facts.

Ashley's basic contention is that theology, "rather than defend itself against contemporary science, or meekly accept the interpretation given science by the Enlightenment, must redeem it in the light of the Word of God."[97] From his evaluation of what science reveals about the human being, Ashley proposes the following "scientific definition" of the human person:

> We human persons are creative, communicating, socially intelligent animals, motivated by unconscious and conscious emotions and purposes, capable of achieving scientific knowledge through which we can control our own behavior,

---

[96] Ashley, *Theologies of the Body,* xviii.

[97] Ibid., xiv.

36

our environment and our own evolution. At any moment of our historical development we are limited by our past, by barriers that divide our human community, yet we continue to strive to transcend these limits and so build a novel future.[98]

From this point, Ashley begins to engage a number of currents throughout the history of Humanism, briefly touching on the Renaissance, and more thoroughly the post-Cartesian era. Of particular importance is his interaction with the process philosophies most readily identified with theologians such as Charles Hartshorne and Alfred North Whitehead in the modern era. Process philosophies, taking cue from ancient Stoics, "wish to reduce physical reality to pure process, to 'events.'"[99] Accordingly, Ashley is critical of process philosophies for a number of reasons. Nonetheless he attempts to "sketch what a process philosophy interpretation of the scientific world-picture which would respect the reality of matter and the human body might be."[100] He appeals to Whitehead's concept of "creativity." For Whitehead, "creativity is the ultimate principle which is embodied in every existent and which brings it into existence."[101] This principle becomes central to Ashley's approach to the body. According to Ashley, the scientific-world picture is a "moving picture." "Process is creativity, and every entity in the world of our experience is in process."[102]

What emerges from Ashley's project is what he terms a "process theology of the body."[103] Because the human intelligence both transcends the

---

[98] Ibid., 40.

[99] Ibid., 262.

[100] Ibid., 264.

[101] Ibid., 268.

[102] Ibid.

[103] "Christian theology has always taught reverence for the human body as the temple of the human spirit and the Holy Spirit, but influenced by dualistic conceptions of the relation of mind to matter it has failed to take full advantage of our increasing scientific self-understanding. There remains the haunting idea that matter, although created by God, is somehow the source of the evils in the world. To overcome this notion, throughout the argument of this book I have tried to show how all human knowledge arises out of matter or is at least expressed only in terms derived from matter, even our loftiest ideas of God and the spiritual world. To summarize all this, I want to state succinctly both the negative and the positive aspects of matter. Matter, in the radical sense of the primary matter, is a negative principle in that it is *pure*

limits of the body yet remains necessarily rooted to it, the intelligence of man has a teleology corresponding to the teleology of matter. The underlying question, one that Ashley posed in the first chapter, "Can we create ourselves?" is answered with a "yes" in his conclusion. The human intelligence, rooted in the human body as God's image, is "present to itself and draws all the past together in memory as it reaches out to plan for the future, to create what has never been."[104]

While it is beyond the scope of this book to extensively address Ashley's conclusions, as they tend to be more philosophically than theologically oriented, his analysis of the history of the body is quite helpful for these purposes. The eschatological implications of a body understood not as "being" but "becoming," will be engaged. He reflects a genuine concern, by many, that theology has tended to be dismissive of the sciences and, in turn, has devalued insights that can be gleaned from the material world about the human body. Recognizing that "caring for the body," as a general theme, must engage what modern science has to say about what is, or isn't, healthy for the body, Ashley's concern to engage a theology of the body through a responsible appropriation of the sciences is worth heeding.

[handwritten: —never more than co-creators and finite in death etc.]

[handwritten: turn to theosis]

Graham Ward

[handwritten: but God has always said "Let us reason together" but the norm is not current theologies but Word.]

If Pope John Paul II's work may be seen as the preeminent critique of a modernist somatology, contemporary theologians representing radical orthodoxy have furthered that critique employing the perspective of postmodernism. Graham Ward articulates what he terms a scandalous "transcorporeality" of the body, engaging the theological relationship "between creation, incarnation, ecclesiology and eucharist."[105] The

[handwritten: begs question of matter created first "five days" of creation account— that matter was not all negative potential]

potentiality which cannot actualize itself, but requires to be actualized by actually existing beings. Therefore, it exists only in existing natural units as their intrinsic capacity to be transformed into other actually existing units, and can never exist in its own right...Because all material things always retain this radical passivity in their materiality, they are all liable to be destroyed by exterior forces. All living things are eventually killed; all non-living things are eventually disintegrated by the action of external agents." Ibid., 694.

[handwritten: it was what it was which was good— alive (animals)]

[104] Ibid., 696.

[105] Graham Ward. "Transcorporeality: The Ontological Scandal," in *The Radical Orthodoxy Reader*, ed. John Milbank and Simon Oliver (New York: Routledge 2009), 288.

[handwritten: all creation is "negative" matter " in this reading, at which point just say All creation hangs on the Word/Will of God...]

This page makes me want to read G. Ward and slap Fouts

eucharistic body, however, becomes the prevailing theme in Ward as he notes that from the words of institution "...the shock-wave in these words emerges from the depths of an ontological scandal; the scandal of that 'is'."[106] This emphasis is not a limiting factor so much as a launching point for understanding "body" in general as a sign of the fuller body (Christ's body) that is signified:

> With transcorporeality, as I am conceiving it theologically, the body does not dissolve or ab-solve, it expands en Christo. While always located within specific sociological and historical contexts, it nevertheless is continually being opened up, allowing itself to open up, in acts of following which affect the transferral, the transduction. Transcorporeality is an effect of following in the wake of the eternal creative Word. Discipleship becomes transfiguring. The body accepts its own metaphorical nature -- insofar as it is received and understood only in and through language. Only God sees creation literally. We who are created deal only with the seeing and understanding appropriate to our creatureliness. We only negotiate the world metaphorically. The body as metaphor, moves within and along the intratextual nature of creation. As such metaphor becomes inextricably involved with participation within a divine economy -- metousia, metexein, metalambanein and metanoia.[107]

groovy, but, lay it out

no, we precisely do not

metaphors ≠ entic being

You cannot introduce this level of complexity and terms and then just leave it ...

The themes developed in radical orthodoxy won't take a preeminent place in this book, but they should certainly be in view. With radical orthodoxy, the Cartesian dualism between body and mind that permeates modernist thought is a foil against which a proper biblical somatology ought to be clearly differentiated. Insofar as the insights of postmodernism and radical orthodoxy may further this goal, it will be taken into consideration.

— why plop it down, then.

Matthew Lee Anderson *orphaned*

---

[106] Ibid.

[107] Ibid., 302.

Matthew Lee Anderson has taken the lead from the former Pontiff's work to address some of the same concerns addressed by John Paul II within the context of evangelicalism. Recognizing that John Paul II's work has largely been ignored within evangelicalism, Anderson hopes to provide "something of a starting point for a life of pursuing the kingdom of God that takes seriously the human body as the place of our personal presence in the world."[108]

Anderson does not dwell on John Paul II"s work extensively, though. His larger concern is the inattention the body has received in evangelical thought. He offers insights from various sources, a Presbyterian,[109] a Baptist,[110] a high-church Anglican,[111] and a proponent of the emerging church[112] who all, while not in universal agreement as to a solution, unanimously agree that evangelicalism has gone awry regarding a Biblical understanding of the body. That said, the history of evangelicalism regarding the body isn't as disparaging toward the body as some have argued.[113]

---

[108] Anderson, *Earthen Vessels,* 234.

[109] "It would seem that the critics of modern American religion are basically on target in describing the entire religious landscape, from New Age or liberal, to evangelical and Pentecostal, as essentially Gnostic. Regardless of the denomination, the American Religion is inward, deeply distrustful of institutions, mediated grace, the intellect, theology, creeds, and the demand to look outside of oneself for salvation...if one is to be saved, one must accept the death of individualism, inwardness, emotional and experiential ladders of ecstasy, merit and speculation." Michael Horton, "Gnostic Worship" in *Modern Reformation* 4 (1995): 13-21. Quoted in Anderson, 37.

[110] "It is my contention that evangelicals at best express ambivalence toward the human body, and at worst manifest a disregard or contempt for it. Many people, often due to tragic experiences with the body (e.g., physical/sexual abuse), abhor their body, and many Christians, due to either poor or nonexistent teaching on human embodiment, consider their body to be, at best, a hindrance to spiritual maturity and, at worst, inherently evil or the ultimate source of sin." Gregg Allision, "Toward a Theology of Human Embodiment," *Southern Baptist Journal of Theology,* 13 no. 2 (2009) quoted in Anderson, 37-38.

[111] N.T. Wright, *Surprised by Hope.*

[112] "Remember, modernity only wants abstract principles, universal concepts, and disembodied absolutes. So we take an expression like 'the kingdom of God' and try to give it meaning without any context. Postmodern theology has to reincarnate; we have to get back into the flesh and blood and sweat and dirt of the setting, because as I said, all truth is contextual." Brian McLaren *A New Kind of Christian: A Tale of Two Friends on a Spiritual Journey,* 1st ed. (San Franciscoo: Jossey-Bass, 2001), 102. Quoted in Anderson, 38.

[113] Reflecting on figures such as D.L. Moody and Billy Graham who speak clearly about the bodily resurrection of the Christian, Anderson argues that while much of the critique of evangelicalism's attitudes

Nonetheless, Anderson identifies certain evangelical responses to modern movements that have reinforced within evangelical circles attitudes about the body that have lurked throughout the history of Christendom. Similar to other authors previously discussed, Anderson identifies the historical problems of Gnosticism (body as a prison) and Cartesianism (body as machine) as contributing factors to the contemporary dilemma.[114] What is more perplexing, though, is that while evangelicals have been largely inattentive to the body in their theologies, the dominant intellectual trends of our time have turned to the physical body in attempt to solve the social and political problems of modernity.[115]

Consider, for example, the emphasis postmodernism has placed on the body. Evangelicals have certainly been eager to address and refute certain claims within postmodernism. While focusing on the ontological problem of "truth" and the epistemological problem of "how we know it," evangelicals have scarcely examined postmodern attitudes regarding the body. Anderson suggests that, while Christians readily recognize the problem of Descartes' "I think, therefore I am," one needs only "swim up the postmodern stream a little" to find a "strong current" of thought focused on the body.[116] Jean-Paul Sartre turned Descartes' axiom on its head, writing "The body is what I immediately am...I am my body to the extent that I am."[117] Thus, drawing a straight line from Cartesian dualism to the contemporary problem is too simplistic. That said, postmodernism (while Anderson affirms that it is a gross oversimplification to speak of postmodernism as a monolithic movement) has presented a new problem with respect to the body.

> The postmodern "body" has been destabilized. In fact, rather than even speaking of the body, we must speak of bodies, for the postmodern critique is that there can be no single narrative

[margin annotation: actually Lutheran wish]

---

about the body has merit, the uncharitable caricature of evangelical thought often assumed doesn't entirely hold up under scrutiny. See Anderson, *Earthen Vessels,* 39-41.

[margin annotation: until we acknowledge there is One sovereign narrator who is catholic and holy and apostolic]

[114] Anderson, *Earthen Vessels,* 54-57.

[115] Ibid., 42.

[116] Ibid.

[117] Jean-Paul Sartre, *Being and Nothingness*, trans. Hazel Barnes (New York: Philosophical Library, 1956), 302. Quoted in Anderson, 42.

of embodied existence. Gay people have one experience of the body, females another, and white males a third. If postmodernism rejects the possibility of objective truth, it also rejects the possibility of an objective body.[118]

but there is a construct possible...

Anderson addresses, in similar vein, the problems of the body in contemporary movements such as feminism and philosophical naturalism. While one would think that the emphasis on the body in contemporary schools of thought would have provoked a healthy somatic emphasis within evangelical theology, the response has been lacking. This has been a missed opportunity to reaffirm the centrality and relevance of the body to the Christian faith and life. "In a world where the body's status is in question, we have an opportunity to proclaim that the God who saved our souls will also remake our bodies; that the body is nothing less than the place where God dwells on earth. It means moving the body to the center of our understanding of what it means to be human, but it is a move that is justified when we remember that the Word himself became flesh."[119]

this is not a novum but so core to apostolic theologies.

While Anderson's above perspectives reflect many of the ideological movements that have colored contemporary attitudes of the body, the popular problem he argues for in the daily life of American culture is the American commitment to the twin problems of consumerism and individualism. While the body's dependency upon the creation for its continued sustenance, and even its pleasure, was once a given, in our late-modern world the human identity in connection with creation has "been distorted to the extent that what we consume has become central to our identity as persons."[120] Value is determined not because something, or even someone, has intrinsic value but is assigned a value in terms of exchange in the literal or figurative marketplace. While this is readily seen in objects, goods or services, this same principle has become an identifier for how people value their own selves, their bodies, as well as the bodies of other

ok — true to unawake folk

In short, we commodify selves, even our selves (Trump does this every time he blinks...)

---

[118] Anderson, *Earthen Vessels*, 43.

[119] Ibid., 50.

[120] Ibid., 74.

[handwritten: this is age-old human sin (Tamar ...)]

people. People are reduced to objects, who are valued from one person to the next, in terms of how much an "exchange" in relationship will add to one's own personal gain or well-being. In terms of a sexual relationship, the relationship is pursued in terms of a pleasurable exchange. Each person becomes an instrument for the other's own pleasure and self-identity.[121] Consider the implications of this problem, further, in terms of the American perspective on abortion. If the value of an unborn child is not intrinsic to the value of the child by virtue of his or her human identity, and is determined instead in terms of what sort of personal gain, or personal difficulty, the child will add (or take away) from the life of a prospective mother, then the child's value is relegated to the woman's choice–her evaluation of whether or not a child would be a personal benefit or detriment. Individualism is in many respects "kissing cousins with consumerism."[122] Individualism affirms self-sufficiency and independence while denigrating dependency.

[handwritten margin: unsubtle slip into pro-life talk.]

The order of creation provides a Biblical foil to the American consumeristic and individualistic personality.[123] The world and every creature is actually created, thus owing their very origins to a Creator. Dependency is affirmed from the start. The first chapter of Genesis, however, also affirms that God arranged the world into various kinds and species. "His creation is orderly–it has a variety of creatures, each with their own unique dignity and value."[124] When creatures presume that they have the choice to determine relative value, as consumerism encourages, the very order of creation is undermined. Human life is granted, in the order of creation, a special value as man is made in the "image of God" and is instructed to be fruitful and exercise dominion over other creatures and the creation itself. Anderson discerns here two "centers" of creation. In relationship to other animals, humans are at the center of creation. In relationship to God, God is at the center of creation. "These two axes–our authority over creation and

[handwritten margin: and did not hesitate in scripture to allow for miscarriage etc.]

[handwritten: Why does husbandry/stewardship always get reduced to power dominance. not really demonstrated in texts.]

[123] The "order of creation," as a theme that certainly carries a lot of baggage in regard to gender roles, is not really how Anderson seems to be employing the term. By "order of creation" it seems that Anderson is really addressing the "natural order" of all creation according to God's design.

[124] Ibid., 77.

[handwritten: In fact, they are last · most contingent on everything being here already so they can carry on...]

God's glory—meet in the person of Jesus Christ, who affirms the goodness of creation and our position as stewards within it."[125] Thus, rather than exploiting creation for man's own consumeristic benefit, man is called to care for creation. "Creation care is human care, and human care is creation care. Because our bodies connect us to others and the world, the resurrection of the body is inextricably linked to the restoration of the cosmos."[126]

While Anderson does much to recover the significance of the body for the Christian life, particularly regarding disciplines to subdue the sinful flesh, he also relegates issues of bodily care, health and fitness to the realm of mere "temporal" benefit that fails to consider a more eschatalogical now/not-yet character to the bodily wellbeing of man here and now.[127] To put it another way, while Anderson fully recognizes the unity of the human creature who is, and doesn't merely "have," body and soul, when it comes to issues of care for the total man he misses how such health and care likewise applies to the total person, rather than relegating issues of physical wellbeing to the mere "temporal" component of man's creaturely identity. Clearly Anderson affirms the value of the body to faith, but he doesn't fully explore that relationship in reverse. What is the significance of faith for the human body? To only explore the interplay of body and faith one direction, from body to faith, inherently undermines the very significance of the unity of both Anderson intends to uphold. In fairness, Anderson is not diminishing the importance of "temporal" benefit, though. Temporal concerns are valid concerns for the life of the Christian who lives in the world. Caring for the body is important. That said, his concern is that if matters of bodily care, fitness, *et al.*, are extended beyond the realm of "temporal benefit," the danger is that Christian theology could be used to further justify the popular notion that views the body as a project, or something to perfect.[128] This is

---

[125] Ibid., 78.

[126] Ibid., 82.

[127] "Bodily health is not sufficient to reverse the power of death, and hence its value is inherently temporal. It is an unqualified good—but it is a good that is subordinate to pursuing the life that we will have in the next. Our pursuit of physical fitness needs to be kept in the context of the rest of our Christian life, with our primary focus being on the formation of our character (building discipline, diligence, self-control) rather than on the pursuit of physical health *per se*." Ibid., 189.

[128] Ibid., 99-101.

certainly a caution to heed. That said, Anderson's insistence that bodily care be relegated to "temporal benefit" does not seem to cohere with his larger argument but is, admittedly, consistent with Calvin's approach to the issue. As such, as this book will focus largely on Luther's theology of the body, the emphasis within Luther on the "locatedness" of God's action in creation adds a profound incarnational/sacramental dimension to the human creature that both avoids Anderson's concern above and furthers the significance of bodily care for the life of God's people. *that's the title ...*

Wendell Berry

he is a stated Christian ...

Wendell Berry, while not a theologian *per se*, has nonetheless contributed to contemporary discussion on the body by understanding it from an agrarian perspective. As indicated earlier, the Cartesian revolution that elevated the "thinking" creature above all else took hold largely because of how the project he set in motion was codified through actual industrial and technological progress. Berry argues that technological advancement bolstered dualistic tendencies that have led to attitudes of the body viewing it more as "machine" than "creature."

Wow, reading this is like reading poetry after garbled speech ...

The danger most immediately to be feared in "technological progress" is the degradation and obsolescence of the body. Implicit in the technological revolution from the beginning has been a new version of an old dualism, one always destructive, and now more destructive than ever. For many centuries there have been people who looked upon the body, as upon the natural world, as an encumbrance of the soul, and so have hated the body, as they have hated the natural world, and longed to be free of it. They have seen the body as intolerably imperfect by spiritual standards. More recently, since the beginning of the technological revolution, more and more people have looked upon the body, along with the rest of the natural creation, as intolerably imperfect by mechanical standards. They see the body as an encumbrance of the mind– the mind, that is, as reduced to a set of mechanical ideas that can be implemented in machines – and so they hate it and long to be free of it. The body has limits that the machine does not

45

have; therefore, remove the body from the machine so that the machine can continue as an unlimited idea.[129]

Particularly in an increasingly urbanized world, where the technological and industrial marvels of man increasingly arrest the attentions of many while the natural wonders of God's creation are obscured or cast off into the recesses of daily human consciousness, the body remains the sole inescapable reminder–or, at least, the most readily obvious one– that we are still creatures. Granted, even all of man's inventions and constructions owe their origins to created matter, but an illusion is more than enough for fallen man to cling to in his desperate attempts to pursue the tempter's original lie: to be "like God," a creator rather than a creature. Wendell Berry's insights are many, and several are reflected in many of the theological works previously examined. That said, Berry's contribution to the discussion cannot be overplayed. Being that his writing is not explicitly "theology," it is no less "theological" in thrust and extends the concerns of creation care, and the orientation of the human creature toward his or her own body, into public dialogue with those who impact the contemporary world in disciplines that are not ordinarily concerned with theological questions. In other words, Berry's emphasis takes a theological concern into the public square in a relevant and profound way that resonates with the common American experience. *he is a faithful and coherent witness*

Current Scholarship and the Monism-Dualism Debate

While much of the above, from John Paul II to others engaged, seeks to move beyond the monism-dualism debate in order to conceive of the essential nature of humanity in terms more consistent with the Biblical narrative many scholars continue to wrestle with the tensions that body-soul dualism and monism present to a thorough theological expression of human essence.

According to Joel P. Green the prevailing perspectives championed today fall along a continuum between reductive materialism and radical

---

[129] Berry, *The Art of the Commonplace*, 75.

dualism—neither extreme being easily reconcilable with Christianity.[130] Green's categories of reductive materialism, radical dualism, holistic dualism, and monism summarily distinguish the various views along this continuum and, for that reason, his categories will be adopted here.

Reductive materialism. Those adhering to this view effectively suggest that anything akin to a human consciousness is only the result of some sort of biological or chemical process—either understood or yet to be understood by science—that belongs solely to a the human being's material body. The reductive materialist argues that "the human person is a physical (or material) organism whose emotional, moral and religious experiences will ultimately be explained by the natural sciences."[131] This view is essentially annihilistic—once a human being dies he or she ceases to exist in any substantial way. The deceased person ceases to be a person and is rendered as only a memory. While reductive materialists place significant stock in the sciences—particularly neuroscience—to eventually explain the human experience the must admit that to-date the sciences have yet to provide comprehensive explanations of the material mechanisms fully responsible for human sensations, memory and consciousness.

Radical dualism. Radical dualists not only argue that an immaterial component of the human being (*i.e.* soul or mind) exists but that the immaterial component of human personhood is entirely separable from the body, "having no necessary relation to the body, with the human person identified with the soul."[132] Those who use metaphors describing the body like an "earth suit" or the soul-body-relationship like a "ghost in a machine" (*i.e.* Descartes) would fall into this category of radical dualism. While radical dualism is incompatible with essential Christian doctrines— *i.e.* the doctrine of the resurrection of the body—many Christians popularly hold to such views believing that their eternal destiny is some sort of bodiless existence (*i.e.* eternity in heaven). Radical dualists view the body as something meaningless or temporary at best and downright evil at worst.

---

[130] Joel B. Green, "Body and Soul, Mind and Brain: Critical Issues," in Joel B. Green, Stuart L Palmer and Kevin Corcoran, eds. *Search of the Soul: Four Views of the Mind-Body Problem.* (InterVarsity Press, 2005): 7-32.

[131] Ibid., Kindle loc. 136.

[132] Ibid., Kindle loc. 152.

Regardless, such radical dualists do more than separate body and soul but tend to elevate the soul or mind over and against the body as the sole essential component of what it means to be fully human.

3. ——>

Holistic dualism. The various manifestations of this view commonly posit that "the human person, though composed of discrete elements, is nonetheless to be identified with the whole, which then constitutes a functional unity."[133] In short, holistic dualists maintain that there is a viable distinction between the body and the soul but nonetheless affirm that both body and soul ought to be held together as necessary components of what it means to be human. Goetz's substance dualism and Hasker's emergent dualism both fall within this category.

It is tempting to classify Stewart Goetz as a radical dualist on the one hand because he clearly prioritizes the soul over the body. It is the soul, Goetz writes, that comprises one's identity: "Because it is a necessary truth that no physical body is able to become or exist disembodied (*i.e.*, a physical body is essentially a physical body), it follows that I am a soul and not identical with my (or any) physical body."[134] Nonetheless, while the body is not identical with one's person in Goetz's view, the body is neither disparaged nor minimized in terms of its importance to the soul. In order to engage the world one's self—his soul—must cohere with a body that occupies space.[135] Put another way, Goetz is rightly viewed as a "holistic dualist" because he affirms that "the soul is present in its entirety at each point in space that it experiences sensations."[136] While Goetz argues that his view coheres most closely with ancient Christian perspectives he does not ground his view primarily through Scriptural argument but philosophical argument consisting of a series of syllogisms.

——> William Hasker's "emergent dualism" might also fall within the category of holistic dualism. Based on the philosophical notion of

---

[133] Green, "Body and Soul, Mind and Brain: Critical Issues," Kindle loc. 152.

[134] Stewart Goetz, "Substance dualism." In in Joel B. Green, Stuart L Palmer and Kevin Corcoran, eds. *Search of the Soul: Four Views on the Mind-Body Problem* (InterVarsity Press, 2005): Kindle loc. 775.

[135] Ibid., 980.

[136] Ibid., 992-993.

emergence, that "when elements of a certain sort are assembled in the right way, something new comes into being, something that was not there before" Hasker affirms that the human being is more than what is material or physical but that his consciousness, what others term the "soul," emerges as a result of man's physical existence.[137] According to Hasker's view no separate divine act to establish man's "soul" or consciousness was required—as a result of the material properties of the human body, particularly the brain, a conscious "mind" emerges that nonetheless bears no physical properties in and of itself. In other words, while the brain is constituted by atoms and molecules that mind itself has no molecular properties. One advantage of this approach is that it "immediately establishes a close connection between the mind/ soul and the biological organism, a connection that in some other forms of dualism is far more tenuous."[138] The view also coheres well with language of Genesis 2:7 which describes how God forms the body from the ground, breathes the breath of life into clay-molded body he designed, and man then becomes a living creature. There is no separate act of God creating a soul here that is infused into the body molded from the ground. In fact, it is God's breath—not a soul at all—that vivifies the body resulting in an emergent and conscious human creature. John Cooper, after surveying a long history of perspectives on body-soul-spirit including an analysis of the Biblical texts—not excluding an analysis of the intertestamental apocryphal writings—also concludes that holistic dualism is both the most consistent position relevant to scripture and remains compatible with the latest developments in science.

Monism. Monists essentially affirm that there is a single component—not necessarily material or immaterial, but one component nonetheless—which constitutes human personhood. Most contemporary monists tend to favor the material component of humanity as the sole substance of what makes one human.[139] That said, such monists need not necessarily be

---

[137] William Hasker, "On behalf of emergent dualism." In in Joel B. Green, Stuart L Palmer and Kevin Corcoran, eds. *Search of the Soul: Four Views of the Mind-Body Problem* (InterVarsity Press, 2005): Kindle locs. 1495-1496.

[138] Ibid., 1551.

[139] Idealists or "idealist monists" have attempted in the past to argue for the primacy of the soul as the sole essence of the human person. That said, few argue for such a perspective in contemporary

reductive materialists. Nancey Murphy's nonreductive physicalism and Kevin Corcoran's constitutional view of human personhood represent two modern monist positions that attempt to reconcile the affirmation of the material as man's essence with Biblical Christianity.

Fuller Theological Seminary's Nancey Murphy has, in fact, denied that the soul exists at all. Murphy's physicalism is evident—though she avoids what she also terms mere materialism: *Clay Schmidt was there explains a lot...*

> ...we are our bodies – there is no additional metaphysical element such as a mind or soul or spirit. But...this "physicalist" position need not deny that we are intelligent, moral, and spiritual. We are, at our best, complex physical organisms, imbued with the legacy of thousands of years of culture, and, most importantly, blown by the Breath of God's Spirit; we are Spirited bodies.[140]

From a physicalist perspective Murphy and those who adhere to similar theories hold that "as we go up the hierarchy of increasingly complex organisms, all of the other capacities once attributed to the soul will also turn out to be products of complex organization, rather than properties of a non-material entity."[141] Accordingly, the sciences factor in heavily to the physicalist perspective even for those, like Murphy, who believe their positions are compatible with Scripture. Murphy points out that during three different epochs of Christian history theologians have had to reevaluate their perspectives on human nature in the light of scientific discoveries. The first reevaluation occurred with the replacement of Aristotelian physics with modern physics and atomism in the seventeenth century leading to a more radical dualism than before. The second came with the Darwinian revolution in biology which led to some theologians committing themselves to dualism even further in an effort to preserve the

---

philosophy or theology.

[140] Nancey Murphy, *Bodies and Souls, or Spirited Bodies? (Current Issues in Theology)*. Kindle edition. (New York: Cambridge University Press, 2006) Kindle loc. 55.

[141] Ibid., 57

privileged place of the human creature over and against animals. The third epoch is currently underway due to rapid advancements in the cognitive neurosciences which have made it "increasingly obvious to many that the functions and attributes once attributed to the soul or mind are better understood as functions of the brain."[142]

Kevin J. Corcoran of Calvin College in *Rethinking Human Nature: A Christian Materialist Alternative to the Soul* proposes what he terms a "constitutional" view of the human person.[143] In short, Corcoran argues that the human being while not identical to his body is nonetheless *constituted* by it much like a marble statue is not identical with the substance of marble even though it is constituted by marble and is inseparable from it.

While all of the above are intriguing and to greater and lesser extents are compatible or incompatible with Christian thought, the fact remains as Green points out that the "biblical writers never explicitly take up the problem of the construction of the human person as a topic."[144] Participants in the monism–dualism debate are advancing mostly philosophical propositions which take into account in varying degrees (depending upon the thinker's own commitments) both biblical and scientific insights. Advancements in neuroscience have been particularly impactful typically bolstering the monism side of the debate. That said, the epistemological constraints of science make it incapable of necessarily excluding an immaterial component, such as the soul, from the human creature's makeup. Even if neuroscience *can* explain the properties of consciousness, as even a physicalist like Nancey Murphy admits, it does not necessarily follow that a "soul" is thereby excluded.[145] The emergence of the term "neurotheology" in recent years suggests a willingness to transcend the

---

[142] Ibid., 40

[143] Kevin J. Corcoran, *Rethinking Human Nature: A Christian Materialist Alternative to the Soul*. (Grand Rapids, Baker Academic, 2006).

[144] Joel B. Green, "'Bodies— That Is, Human Lives': A Re-examination of Human Nature in the Bible," in *Whatever Happened to the Soul? Scientific and Theological Portraits of Human Nature*, ed. Warren S. Brown, Nancey Murphy and H. Newton Malony, Theology and the Sciences (Minneapolis: Fortress, 1998), p. 154.

[145] Murphy, *Bodies and Souls, or Spirited Bodies?*

science-religion divide and explore how theological propositions and religious experience is experienced biologically.[146] Such materialistic explanations, however, neither prove nor disprove the existence of a soul. If anything, the conclusions drawn according to such theories and neuroscientific observations could be cited to argue *for* an immaterial component of man with which the brain is naturally "wired" to cooperate. In other words, neuroscientific explanations of consciousness or religious experience do not necessarily lend themselves to materialism. On the contrary, the presence of such mechanisms offers a biological signal, in fact, that the material body is designed to cohere with something akin to a soul. At the very least, such advancements lead to the acknowledgment that something "more" than the material body is something that the human being is *naturally* cognizant of. If St. Paul was correct in Romans 1:20 that the presence of God within the world is evident from the things that have been made—thereby rendering unbelievers without excuse—it should not be surprising that biology and neuroscience (the body and brain fall under the category of "things that have been made") offer such a testimony as well as geology or physics might. Thus, while scientific advancements in subjects like neuroscience might lead some to ponder the spiritual dimension of the body more thoroughly, such premises do not lead to the conclusion that the body is necessarily the sole component of the human being. A holistic approach, in fact, accounts for such evidences just as well if not better.

Materialism—if gleaned from the notion that scientific research in to the brain can explain consciousness and religious thought—is left with little recourse but to explain such phenomena as little more than a coping mechanism wired into the brain through millennia of evolutionary development. Even this interpretation, however, is problematic. If evolutionary thought suggests that such features would develop in a species' quest for survival, one is at a loss to explain how the emergence of such a

---

[146] See, for example, the work of Andrew Newberg and Mark Robert Waldman—*i.e.* Andrew Newberg and Mark Robert Waldman. *Born to Believe: God, Science, and the Origin of Ordinary and Extraordinary Beliefs*. (Simon and Schuster, 2007); Andrew B. Newberg. *Principles of Neurotheology*. (Ashgate Publishing, Ltd., 2010); "The Neuroscientific Study of Spiritual Practices." *Frontiers in Psychology* 5 (2014): 215; *How God Changes Your Brain: Breakthrough Findings from a Leading Neuroscientist*. (Ballantine Books, 2010).

52

coping mechanism would offer a significant enough biological advantage to become such a universal neurological phenomenon within the human species. A better explanation is, in fact, that the religious machinations of the brain are in fact evidence that the human creature is *naturally* religious— created in such a manner by his very nature, so that man is intended to live in relationship to God.

thesis of the God spot guy

In short, the monism–dualism debate is one that emerges more from *exactly* philosophy than biblical theology *per se*. Dogmatic theological commitments pertinent to the relationship of body and soul are not necessarily warranted if one accepts that Scripture alone is the norm and rule of Christian belief.

P. Ko Bedr

At the same time, some of the perspectives outlined above are more or less compatible with Scripture and warrant either consideration or rejection accordingly. That said, it should be recognized at this point that this author finds the perspectives beneath the heading of *holistic dualism* the most biblically compatible and for many of the reasons outlined in the prior paragraph does not find the Christian materialist perspectives altogether convincing in spite of some of the advantages they offer. At the same time this author believes that the terms of the monism–dualism debate are not biblically derived and, therefore, are not the primary schema through which Christians ought to understand the essence of the human creature. In many respects, "Who Cares?" really is the biblical answer to the monism–dualism debate. What the biblical narrative suggests—as will be shown in Chapter 2 below—is not a primary concern with how the components of the human creature relates to himself, but how the human creature as a whole relates to both the Creator and the rest of creation. *methodology i.e.,*

no! WHY we relate. Gods' purpose of us.

So Luther would say Do not speculate on things above

The Methodological Procedure to Be Employed

It is a reasonable question to ask why Luther would be chosen as the figure to bring into the larger conversation regarding theologies of the body. This book will seek to discern Luther's theology of the human creature, not necessarily a "Lutheran" theology of the body. The reason for this is multifaceted. First, Luther is a figure who speaks into many theological traditions beyond Lutheranism, including most Reformed churches. He is a figure more universally respected than the later theologians within Lutheranism. Luther is a widely hailed figure even in protestant

more primary that Luther identified the self and to give moral self... the shaky conscience, and self-consciousness See Luther and the Modern self

denominations which do not owe their heritage directly to the Lutheran reformation. Even Roman Catholics, who still formally consider Luther a heretic, frequently engage his works. It is the desire of this author to contribute to discussions regarding the body beyond the borders of those churches with a Reformation heritage. Second, Luther offers a unique voice to the discussion that has not been fully engaged in current theologies of the body. Luther's "earthy" theology makes him a more natural import into somatic discussion than other protestant reformers who tended to spiritualize the physical world. This is evident particularly in his sacramental theology and in his pre-sacramental emphases in his works on the Old Testament. The insights here, however, need not necessarily touch upon or breach controversies of sacramentalism that continue to divide the Lutherans from the other churches of the Reformation today.

Most of the insights relevant for these purposes that are gleaned from Luther may also be embraced by Covenant theologians who embrace the "earthy" and physical phenomena related to covenant signs. Further, many of Luther's themes regarding the creaturely identity of man simply are not as prominent in post-Reformation Lutheran theologians. This book will navigate these tensions while avoiding the temptation to get caught up in debates over sacramental "presence" that separate these traditions. There are plenty of other works that rehearse and rehash that centuries' long debate.

The problems presented by various dualisms in the western world of thought have been widely addressed. Many Biblical theologians have thoroughly examined the disparity between the Hellenistic and Hebraic views of man. As an Old Testament theologian, himself, Luther's thought is mostly consistent (or, at least comparable) with what contemporary theologians have said about the relationship of body, soul and spirit to human identity. While sometimes employing dichotomous (body and soul) and at other times a trichotomous (body, soul and spirit) categories, what is clear is that while Luther certainly distinguishes these parts of man according to his Biblical insight, he nonetheless holds them together as essential to components of human identity—*totus homo*. This will have to be discussed in further detail.

Primary Source Material

Luther's Genesis Lectures (1535-1545) will serve as an "entry point" into Luther's greater corpus on the topic. There are two reasons why these lectures will take center stage in this book. First, being that this book will bring Luther's theology into conversation with contemporary discussion on the body, Luther's comments on Genesis have to be considered. John Paul II, as indicated earlier, elucidates the most fundamental categories concerning his theology of the body from the first two chapters of Genesis. In order to adequately bring Luther's insights into conversation with John Paul II, Luther's own reflections on Genesis have to be given primary consideration. Second, as Johannes Schwanke has persuasively argued, the Genesis lectures reflect the "mature testimony of the late Luther, and one could even say that they represent his Summa."[147] Robert Kolb has further bolstered Schwanke's position by demonstrating how Luther's earlier sermons on Genesis reflect Luther's primary paradigmatic understanding of the human creature according to two kinds of righteousness.[148] Having considered Kolb's argument, this author believes that similar insights regarding the two kinds of righteousness are maintained in the *Genesisvorelesung* from Luther's later years.

Relying so heavily on Luther's *Genesisvorelesung* has both some advantages and challenges that should be noted at this point. Beyond serving as a testimony of the "mature" Luther it is also a work that spanned the greater part of a decade. The final day of May, 1535, when concluding his lectures on Psalm 90, Luther gave notice to his students of this new final project.[149] Throughout the lectures Luther freely engages other topics of his own theological emphasis, even when the text does not seem to directly warrant it. What Luther views as Old Testament "means of grace," such as the tree of the knowledge of good and evil, Noah's entrance into the Ark, the

---

[147] Johannes Schwanke, "Luther on Creation," In *Harvesting Martin Luther's Reflections on Theology, Ethics, and the Church*, ed. Timothy J. Wengert, (Grand Rapids: Eerdmans, 2004) Kindle Edition. Kindle loc. 873.

[148] Robert Kolb, "God and His Human Creatures in Luther's Sermons on Genesis: The Reformer's Early Use of His Distinction of Two Kinds of Righteousness," *Concordia Journal* 33, no. 2 (2007): 166-84

[149] "*Postea suscipiam praelegendum Genesis, ut operemur quidquam et ita in verbo et opere dei moriamur.*" *WA* 42, vii.

flood, or circumcision, frequently evoke ad hoc discussions on Baptism or the Lord's Supper. This is not a feature of Luther's lecturing that indicates a man who frequently went off-topic so much as it indicates Luther's view on God's consistency. God continues to engage his creatures in the same manner, particularly in corporeal forms, across both testaments and still does so in Luther's own day.

Accordingly, Genesis is not of mere scholarly or historical interest for Luther, but is paradigmatically and practically relevant for God's people in all times and places. Luther's emphasis on the corporeality of man, particularly as God engages man's bodily senses through the means of grace, is especially pronounced in his *Genesisvorelesung*. Nonetheless, as Genesis is not the locus for all of Luther's major doctrines, including the two kinds of righteousness and the sacraments which will be prominently featured in this book, other works will need to be regularly engaged. One should not necessarily expect a fully nuanced theology to emerge in every instance that a doctrine is cited. For Luther's students, who were well versed with Luther's theology in general, the context of his more nuanced theological positions could have been assumed and read in to his comments on Genesis. As such, when the discussion calls for it, engaging Luther's fuller corpus is appropriate and sometimes necessary. Certain writings will thematically emerge to the fore when appropriate to further elucidate Luther's commentary. For example, Luther's *The Magnificat* (1521)[150] offers one of his clearest expositions of the relationship between body, soul and spirit within the human creature. His *Commentary on 1 Corinthians 15*[151] offers the fullest expression of Luther's theology of the resurrected body and will have to be consulted.

Luther's additional writings will also need to be consulted due to the questionable accuracy of the Genesis lectures themselves. While this author finds the lectures to be mostly consistent with Luther's thought and likely close-to-true to Luther's original lectures, it should not go unstated that the veracity of the text that is extant today is not without its critics. In the 1930s

---

[150] Martin Luther, *Luther's Works* (Saint Louis and Philadelphia: Concordia and Fortress, 1958-1986) [henceforth *LW*] 21:1-294.

[151] *LW* 28:59-213

Erich Seeberg and, more thoroughly, his student Peter Meinhold published some seemingly devastating source-critical analyses of Luther's Genesis lectures. Some of Meinhold's initial concerns should be granted. Luther never published these lectures nor were his lecture notes preserved for posterity. The lectures, as presently presented, were chiefly edited together by Veit Dietrich (along with Hieronymus Besold, Caspar Cruciger and Georg Rörer) from the notes of Luther's students. Basing his results on a study of the theology of Veit Dietrich in relation to both Luther and Melanchthon, Meinhold concluded that the lectures presented "traces of an alien theology" sometimes reflecting the "Melanchthonian" voice of its editors often more prominently than Luther's.[152]

What should be made of Meinhold's conclusions? First, it is true that the text reflects certain editorial liberties.[153] That said, such instances are not difficult to identify and typically do not interfere with the prevailing theological or exegetical point the text is making. Some editorial liberty, particularly when editing together a variety of notes that lack continuity, should be expected. Meinhold's conclusions, following other early 20th Century perspectives, also rest on an exaggerated disjunction between Luther's and Melanchthon's thought that has since been ameliorated by more recent scholarship. The attempt to somehow divorce Melanchton's thought from Luther's was a construction of the Gnesio-Lutherans who were unwilling to admit that the Luther who accepted Melancthon's *Variata* of the Augsburg Confession—the very version signed by John Calvin—could have been the real Luther. The evidence suggests—including the evidence of the *Genesisvorelesung* that the "mature" Luther was more open to diversity in theological expression than he was earlier in his theological development. While there were substantive differences between Luther and Melanchthon, more frequently than not their differences in terms of style, emphasis, intention for writing, and terminology when carefully considered reveal that

---

[152] Erich Seeberg, *Studien zu Luthers Genesisvorlesung* (Gütersloh: Bertelsmann, 1932); and Peter Meinhold, *Die Genesisvorlesung Luthers und ihre Herausgeber* (Stuttgart: W. Kohlhammer, 1936).

[153] For example, lecturing on Gen. 4:10, probably during 1536, a reference is made to the martyrdom of the Englishman Robert Barnes who died in 1540. *LW* 1:288. The work of the editor is also evidenced in occasional references to the "dear reader" (for example, *LW* 1:184).

the gulf between Luther and Melanchthon is not as wide as some have supposed.[154]

While Meinhold identifies certain hallmark "Melanchthonian" teachings, such as a symbolic interpretation of the sacraments and the psychological impact of the sacraments on the recipients, Meinhold is straining for gnats when he substantiates his claims according to the *Genesisvorelesung*.[155] His view relies upon a "Gnesio" understanding of the late-Luther that might not have been true to fact. Meinhold's method is also problematic as he expressly attempts to judge the *Genesisvorelesung*, a document incomparable in size and importance from this period of Luther's life, by comparing the content nearly exclusively to the *younger* Luther.[156] Again, this was a tendency of the so-called Gnesio-Lutherans who largely carried the Lutheran banner forward into the next generation. Even if there is some "Melanchthonian" influence in Veit Dietrich's final edit of the lectures such impact is doubtfully significant and likely was intended to corroborate with rather than differ from Luther's original content. Veit Dietrich was well acquainted with both Luther and Melanchthon and, in the course of his edits, may have needed to "fill in the gaps" that the extant notes on Luther's original lectures did not fill in for him.

This is not the result of malicious intent but the result of a conscientious editor who strove to remain faithful to Luther's original

---

[154] For example, see Robert Kolb, *Bound Choice, Election, and Wittenberg Theological Method: Martin Luther to the Formula of Concord,* (Grand Rapids, MI: Eerdmans, 2005).

[155] See Meinhold, 389f. Meinhold cites, to substantiate his claim, *WA* 43:305 (*LW* 4:236). Commenting on Gen. 24:1-4 Luther suggests that the sacrament of the Lord's Table was instituted by Christ in order that " we might eat and drink his body and blood in order to buoy up our consciences and to strengthen our faith." How this reflects a symbolic interpretation of the supper is difficult to discern and even more the claim that such a reference to Christian conscience is a psychological assessment imported from an "alien" Melanchthonian theology is a stretch. Luther regularly appeals to Christian conscience in works that he himself had published during his life, even within the context of the Lord's Supper. For example, *LW* 26:44, 36:172.

[156] "*Das sachliche Kriterium für sein Authentie blidet hier die Theologie des jungen Luther, die überraschend stark in all ihrer Grundgedanken in dem großen Alterswerk wiederkehrt.*" Meinhold, 427. This is a grave methodological problem on Meinhold's part. Even Luther, himself, prefacing the German edition of his works (first published in 1539, at the same time he was lecturing on Genesis to his students) indicated a significant disjunction between his current and earlier works. *LW* 32:283. He made this point even more poignantly when prefacing the Latin edition of his works in 1545. *LW* 32:328. Pelikan also rightly criticizes Meinhold's over-reliance upon the young Luther for his analysis. See *LW* 1:xii.

lectures while also rendering the final product palatable to the reader. It is the estimation of this author, then, that Luther's *Lectures on Genesis* (1535–1545) accurately reflect Luther's own thoughts. That said, due to the fact that it is an edited work with clear editorial liberties taken on occasion by Dietrich and company, the lectures will not be the exclusive fount from which this book draws. By considering the greater body of Luther's works in conjunction with his lectures on Genesis it should both serve to further substantiate the claims this book will make while also bolstering the reliability of the published lectures themselves.

Luther's two kinds of righteousness serves as a defining paradigm in Luther's thought allowing him to conceive of the human creature, not primarily as a sum of his various parts, but relationally and holistically.[157] This relational conception of the human creature holds man "together" as a total human, in proper relationship with both God and the world. It is not as though the soul is the component of man that relates to God, while the body relates to the world. For Luther, it is always the total human being, in both relationships, that is considered. As such, understanding the "body" through Luther as the primary focus of this book will have to account for how it is to be properly understood in relationship before God, as well as before the world. While the "body" is not explicitly addressed in any particular treatise of Luther's, it is dealt with frequently as a component of Luther's larger concern to understand the relationship of the human creature before God, and before the world. Luther's writings dealing with the two kinds of righteousness will serve as a sort of "lens" through which Luther's other occasional insights on the body are best understood. Accordingly, Luther's writings on the two kinds of righteousness will be given significant attention.[158] Among those, his *Galatians Commentary* (1535)[159] which represents "the culmination of his thinking on the two kinds

---

[157] Kolb and Arand, *The Genius of Luther's Theology*, 95.

[158] For example, "The Heidelberg Disputation" *LW* 31:35-69; Luther's sermon entitled "Three Kinds of Righteousness" (1518), found in *Dr. Martin Luther's Werke* (Weimar: Bohlau, 1993–) [henceforth, *WA*] 2:41-47; "Two Kinds of Righteousness" (1519), *LW* 31:293-306 ; "On Monastic Vows," *LW* 44:243-400 ; and Luther's sermons on Genesis (1523/1527), *WA* 24:1-710.

[159] *LW* 26, 27.

of righteousness"[160] will take center stage. Though not written by Luther, the *Augsburg Confession*, and particularly the *Apology*, follows the two kinds of righteousness paradigmatically,[161] and will also be considered on occasion. That said, there are particular writings of interest where the subject of man is explicitly engaged, such as *The Disputation Concerning Man* (1536).[162] This piece will be of particular significance, as written not long after fully articulating the two kinds of righteousness in his *Galatians Commentary*. In it, Luther argues for a theological understanding of man that cannot be fully understood or embraced by the philosophers, rejecting particularly Aristotle's conception of man. As this book's title suggests, however, Luther's *Small Catechism* and *Large Catechism* reflect his theology of the human creature in meaningful, and practical ways for the life of the common Christian. Intending to engage a holistic approach to human creatureliness, the catechisms must factor in prominently to this work. Other writings within Luther's works will be cited, when appropriate, and engaged occasionally. The above, though, will serve as the "guiding" texts to define Luther's theology of the human creature.

When Luther's writings are consulted this author will examine his words according to the original Latin and/or German on the basis of the *Weimarer Ausgabe* (WA), the critical edition of Luther's writings begun in 1883. When translations are available from the "American Edition" of Luther's works (LW) those translations will be quoted and cited. In the event that the translations from the "American Edition" need amendment or further commentary according to their original languages such will be indicated as appropriate. The original languages will only be quoted when necessary to elucidate Luther's point beyond what the English translation is capable. Unless otherwise indicated, translations from the WA will be this author's own.

---

[160] Kolb and Arand, *The Genius of Luther's Theology,* 25.

[161] See Charles P. Arand, "Two Kinds of Righteousness as a Framework for Law and Gospel in the Apology," *Lutheran Quarterly* 15 (2001), 417-439.

[162] *LW* 34:133-144

Theological Method and Structure

While Luther's reputation and influence is undoubtable, he was far from inerrant. A responsible examination of the topic must begin where Luther also began in his theological method—with a responsible exegesis of Holy Scripture. Luther himself lamented how many took his own writings as if they were only a little lower than the Gospels in authority. He recognized his own fallibility and hoped that subsequent generations would consistently hold his own insights accountable to Scripture. True to Luther's wish, and to sound theological method, we will engage a relevant exegesis of relevant passages and biblical themes before diving headlong into Luther's comments on the topic. This will provide a standard by which Luther's writings, too, while mostly received favorably by this author must also be compared and, at times, appropriately critiqued in light of the Word of God. While Luther is helpful—this author's concern is not merely to offer interesting insights into Luther's thought, but by applying a helpful perspective from Luther to better articulate what Scripture has to say about the Christian's relationship to his or her body today. *So a Luther hermeneutic?*

Particular themes within Luther's theology, albeit understood through the "lens" of his paradigmatic understanding of the "two kinds of righteousness," will individually emerge as they appropriately engage bodily existence. As a prevalent theme, Luther's understanding of Christian vocation will be addressed in chapters two and three. The "original vocation" *vocation* of Edenic man, the subsequent curse post-fall whereby the ground is worked with toil and pain, factors into Luther's *Genesisvorelesung*. The relationship of man, having been fashioned from the ground itself which becomes the very object he is called to work in, will prove worthy fodder for consideration. In what respect is vocation, be it "working the ground" directly, or serving one's neighbor, both a fulfillment of man's original Edenic call and also a participation in the eschatological age to come? Such questions will lead to more fundamental questions regarding the discipline of the body as well. If *too literal* the ground is unruly after the fall, and can only be disciplined with painful toil, how should the body be considered that was fashioned originally from the ground also? Luther's writings on monastic vows frequently engage matters regarding the discipline of the flesh, both in terms of its care and also for subduing the sinful nature. The corporeal nature of Luther's

61

theology of the means of grace, particularly as it relates to man's own bodily existence, will frequently emerge. The unity of man in body and soul, *totus homo*, is a necessary theme to engage. Regin Prenter's landmark study, *Spiritus Creator*, will be consulted in chapter five as Prenter demonstrates through Luther's pneumatology the unity of spirit and flesh which also has bearing on Luther's understanding of man.[163]

These "themes" will naturally engage relevant questions of contemporary concern. How does Luther's understanding of the Spirit–Flesh union of man, *totus homo*, speak to dualistic conceptions of man today? As such, how does "caring for the body" of oneself and of one's neighbor, properly embrace the creaturely identity of man according to contemporary vocation? How do the challenges of a contemporary world, where man's inventions often "work the ground" on our behalf, challenge our understanding of the human being as a "creature" and how should these challenges be addressed? Where manual labor can no longer be an assumed component of human survival, how has physical fitness emerged as a way to address the need of man as he was created to be working and active? How can the body be properly cared for, in a manner that accords with God's design for the body to function optimally, without pursuits of vanity dominating the physical fitness enterprise? How do such questions of the disciplined flesh likewise challenge libertine approaches to the body in American culture today? Further, as the matter of human sexuality factors prominently in the discussions of the body both in John Paul II and also in Luther, such matters will have to be engaged. How is the human creature *essentially* a sexual being? What is God's original design for the body, in terms of the sexual relationship between man and woman, properly upheld? How might contemporary questions regarding sexuality, from divorce and remarriage to the matter of homosexuality, be reframed from the perspective of a theology of the body that understands the beauty of human sexuality as

---

[163] "In all Luther's difference with the enthusiasts we are concerned with only one thing: the exclusive understanding of the Spirit as the Spirit of God. Over against this is the idea of the enthusiasts about spirit and spirituality, which is oriented from the point of view of a spiritualistic, metaphysical dualism between the body and the soul, between the visible and the invisible, between matter and thought. To Luther the Spirit is not 'something spiritual.' The Spirit is the Triune God himself in his real presence as our sphere of life. Everything pertaining to the Spirit is brought into the unbroken, creative-redemptive work of the Triune God, and therefore it is spiritual." Regin Prenter, *Spiritus Creator*, translated by John M. Jensen, (Eugene, OR: Wipf and Stock, 1953), 288.

a component of human identity from the beginning? This book could engage any number of themes regarding the body. For the sake of brevity, however, this book is limited to the above concerns. The reason these themes, as opposed to others that could be chosen, have been selected is that it is this author's judgment that these themes reflect the most pressing concerns in contemporary society that can be addressed most immediately from the theological questions that this work intends to engage.

Attempting to structure a work on a particular subject, such as the body, according to the two kinds of righteousness alone is difficult. As already mentioned, the two kinds of righteousness functions in Luther not as a particular article of faith but as a norming distinction that is woven throughout the vast tapestry of his works. Luther's two kinds of righteousness functions much like covenantal distinctions function in Reformed theologies. In fact, it can be argued that Luther's distinction between the two kinds of righteousness is an approximate affirmation of Covenant theology articulated in other terms. *but you do not demonstrate this*

Luther's thoughts on the body, specifically, are nuanced according to *context* the context of the body prior to man's fall into sin, after the fall, and *pre* according to man's bodily redemption in Christ. Accordingly, the following *ante* pages will address the body according to these three specific contexts and *redeemed* conditions. This will also more closely parallel the structure John Paul II employed in his lectures. As Luther does himself throughout his works, the two kinds of righteousness will also be woven into the content of this examination according to the above three situations.

While Luther certainly factors into this book in a prominent way, it should be noted that this work does not intend to *primarily* contribute to Luther studies in general. The purpose, rather, will be to introduce Luther's *categories* theological categories relevant to his understanding of the human creature into contemporary discussion on the topic of the body. As such, while Luther's writings will be considered historically and contextually, it would be beyond the scope and purpose of this book to dive into various schools of thought, or interpretations, of Luther. Luther scholarship will be consulted, and insights gleaned therein will be heeded accordingly, but they will not factor prominently into this book. Further, the thesis of this book is not that Luther has thoroughly developed a theology of the body, *per se*, but that his theology bestows us a guiding framework for understanding the human creature by which a theology of the body can be developed that will engage contemporary theologies of the body as well as general concerns of the body in contemporary culture.

At times, we will have to engage contemporary themes that Luther had never imagined. While many issues that are faced today were similarly issues in Luther's day, other issues that have arisen regarding the body never could have been predicted much less expounded upon from Luther's position in the Sixteenth Century. This is another reason why Luther's paradigmatic categories, not his writings *per se*, will govern the presentation below. While Luther may never address at length, for example, the contemporary problem of sedentary living and the rising obesity epidemic in America, his theological categories can nonetheless serve as a helpful "lens" through which such contemporary matters can be engaged.

Because it is the intention of this author to bring Luther into conversation with contemporary discussion regarding the body, however, many of the contemporary writers cited above will continue to be engaged at more depth according to various subjects as they arise. Looming the largest in somatological discussion, John Paul II's works will be most prominently featured. Luther will serve, then, to provide a perspective on many of the themes being engaged today that is often lacking in contemporary somatology. As such, as the various chapters evolve, addressing the human creature in the prelapsarian Edenic, post-Edenic sin and redemption contexts, the most relevant contemporary authors who similarly engage such topics will be addressed. Luther will serve, then, as a sort of conversation partner with these authors at times offering critique of their perspectives, and at other times furthering their arguments through a different framework.

The Outcome(s) Anticipated

Luther's theology offers an emphasis on the creaturely dimension of the human creature, particularly through his paradigmatic distinction between the "two kinds of righteousness," that can enter into contemporary dialogues on theologies of the body. Examining Luther's theology as proposed above will provide a foundation for articulating a theology of the body that will add a profound dimension to contemporary discussion. His emphasis serves to add a dimension to dialogues within Roman Catholicism that moves beyond the sexual dimension of human personhood and expands the "relational" character of man into daily life. This theme will ring true particularly as Luther's response to monasticism in his own day engages the daily, vocational, life of the common person. Luther's "means of grace" theology, regardless of whether or not evangelicals will embrace it entirely, nonetheless can lead evangelical thinkers to ponder more thoroughly how caring for the body, in general, has profound implications on the life and faith of the Christian. What further emerges, from Luther, allows a theology of the body to be articulated that is not purely theoretical, but also immensely practical. As Luther rejoices, "I am God's creature!" he proclaims into daily life a profound insight that can impact how one identifies with his or her body over and against the trappings of the contemporary world.

CHAPTER 2:
AN EXEGETICAL STUDY

AS ARTICULATED ABOVE THE PURPOSE OF THIS BOOK is not merely an exploratory study into Luther's thoughts on the body. Rather, Luther offers insights discerned from Holy Scripture which can help elucidate a Biblical theology of the body that will contribute to matters of crucial importance facing the church today. Luther was not infallible. He begged his own students and readers to test his teachings according the Word of God. Accordingly, a responsible appropriation of Luther's thought into matters of such importance must be accompanied by an obligatory study of the pertinent Biblical texts which speak to the topic at hand. This chapter, through a careful exegesis of pertinent texts, will present a Biblical theology of the body by which Luther's insights in latter chapters can be evaluated.

The Body in the Old Testament

Contemporary theologies of the body rightly place a great deal of emphasis on the creation of the human being in Genesis 1–2. It is here where the formation of the body, the infusion of the body with God's breath of life, and the emergence of the human being as a bearer of God's image and steward over the created order is established. John Paul II's *Man and Woman He Created Them: A Theology of the Body*, which will be engaged at length throughout this book, begins with the Genesis account of creation as pivotal for understanding the body's role in both testaments and while engaging contemporary concerns, particularly involving human sexuality. The greater theme of this book will engage Luther's reflections on the body primarily through his Genesis lectures and, more specifically, in his commentary on the creation account. If the Old Testament presents a "theology of the body" at all it does so inseparably from its theology of creation.

Even this point, however, begs the question regarding the role of creation as a theme within the Old Testament. If the Old Testament perspective on the human body is dependent upon an Old Testament theology of creation, it follows that the Old Testament theology of creation must, itself, be solidified before proceeding to relevant insights concerning the body becomes possible. The centrality of creation as a formative principle *dash —* for the theology of the Old Testament cannot be taken for granted. *only way we are / have to be able*

In fact, for most of the last century-plus the theology of creation has *to be* been exorcised from Old Testament theologies as a matter of mere tangential *reflecting / on* importance. As Rolf Rendtorff put it, the theme of creation has been little *and* more than one of many "'proverbial step-children in the recent discipline of *Solver,* Old Testament theology."[164] Many Old Testament theologies have effectively skipped past the first eleven chapters of Genesis as a casual reader might skip past a book's preface; instead, these theologies have tended to begin with the call of Abram in Genesis 12.[165] This trend coincides with the notion that the history of God's Old Testament people began, in fact, with Abram rather than Adam—the former being the originator of the Israelite faith while the later marked its beginnings in myth alone.

Perhaps the most pivotal influence on relegating the doctrine of creation to the periphery of Old Testament theology was Gerhard von Rad. In a 1936 essay entitled "The Theological Problem of the Old Testament Doctrine of Creation," von Rad summarily argued that the Old Testament presents no comprehensive doctrine of creation, *per se*, or any perspective on Yahweh as Creator, except insofar as either theme emerges subserviently to the Old Testament doctrine of redemption.[166] As von Rad put it, the

---

[164] Rolf Rendtorff, "Some Reflections on Creation as a Topic of Old Testament Theology," in Eugene Ulrich, *et al.*, eds., *Priests, Prophets and Scribes. Essays on the Formation and Heritage of Second Temple Judaism in Honour of Joseph Blenkinsopp* (Sheffield, England: Sheffield Academic Press, 1992), pp. 204-212.

[165] Ibid., 204.

[166] Gerhard von Rad, "The Theological Problem of the Old Testament Doctrine of Creation, 1936," in *The Problem of the Hexateuch and Other Essays*. Translated by E. W. Trueman Dicken. (New York: McGraw-Hill, 1966): 131-143

because it was a given category (the category is God)

"Yahwistic belief in the doctrine of creation never attained to the stature of a relevant, independent doctrine...[but it was found to be] related, and indeed subordinated, to soteriological considerations."[167] That said, beyond Genesis' first two chapters the remainder of the Old Testament concerns postlapsarian people—and all of it was composed, originally, with the concerns of a postlapsarian people as its audience. How else should von Rad suppose that a theology of creation would function if not within a redemptive context? It appears that von Rad puts the egg before the chicken, and does so with more dogmatic conviction than the debate truly warrants. Even the notion of redemption *implies* some sort of fall from which man must be redeemed. In other words, a theology of redemption presupposes a theology of creation. Redemption, by definition, suggests a theology of creation which precedes it both temporally and conceptually.

Brueggeman credits von Rad's position to a debt owed to Karl Barth whose dialectical theology emerged from an antagonism between revelation and natural theology, or between faith and religion. This struggle has been reflected particularly in the theologies of the German churches, both Lutheran and Reformed, in the 20th century. As Brueggeman put it,

> *ironically the emphasis on the kind creation was ungoen and not sopial...*
>
> Von Rad's framing of the problem transposed the opposition of Baal versus Yahweh, Israelite faith versus Canaanite religion, into the church struggle in which the opposing religion came to be regarded as natural religion. This transposition alerts us to the likelihood that from the outset, von Rad's understanding of creation in the Old Testament was shaped by the German church struggle. Von Rad's cultural context caused him to pose the question as he did, because Canaanite Baal religion with its accent on fertility was easily paralleled with "Blood and Soil" religion in Germany. In so doing, he made creation a quite marginal matter in Old Testament theology, and his decision had far-reaching consequences.[168]

---

[167] Ibid., 142.

[168] Walter Brueggeman, *Book that Breathes New Life (Theology and the Sciences)*. (Minneapolis: Fortress Press, 2005): 84.

In a similar vein, Brueggeman has identified in G. Ernest Wright a similar Barthian dialectic between nature and religion, exacerbated by his otherwise worthy attempt to demonstrate the uniqueness of Yahwism against Canaanite religion. Wright demonstrated that Yahweh is *sui generis* with no part of his essence or identity derived from such other gods. While Wright effectively countered the claim that the Old Testament emerged with similitude to the mythologies of Canaanite religion, he and a full generation of Old Testament scholars who followed suit pursued the nature versus religion dichotomy yielding "a form of faith that is removed from human birth, suffering, and dying—bodily and communal processes in which the mystery of human life is lodged."[169] While the perspective of Wright and those thereafter effectively prevented the reduction of the divine to the mere natural, it also became a reiteration of Cartesian dualism "that served masculine logic while not appreciating the femininematernal hosting of the mystery of God-given life as an important theological datum."[170]

The theses of von Rad, Wright and other critics, however, began to be seriously questioned by Old Testament exegetes in the 1970s. James Barr's 1961 publication of *The Semantics of Biblical Language* became a sort of Copernican revolution in Old Testament studies. Barr challenged the then in-vogue approach of etymology-based word study and an over reliance upon word equivalents in other Semitic languages, such as Ugaritic, to decipher the meanings inherent in many Old Testament words.[171] Others followed suit in subsequent decades, such as Brevard Childs, who published a number of studies demonstrating that an overreliance upon history while neglecting literary context leads to untenable interpretations of Old Testament passages.[172]

In 1971 Claus Westermann wrote an essay seeking to revive the theology of creation as a prominent Old Testament theme. According to

---

[169] Ibid., 85.

[170] Ibid.

[171] James Barr, *The Semantics of Biblical Language* (Oxford: Clarendon Press, 1961).

[172] See Brevard S. Childs, *Biblical Theology in Crisis* (Philadelphia: Westminster, 1970), and *Biblical Theology of the Old And New Testaments: Theological Reflection on the Christian Bible* (Minneapolis: Fortress, 1992).

Westermann, "The acting of God in creation and his acting in history stand in relation to one another in the Old Testament; the one is not without the other…Creation and history arise out of the same origin and move toward the same goal."[173]

Frank Moore Cross in *Canaanite Myth and Hebrew Epic* proposed that the separation of creation from redemption in von Rad and others amounted to an either/or fallacy arguing, instead, that the two are linked—acts of redemption have creation-oriented ends.[174] More recently, Terrence Fretheim has argued that the very impetus of redemption comes from God's desire to restore his threatened creation. He wrote: the fact that "the Bible begins with Genesis, not Exodus, with creation, not redemption, is of immeasurable importance in understanding all that follows."[175] The Lord redeemed Israel not solely for her own sake, but for the sake of all creation (Ex 9:16). When the Lord intervenes on behalf of Israel he does so not as an end in itself, but in service of all of creation.[176] Accordingly, following Fretheim's impetus, a theology of the body's redemption—including its inherent meaning and value for human life—should begin in creation as well.

Genesis 1-2: Origins and Order

When the contemporary reader approaches Genesis 1-2, or the topic of creation in general, he is likely inclined to think in terms of the *material* origins of the world and all it contains—including human bodies. In other words, how did the material world come to be? The things that one can see, or touch, or otherwise comprehend with one of the five senses—how did these things come to exist? With respect to human beings, the question becomes "What *material* makes up the constituent parts of man?" These questions preoccupy the modern mind. As such, when approaching these

---

[173] Claus Westermann, "Creation and History in the Old Testament," in *Creation*, trans. John J. Scullion (Philadelphia: Fortress, 1974), 24, 34.

[174] Frank Moore Cross, *Canaanite Myth and Hebrew Epic: Essays in the History of the Religion of Israel* (Cambridge, MA: Harvard University Press, 1973).

[175] Terrence Fretheim, *God and the World in the Old Testament: A Relational Theology of Creation* (Nashville: Abingdon, 2005), xix.

[176] Lessing, "The Good Life: Health, Fitness, and Bodily Welfare," 37.

texts modern concerns for material origins are often read into the text. The question, however, that must be asked is whether or not this is the *primary* question the text intends to answer. *and the answer is no, it is a mythic narrative that means to God.*

It is not merely the preoccupation of materiality in modernity, however, that has led to an overemphasis on material origins in interpretations of Genesis 1-2; *Dogmengeschichte* must also share the blame. Indeed, *creatio ex nihilo*, has loomed thematically large in the history of dogma. As will be demonstrated later via the work of Johannes Schwanke it was a major theme in Luther's theology of creation as well.[177] The proposition that God created the material world from nothing, *ex nihilo*, is a biblical doctrine with its *sedes doctrinae* resting not only upon Genesis 1-2 but upon texts like John 1:3, Colossians 1:16 and Hebrews 11:3. The importance of *creatio ex nihilo* as a refutation of materialistic, Gnostic and pantheistic worldviews is affirmed. John 1:3, for example, was likely targeted by the beloved Apostle against Gnostics who viewed the material world as a sort of aborted mistake.[178] This was not the worldview against which the Mosaic creation narrative was penned.

While *creatio ex nihilo* is not explicitly affirmed it is undoubtedly implied in Genesis 1:1 by the use of the Hebrew verb . A survey of the uses of בָּרָא throughout the Old Testament shows, in each instance, that God is the *KEY* subject of the verb. It is God, alone, who creates in the technical sense—and God creates freely and unimpededly. The word also denotes, throughout its Old Testament use, the "initiating of something new" or "bringing into existence."[179] That said, the materiality of creation out of nothing cannot be considered the prevailing theme of Genesis 1-2.[180] What the Mosaic account

---

[177] Johannes Schwanke, "Luther on Creation," In *Harvesting Martin Luther's Reflections on* *[Read]* *Theology, Ethics, and the Church*, ed. Timothy J. Wengert, (Grand Rapids: Eerdmans, 2004) Kindle Edition.

[178] For a brief discussion of Valentinus' Gnostic mythology see the introductory chapter of this book, as well as Brown, *The Body and Society: Men, Women, and Sexual Renunciation in Early Christianity*, 108.

[179] *TWOT,* 1:127.

[180] In a word study of all the Old Testament uses of the word בָּרָא John Walton has concluded that while the word always has God as its subject—either explicitly or implicitly—the object of the verb can possibly indicate material origins but, almost always, includes a functional meaning. In other words, if Walton's analysis is correct, what God sets out to do when he creates (בָּרָא) is preeminently concerned

affirms by declaring that God created, בְּרָא אֱלֹהִים, is not the materiality of the world and its origins, *per se*, but the *relationship* of all God's creations—animate and inanimate—to Himself.[181] Thus, as Weinrich argues, *creatio ex nihilo* has traditionally been understood —even in its New Testament and patristic contexts—as a statement less about materiality *per se* and, instead, an as affirmation of God's free and sovereign relationship to creation.[182] *Creatio ex nihilo* is not, primarily, a statement about the creation but the Creator. In this sense, בְּרָא in Genesis 1:1 affirms, if not *creatio ex nihilo per se*, the same conclusion drawn from a different premise. If based on Hebrews 11:3, et al., *creatio ex nihilo* affirms God's sovereign status beyond materiality then בְּרָא in Genesis 1:1 affirms the same by emphasizing God's *activity* through His uniquely divine prerogative of creating all things.

This falls perfectly in line with Mosaic Pentateuchal authorship. It is the God who creates (בְּרָא) through speaking whose voice thundered from Sinai conversing "face-to-face" with Moses, who spoke of Israel's promised land inheritance, who initiated the covenant with Israel through Moses as the covenant representative and who spoke the ten words (דְּבַר) of law/Torah that explicated the terms of Israel's covenant obedience. Post-exodus Israel likely had very little curiosity about the material origins of the cosmos, but they were intimately concerned with the nature of the God who had rescued

---

with the functions and roles of every material object created. To put it plainly, God does not create the physical world randomly without purpose, but everything created serves a particular function in God's ideal order. See John Walton, *The Lost World of Genesis One: Ancient Cosmology and the Origins Debate* (Downers Grove, IL: InterVarsity Press, 2010), 38-45. That said, Walton goes too far by equivocating between the material origins of creation and the function of the objects created. If the most authoritative interpreter of Scripture is Scripture itself, the insights of various New Testament passages such as John 1:3, Colossians 1:16 and Hebrews 11:3 suggest that what Genesis 1 implies by בְּרָא is both material origins and function—even if "function" is the primary concern that Genesis 1 seeks to address. While Walton does a great service to the text by bringing out the functionary dimension of the creation narrative, it is likely his intention to reconcile the Biblical narrative with contemporary evolutionary perspectives that leads him to favor his functional read of the text to the exclusion of the text's affirmation of God's act of *creatio ex nihilo* in Genesis 1.

[181] "*Creatio ex nihilo* is not pure protology, a statement about the world's beginning. It is first and foremost a statement about God and how he relates to the world at all times and in all places. *Creatio ex nihilo* is also a statement about the nature of the creature and how it relates to God the Creator at all times and in all places. In short, the *creatio ex nihilo* makes the necessary distinction between God and the creature, especially man." William Weinrich, "Creation *ex Nihilo*: The Way of God," *Logia* 4, no. 2. (April, 1995): 38.

[182] Ibid.

them from Egypt and who was bidding them to enter a new land inhabited by hostiles who worship impotent gods. At the same time, however, while the creation narrative is not explicitly preoccupied with materiality, *per se*, materiality is nonetheless assumed. There is <u>nothing</u> present within the narrative <u>detailing any great difference between</u> spiritual and material realities. What is at stake is the existence of the material world, the order and form in which it is made, and the relationships between the major players—particularly between God and man, but also between man and the other creatures.

"Let us make man in our image..." (Gen. 1:26)

Throughout the history of Christendom a number of interpretations regarding the significance of the image and likeness of God in man have been proposed. This author believes, however, that the meaning of this elusive but important title vested in man should be understood within the textual context of Genesis 1 itself.[183]   Many attempts to try and assign various attributes of God upon man by virtue of this image, without any warrant in the text itself, have been frequently proposed. God speaks in the plurality of the divine counsel: "let us make man in our image (צֶלֶם), after our likeness (דְּמוּת)." Defining and distinguishing these two Hebrew words can be a bit of an elusive endeavor. While "image" (צֶלֶם) makes twelve other appearances in the Old Testament ten of the occurrences involve a physical representation

---

[183] It should be noted that the concept of the image/likeness of God is evoked in the New Testament (*i.e.* Ephesians 4 and Colossians 3). Employing the hermeneutical principle that Scripture interprets Scripture, these texts can be enlightening in authoritatively interpreting and defining the *imago Dei* as originally expressed in Genesis 1. In each of these New Testament evocations of the concept, the image of God is inextricably linked to Christ in and through whom the image of God is restored in man. It does us very little good to look to the first Adam to attempt to understand what the image of God truly is when our only way of participating and embracing the image of God is through the second Adam, Jesus Christ. In each of these New Testament occurrences, the image of God is evidenced in terms of external righteousness. In Colossians 3, the "new self" which is "renewed in knowledge after the image of its creator" is explicitly tied to the identity of the Christian as "holy and beloved" who in turn embraces the virtues of compassion, kindness, humility, meekness, and patience. (Col. 3:9-13). In Ephesians 4, similarly, the "new self" is "created after the likeness of God in true righteousness and holiness" (Eph. 4:22). Similar virtues are also cited within the broader context of Paul's discussion here. Thus, the "image of God" is first and foremost righteousness and holiness. This presumes, still further, that the bearer of God's image recognizes his relationship to His creator who is responsible for our new selves, and completes his work of creation by redeeming man in Jesus Christ, the truest divine image bearer. Only by looking to Christ, then, can the Christian truly behold the image of God as we are intended to experience it in the life of redemption.

of something—i.e. the image (צֶלֶם) of Canaanite deities occurs in Numbers 33:52 and 2 Kings 11:18. While the word "likeness" (דְּמוּת) might be understood to connote similarity, in a sense weaker than "image," in many instances its usage is practically identical to "image" and is even used in isolation in Genesis 5:3 referencing Adam's offspring. Due to such a significant semantic overlap several exegetes believe that the two words are evoked not to say anything different from one another, but to reflect together the nature of the relationship between God and his favored creature in "representation" or "resemblance" of His divine presence and authority within the created order.[184]

If these words, "image" and "likeness," tend to reflect a physical resemblance or representation of the object of which they are derived, how does this pertain to the physical nature of man, namely, the body? Keil and Delitzsch deny that it pertains to the body at all, arguing that since God possesses no physical body there can be no correlation between the image and likeness of God with man's body. According to Keil and Delitzsch, "man is the image of God by virtue of his spiritual nature."[185] Evoking the verses from Genesis' next chapter, that "man became a living soul" (Gen. 2:7) Keil and Delitzsch argue that it is this "soul," not man's body that bears God's image and likeness. Gerhard von Rad, however, argues precisely the opposite:

> The marvel of man's bodily appearance is not at all to be excepted from the realm of God's image. This was the original notion, and we have no reason to suppose that it completely gave way, in P's theological reflection, to a spiritualizing and intellectualizing tendency. Therefore, one will do well to split the physical from the spiritual as little as possible: the whole man is created in God's image.[186]

---

[184] Terence E. Fretheim, "Image of God," in *NIB* 3:21.

[185] C.F. Keil and F. Delitzsch, *The Pentateuch,* Commentary on the Old Testament 1. (Edinburgh: T&T Clark, 1866-91), 39.

[186] Gerhard von Rad, *Genesis: A Commentary*, translated by John H. Marks, The Old Testament Library (Philadelphia: The Westminster Press, 1961), 56.

[handwritten: — why is what is at stake — Δ identity]

While von Rad's argument is based, in part, on the documentary hypothesis which separates the first two chapters of Genesis as separate accounts his argument does not hinge, entirely, upon this point. The text says very little pertinent to the *nature* of the image of God, but speaks almost exclusively to its *purpose*. In order for man to exercise dominion over creation it cannot be merely a component of his soul, or spiritual component. The dominion man is commanded to exercise, including the component of procreation, is a commandment fulfilled by the total man, including especially his body.[187]

[handwritten: — imago dei]

John Walton has deciphered four concepts from the Old Testament that can be attributed to the notion of the image of God: (1) pertaining to the *role, or function*, God bestows upon man to "subdue" and "rule," i.e. Gen 1:28; (2) pertaining to the *identity* of mankind; (3) pertaining to the manner in which man serves as God's *substitute* by representing his presence in creation; and (4) indicating the *relationship* God intends to have with mankind.[188] Fretheim attributes to the nature of the image of God in man both creativity and relationality while attributing to the purpose of the image of God multiplication, dominion, and subduing the earth.[189] While the attributes Fretheim attributes to the nature of man are arrived at inductively by the text the purposes of the image of God are stated explicitly.

What makes man unique from the rest of God's creatures is precisely the creaturely vocation given man as God's representative in the world. The image of God in man expresses man's connection to God and also defines *[handwritten: be careful]* the terms of man's responsibility within creation itself. Thus a vertical and horizontal dimension of man's dual-relationship between God and creation is written into the unique character mankind bears in the image and likeness of God. As Bruce Waltke puts it, while many argue that the Bible frequently depicts God anthropomorphically, more accurately "a human being is theomorphic, made like God so that God can communicate himself to *[handwritten: sanctnes]*

---

[187] See Psalm 8:5ff.

[188] John H. Walton, *The Lost World of Adam and Eve: Genesis 2-3 and the Human Origins Debate.* (Downers Grove, IL: IVP Academic, 2015), 42.

[189] Fretheim, "Image of God," in *NIB* 3:21-22.

people."[190] What is emphasized through the image of God is not the creator-creature distinction *per se*—though this is dealt with elsewhere in Scripture and is no less implicit here—but the creator-creature connection.

Having created both man and woman in His image and likeness, God immediately exhorts the jewels of his creation to procreate. The initial command to be "fruitful and multiply" alone says nothing particular to mankind that does not apply to any living creature—the same command was spoken over the creatures of the sea and the birds God had previously created (Gen. 1:22). While the fish and the birds are called to procreate simply to inhabit the seas and the air respectively, however, the fruitfulness of man is commanded for a distinct purpose—to subdue the earth. The command for mankind to be fruitful and multiply takes on special significance explicitly because it is the human creature who is created in the image and likeness of God, which gives man dominion everything else God made (Gen. 1:26-27). It is the dominion, particularly, that bears a special connection to the image of God—sexuality is not proper to God, *per se*, even though the sexual bond between man and woman reflects the relationship God has for his beloved creatures. Brueggemann summarizes the matter effectively:

> Sexual identity is part of creation, but it is not part of the creator. This text provides no warrant for any notion of the masculinity or feminity or androgyny of God. Sexuality, sexual identity, and sexual function belong not to God's person but to God's will for creation. Because humankind is an image, a modeling, an analogy of God, sexual metaphors are useful for speaking of the mystery of God. But they are ways of reference and not descriptions. The slippage between God and image of God is apparent in sexual language here and elsewhere in the Bible. Sexuality is ordained by God, but it does not characterize God. It belongs to the goodness God intends for creation.[191]

---

[190] Bruce K. Waltke, *Genesis: A Commentary.* (Grand Rapids, Zondervan: 2001), 65.

[191] Walter Brueggemann, *Genesis: Interpretation: A Bible Commentary for Teaching and Preaching.* Kindle edition, (Louisville: Westminster John Knox Press, 1982), locs. 845-850.

To put it another way an image (צֶלֶם) is not essentially identical with the individual, deity or object the image represents. There is both continuity and discontinuity between the vessel bearing the image and between whom or what the image emanates. While mankind expresses God, even in his bodily existence, it does not follow that man necessarily depicts God's appearance.[192] When the serpent tempts the woman that she could "be like God," this is not merely an appeal to the image of God. It, in fact, mistakes the relationship between the subject and the object of the image and falsely imagines that the image-bearer should be equal to the image-originator.

In this instance, because man's dominion—clearly connected to the image of God—is reflected first and foremost through the fulfillment of the command to be fruitful and multiply, human sexuality cannot be entirely divorced from the concept of God's image even though sexuality is not proper to God *per se*. Human sexuality reflects, within the context of the command to be fruitful and multiply and the narrative which follows in Genesis 2, a relationship and union which results in new life. As already addressed, however, even the animals are commanded to be fruitful and multiply. It is not procreation alone that signifies the image of God in man. It is, rather, the act of procreation as it becomes part and parcel of subduing the earth and exercising dominion over creation that human sexuality takes on a special significance different than the animals.

That said, the command to be fruitful and multiply and its accompanying blessing as spoken to the animals is only spoken to the creatures of the sea and the air. The "creeping things" and the "beasts of the earth" are not given such a blessing. While the fish are blessed to rule the seas and the birds are blessed to rule the air, only mankind is blessed over the land.[193] The division of spheres, however, does not limit man's dominion within the larger created order. Even though man inhabits the

---

[192] "First, the term *image* refers to a statue in the round, suggesting that a human being is a psychosomatic unity. Second, an image functions to express, not to depict; thus humanity is a faithful and adequate representation, though not a facsimilie." Waltke, *Genesis: A Commentary,* 65.

[193] "The absence of the blessing on the land animals is striking. They are not to have dominion over humanity, who is blessed to rule them. The fish and birds, however, receive blessing sine they inhabit different spheres and pose no threat to people." Ibid., 64.

land, man is charged "have dominion over the fish of the sea and over the birds of the heavens and over every living thing that moves on the earth" (Gen. 1:28).

"...and man became נֶפֶשׁ חַיָּה" (Gen. 2:7)

Among the first descriptors of humanity—what one might call man's essence—emerges immediately upon God's creation of man from the dust. Having breathed the breath of life (נִשְׁמַת חַיִּים) into man's nostrils, man becomes נֶפֶשׁ חַיָּה, which the King James Version translates as a "living soul" (Gen. 2:7). The English Standard Version, reflecting concerns that emerged in the decades preceding its publication that the Hellenistic notion of a Neoplatonic "soul" not be read into the text, translates it instead as a "living creature." Indeed, the LXX renders נֶפֶשׁ as ψυχή, the same word Plato employed in the *Phaedo* to describe "the seat and center of life that transcends the earthly."[194] Interpreting this clause, however, becomes complicated by the fact that the same phrase is employed in Genesis 2:19 with respect to the animals which Adam named. In other words, there is nothing explicitly unique to humanity, in contrast to other living creatures, supposed by the phrase נֶפֶשׁ חַיָּה. Joel Green suggests that across the Old Testament the term נֶפֶשׁ "is used with reference to the whole person as the seat of desires and emotions, not to the 'inner soul' as though this were something separate from one's being."[195] R. Reed Lessing concurs:

> The נֶפֶשׁ is primarily a person's vitality, their life; it never denotes a separate part of a person. This means that people are a body-soul. They are not a soul or spirit which now inhabits a body and will at death forever desert the body. None of the Hebrew terms translated "soul (נֶפֶשׁ)" or "spirit (רוּחַ) refers to the nonphysical part of a human being. In Hebraic thought, "soul" or "spirit" refers to the whole person of the individual as a living being. It stands for the person himself. Human beings live as souls; they do not "have" souls.[196]

---

[194] *BDAG*, "ψυχή," 1099.

[195] Green, *Body, Soul and Human Life,* 56.

[196] Lessing, "The Good life; Health, Fitness, and Bodily Welfare," 35. C.f. William Dyrness,

James Barr, conversely, has argued for a more nuanced meaning of נֶפֶשׁ with respect to the human person. Per Barr the term refers to "a superior controlling center which accompanies, expresses and directs the existence of that totality and...provides the life to the whole."[197] While Barr's understanding avoids the temptation to make נֶפֶשׁ coterminous with the totality of man, it nonetheless affirms an essential unity within the human person that is proper to human identity. That fashioning man into a "living creature" involves more than the breath of God, but also the dust of the ground and such crude, bodily terms as man's nostrils makes any attempt to spiritualize the essence of man wholly impossible if based on the creation narrative. It is neither the act of fashioning a body from the dust nor God's act of breathing his life alone that results in man becoming a living creature—it is the unity of the body, created from the dust, which encounters God's breath as it enters into man's nostrils that makes man not just living, but a creature, or נֶפֶשׁ. There is no room for a Hegelian division of spirit and matter here, nor is there room for elevating either the soul or the body over the other as if one or the other was the essence of man. It is a body-soul unity, a totality of man's physical and spiritual reality, which fully defines the essence of the human creature.

(margin note: at least the Y version)

Genesis 3: The Body and Sin

The original sin not only occurs through a bodily act—forbidden eating—but sin is first recognized when Adam and Eve discover shame in their nakedness. The curses and penalties imposed upon the first couple are bodily in nature—particularly as man's labors to till the ground, the very ground from which man was first made, becomes characterized by pain and toil. Man's task to subdue the earth will now be challenged by an earth which resists man's dominion. An additional dimension to the challenge emerged as being "fruitful" and "multiplying" in fulfillment of God's command will now be accompanied by pain. In short, fulfilling God's plan and purpose will no longer resemble a peaceful walk through a blissful garden, but man's very

---

Themes in Old Testament Theology (Downers Grove, IL: InterVarsity Press, 1979), 85.

[197] James Barr, *The Garden of Eden and the Hope of Immortality* (Minneapolis: Fortress Press, 1993) 42-43.

body will resist fidelity to the Creator. The fact that man will die as a result of sin is the effective result of man's rebellion. Accordingly, the fall into sin cannot be characterized as purely either a bodily fall or a spiritual fall. Sin pervades the total person and is expressed not merely in disobedience, but by a fracture in the essential relationships that defined mankind in Creation.

The recognition of the first couple's nakedness—expressed through the Hebrew adjective עֵירֹם—deserves significant comment because this word makes several appearances in the narrative of man's creation and fall. The first occurrence is in Genesis 2:25 when man and woman recognize they are naked but are unashamed. Clearly, nakedness alone is not the cause of shame. That said, when the serpent appears on the scene only one verse later in 3:1 the text employs a Hebrew adjective with the same consonantal structure—the serpent is more crafty, or cunning, (עָרוּם) than the other animals. The proximity of these words in two successive verses cannot be purely accidental. What this suggests, however, is not necessarily a semantic equivalent between "nakedness" and the serpent's craftiness, but that when man and woman fall into sin and find shame in their nakedness (עֵירֹם) the use of Hebrew pun suggests that in this condition mankind now is now more aligned with the serpent than their Creator. The relationship between Creator and creature was wrecked when man chose to depart from God's command and heeded the serpent's "cunning" words instead.

E.J. Young suggests that when man and woman seek to cover up their nakedness it marks the very first attempt of man to try and accomplish his own salvation by his works.[198] If this is true, then God's act to provide coverings for man's nakedness is the first expression on God's part that salvation will occur by grace. It is intriguing that man's attempt to sew together fig leaves fails to accomplish the purpose of adequately covering their shame in nakedness. Even after making their own loincloths (Gen. 3:7) the fallen couple hides from God when he comes strolling through the garden in the cool of the day. When discovered, in spite of the loincloths they had made, man explains, "I was afraid, because I was naked, and I hid myself"

---

[198] E.J. Young, *In the Beginning: Genesis 1-3 and the Authority of Scripture* (Carlisle, PA: The Banner of Truth Trust, 1976), 103.

(Gen. 3:10, ESV). These manmade loincloths clearly did not satisfy the shame and fear man experienced on account of his nakedness. While sin was recognized, first, in terms of bodily nakedness it was soon discovered that man's "nakedness" represented a vulnerability that encompassed his entire person and could not be resolved by merely covering it up through his own efforts. As man shifts his blame upon the woman, and she upon the serpent, the fracture of the relationship between man and woman, and man and woman together with other creatures, is evident. When man felt shame he sought to address his fallen condition through bodily means—while God provides coverings for man and woman, these coverings are not merely coverings for the couple's bodies but suggests, through a physical sign, God's spiritual concern for man's ultimate redemption. Man's attempt to cover himself, in some sense, could be said to be man's first attempt to sever the components of the human person, to isolate the condition of the body from that of the entire man. This experiment, of course, was unsuccessful. God intervenes in his grace and addresses man's total condition—a body-soul unity that is now both totally depraved in sin, and totally the object of God's redemptive promise.

God's intervention also speaks to God's sovereignty—man's rebellion and fall will not hijack the destiny of God's entire creation. While man did not represent the image of God in concert with man's created purpose, this image was not lost. Man will continue to bear this image as he subdues the earth and multiplies in "toil" and "pain." Whereas man's representation of God is now fully tainted in sin, God will nonetheless continue to intervene in history to bring about his will and purpose for his world and his creatures, including humanity. More than that, God's intervention will occur preeminently through the means now cursed by man's disobedience. Man's sin cannot thwart God's sovereign will and plan—instead, God's will transcends man's fall, even employing the very cursed means of man's embodied life in order to bring about the redemption of man and all of creation. The "seed" of woman is promised, a perfect image-bearer, who will redeem embodied life and restore the right relationships for which man was created—between man and woman, between humanity and creation, and especially between mankind and his Creator.

The Flood and God's Covenant with Noah

The naming of Noah links this man with God's purposes in redemption: "Out of the ground that the LORD has cursed this one shall bring us relief from our work and from the painful toil of our hands" (Gen. 5:29, ESV). In naming his son, however, Lamech fails to see that this relief will come only after the world will pass through a great judgment. Within the context of a genealogy, however, including the naming of Noah's sons, this passage suggests that total fulfillment of the meaning behind Noah's name will likely occur in a subsequent generation, as the "seed" of woman continues to unfold and the genealogy of salvation history expands. This is explicitly stated when God initiates the postdiluvian covenant: "Behold, I establish my covenant with you and your offspring after you" (Gen 9:9, ESV).

This covenant, however, is linked directly to the covenant of creation by the repetition of the command that man, along with all the animals, should procreate. After the flood waters recede God charges Noah and his family to "be fruitful, and multiply, and fill the earth" (Gen. 9:1, 7). With these words O. Palmer Robertson explains that it's the covenant made with Noah which links together God's purposes in creation and redemption as one and the same.

> The explicit repetition of these creation mandates in the context of the covenant of redemption expands the vistas of redemption's horizons. Redeemed man must not internalize his salvation so that he thinks narrowly in terms of a "soul saving" deliverance. To the contrary, redemption involves this total life-style as a social, cultural creature. Rather than withdrawing narrowly into a restricted form of "spiritual" existence, redeemed man must move out with a total world-and-life perspective.[199]

To put it in terms more pertinent to these purposes, the covenant with Noah explicates embodied life as the very life the Lord promises to redeem. It makes an important bridge from the covenant of creation to the covenant of redemption drawing upon insights derived from creation as

---

[199] Robertson, *The Christ of the Covenants*, 110.

relevant to understanding life in the world and in the world yet to come. The covenant with Noah effectively weaves a golden thread between the articles of creation, redemption and eschatology encompassing, in turn, every dimension of human life in creation.

Whereas the image of God was evoked in Gen. 1:26 with regard to man's call to rule over creation—fish, birds and animals—in Genesis 9:6 the image of God in man suggests a responsibility man has to his fellow man that is different than his relationship to mere animals. Man is granted permission to shed the blood of animals, albeit with the consequence that fear and dread will exist in the relationship between man and beast. While the blood of animals may be shed, however, man is forbidden to shed the blood of another human being lest, in so doing, he should forfeit his own life as a consequence (Gen. 9:5). While contemporary opponents evoke the value and dignity of human life in an argument against capital punishment it is precisely *because* man's bodily life has value in connection with God's image that a murderer's life should be taken.

Robertson's point, quoted above, is bolstered by the language within the covenant that it both (1) applies to all creatures and (2) that it explicitly uses the language of a covenant made with "all flesh" (בָּשָׂר) (Gen. 9:15). Those prone to imposing a dualistic division of soul from body within the Pentateuch are likely to set בָּשָׂר in opposition to the previously studied נֶפֶשׁ. Just as נֶפֶשׁ can denote the entire person, however, בָּשָׂר likewise may refer to the totality of man in body-soul unity.[200] This is the case in Leviticus 17:11, for example, which states, "For the life [נֶפֶשׁ] of the flesh [בָּשָׂר] is in the blood [דָּם]." As the blood courses throughout the body the life of man is inexplicably linked to both נֶפֶשׁ and rf'B. This is not the first relevant occurrence of בָּשָׂר in Genesis. When Adam exclaims that Eve is "flesh of my flesh," it is literally "וּבָשָׂר מִבְּשָׂרִי" and when man and woman leave their parents and cleave to one another they become one flesh/ בָּשָׂר (Gen. 2:2-24). The next occurrence in Genesis is the beginning of the Flood narrative where the Lord states that his breath (רוּחַ) will not abide in man indefinitely, "for he is flesh (בָּשָׂר)" (Gen. 6:3). Accordingly, the judgment of the flood will be

---

[200] Edmond Jacob, "ψυχή" in *TDNT*, 9:622.

incurred against "all flesh" (Gen. 6:12-13), and the postdiluvian covenant will also be granted for the sake of all flesh.

What all of this reveals, relevant to these purposes, is that the body cannot be exorcised from God's overarching concern for the world and mankind. On account of the flesh, the Lord grieves over man's corruption while at the same time, in his compassion, he willfully and unilaterally establishes a covenant with "all flesh," emphasizing particularly the flesh of mankind. The covenant, in such terms, prevents a spiritualizing of the Lord's relationship with man in any way which would exclude the body from the covenant bond. What man does in the body has an impact on his spiritual wellbeing and, one could argue in turn, that one's spiritual condition affects his bodily life. Man's spiritual degradation before the flood, much like when Adam and Eve chose to align their commitments to the Serpent's cunning in lieu of God's promise, had consequences experienced in the flesh. Likewise, it is through fleshly activity that this relationship with God is both severed (*i.e.* eating from the forbidden tree, the depravity exhibited by the prediluvian people, etc.) and also restored (*i.e.* from the promised seed that will crush the serpent's head, or the covenant that God makes with creation after the flood).

Body, Soul and Spirit

At this point it is worth exploring the link between breath, or spirit (רוּחַ) and flesh (בָּשָׂר). If a trichotomous view of man—seeing the human being divided essentially between body, soul, and spirit—were read into the Old Testament one would typically equate body with בָּשָׂר, soul with נֶפֶשׁ, and spirit with רוּחַ.[201] While distinctions can, and should, be made between these terms and they do sometimes bear a rough similitude to the traditional components of "body, soul and spirit," there are nonetheless distinct Hebraic notions of each of these that encompass the entirety of the human being not as a summation of parts, but in a holistic sense. While בָּשָׂר and נֶפֶשׁ have been partially addressed above this section will address the Old Testament use of רוּחַ in relation to the other two terms.

---

[201] *TWOT*, 2:837.

Typically, רוּחַ is translated at either "breath," "wind" or "spirit."[202] Frequently, when applied to man it coheres either with his status of being alive or dead—it is practically interchangeable with נֶפֶשׁ in this respect—or can be used to describe an attitude, disposition, or even an emotional state such as anger, depression or jealousy.[203] Under the harsh conditions of Egyptian slavery the people of Israel are said to have a broken spirit (רוּחַ) (Ex. 6:9). For the sake of constructing the tabernacle Yahweh tells Moses that he has filled Bezalel with the Spirit (רוּחַ) of God, equating the bestowal of God's רוּחַ upon an individual with particular talents such as innate ability, knowledge and craftsmanship (Ex. 31:3). There are other "spirits" however that could be associated with a vice, such as the spirit of jealousy, רוּחַ־קִנְאָה (Num. 5:14, 30). Joshua is said to possess a "spirit of wisdom" (רוּחַ חָכְמָה) after Moses laid his hands upon him (Deut. 34:9). Previously, however, the Lord commanded Moses to lay his hands upon Joshua because the רוּחַ was already within him (Num. 27:18). Hosea speaks of a spirit of "whoredom" (רוּחַ זְנוּנִים) that has led God's people astray (Hos. 4:12). The Lord stirs up the "spirit" (רוּחַ) of foreign kings to exact judgment against Babylon (Jer. 51:16-17). Jeremiah also criticizes purposeless idols as foolish and stupid, because they have no רוּחַ within them (Jer. 28:17).

At first glance all of the above might suggest that רוּחַ possesses a variety of unrelated meanings not only spanning the Old Testament but even within the Pentateuch alone. If the most basic and all-encompassing definition of רוּחַ is "air in motion" as has been suggested[204] one might add to that the qualification that such "moving air" if possessed or originated by either God or man always has a purpose. As applied to man, one might say that the רוּחַ does more than vivify the body, but it gives the entire life of man ″an orientation or dedicated purpose.″ Such a purpose can be either noble or natural (cohering with the purpose for which God initially blew his רוּחַ into man's nostrils) or it can be sinful or vain, militating against God's dedicated purpose for man. To put it colloquially, why does one get out of bed in the morning? What is it that defines one's being, orients one's behavior and

---

[202] *BDB*, 924.

[203] Ibid.

[204] *TWOT*, 2:836.

pre-destined? or unbreathed for a freedom. that we break?

85

characterizes one's loyalties? While one's orientations are not equated with רוּחַ it is impossible to conceive of רוּחַ apart from some sort of orientation, worldview, or motivating principle. While רוּחַ is spoken of internally, as something within man, when applied to man there is always an *extra nos* dimension of רוּחַ that unites the human being to an external loyalty or *raison d'être*. Enslaved Israel is said to have a broken רוּחַ because under the chains of Pharaoh they are unable to live according to their prescribed purpose. Yet those committed to a spirit of jealousy or another vice are equally enslaved— such an orientation of one's רוּחַ is neither wise nor prudent and ultimately leads to death. Thus, the principle of God's "breath" giving life to man from the beginning persists even as man's "spirit" often finds itself misappropriated or enslaved. True life has a God-oriented origin and directive.

In fact, in Hebrew terms, dimensions of human personhood understood in modernity and, even more so in postmodernity, as "inner" or "inward" experiences are often associated with bodily organs and physical action. Di Vito has argued, in fact, that the very notion of "self" is entirely foreign to the Hebrew way of thinking about human life.[205] Particular body parts frequently become the centers of human feeling and activity, though never separate from the entire person. What one "part" or organ of the person does, the entire person does. Thus, the blood of Abel has a voice that calls out God from the ground (Gen. 4:10). Bones can sometimes speak (Psalm 35:10) and eyes can testify what they have seen just as ears can declare one "happy" based on what is heard (Job 29:11). Even the kidneys exult when the lips speak "what is right" (Proverbs 23:16). The Psalmist says "my נֶפֶשׁ longs, yes, faints" even as "my heart and flesh" (לְבִי וּבְשָׂרִי) "sing for joy" (Psalm 84:2). This use of נֶפֶשׁ, however, cannot be presumed to be reflective of a modern "inner self." Psalm 42:6 reads, in the ESV, "my soul (נֶפֶשׁ) is cast down within me." While other translations, such as the RSV, NRSV, and NAB similarly translate the direction of the soul's casting to "within," the preposition and pronominal suffix עָלָי carries with it a more external dimension, "upon me" rather than "within me."

---

[205] Di Vito, "Old Testament Anthropology and the Construction of Personal Identity," 219.

[margin note, top right:] Touts disregards the self-reflexive character of conscience which is an aspect of soul — he literalizes the "upon" which is not literal but a metaphor

Accordingly, if נֶפֶשׁ is translated as "soul" it cannot be identified with "inner self" in the modern sense. According to Di Vito, "the preposition is used here to indicate the oppressive force or weight of the 'soul,' not *within* the person but, from the Hebrew point of view, *upon* the victim who is suffering, as if from the outside."[206] Thus, even if נֶפֶשׁ is understood as one of many components of the person responsible for emotions, it cannot be identified with a person's "inner life" in the sense of post–Enlightenment "self." It functions in many respects like other bodily organs—sometimes responsible for or the "seat" of an emotion, but never a comprehensive term for human identity that can be separated from the rest of the body. In fact, that there should be a discussion of נֶפֶשׁ, בָּשָׂר, and רוּחַ correlated to body, soul and spirit respectively is anachronistic in a sense. There is no reason why these three words should be considered the three primary dimensions of human personhood—other words like "heart" (לֵב) factor in just as prominently relative to the person as previously mentioned three. Thus, contra Kierkegaard, there is no mention of Abraham's "fear" or "trembling" in Genesis 22 as he heeds the Lord's command to prepare his son Isaac for sacrifice. Instead, it is the action itself not Abraham's emotional state that proves his fidelity. Likewise, involuntary body flows can rend an individual ceremonially unclean in the Old Testament (Lev. 15:1-33) and a physical defect can render someone unfit to serve as a priest (Lev. 21:16-24). A male with damaged genitals cannot enter the assembly of the Lord (Deut. 23:2). As Di Vito explains, "one cannot easily dissociate who one is from one's bodily integrity, because there is no 'center' within a self and apart from the body to be set over against the body as a 'real' self in contrast to the one that is apparent."[207] It is in this context—where even one's body can expose a fractured relationship between God and man—that Jesus takes particular concern for restoring bodily defects through healing in the Gospels and ultimately vicariously restores the body itself in His resurrection. The Old Testament reality of one's bodily impact on his spiritual well-being indicates, without any doubt, that the totality of man's depravity is not merely a matter of his "soul," but encompasses the entire person—the body

[margin note, right:] the 'weight' of self-awareness ≠ oppressive-ness

[margin note, right:] — not a nuanced understanding of self-awareness

[margin note, bottom right:] yes —

---

[206] Ibid., 229.

[207] Ibid., 233.

in particular. Laws and rites directed at the body's faults, including the priestly postures in Levitical rites, reflect this reality in the Old Testament and finally finds their resolution through the bodily intervention of the Christ in the New Testament.

Circumcision and the Abrahamic Covenant

It is hard to imagine how anything more central to the religious life of Old Testament Israel could be any more "fleshly" or "bodily" than circumcision. Circumcision, as a "sign of the covenant" (Gen. 17:11) was to be administered to every male eight days old, including every male of every generation be he native-born, a servant or a foreigner. Accordingly, God declares "so shall my covenant be in your flesh (בְּשַׂר) an everlasting covenant." (Gen. 17:13). Why circumcision? There are a number of reasons why one might suspect that circumcision is an altogether inefficient, not to mention strange, sign whereby an Israelite might recall his belonging to the covenant community. First, circumcision is not a readily visible sign meaning that it serves very little purpose as an "outward confession" of one's faith, if one were to consider it as such. Second, even though as has been affirmed earlier that man and woman are together created in the image of God and the Lord extends his promise to both genders, women are inherently excluded from bearing this sign of the covenant in their flesh. At first glance circumcision seems an odd choice, particularly since the promised "seed" in Gen. 3:15 is affixed with the feminine suffix, זַרְעָהּ, "her seed" while circumcision deals exclusively with the male's reproductive organ. That circumcision is chosen as the preeminent sign of one's belonging to the covenant community is suggested by some to be an implication of an androcentric Hebrew religion.[208] This argument, however, can easily be turned on its head. That the earlier promise (Gen. 3:15) is attributed directly to women and circumcision is a male-only symbol emphasizes the opposite—the male is not somehow excluded from the fulfillment of the promised seed and he now bears a mark on his reproductive organs to drive home the point. God's design for mankind was a spousal unity between man and woman and it is through marriage,

---

[208] See Shaye JD Cohen, *Why Aren't Jewish Women Circumcised?: Gender and Covenant in Judaism.* (Univ of California Press, 2005) 138.

88

particularly through reproduction in marriage, that God brings about redemption. It is neither the loins of man nor the womb of woman alone that is responsible for the fulfillment of the Lord's covenant promise. His promise will be brought about through the intimate union of male and female. The covenant of marriage binds man and woman together in the covenant of promised redemption. In other words the Lord chooses to deal with man in spousal unity—not as male or female, but as <u>male *and* female</u>. *Elohist account* That the covenant extends beyond the explicit lineage of the promised seed—*i.e.* that one need not be in the messianic lineage in order to be an inheritor of the covenant promise—suggests likewise that God also intends to deal with families.[209] *or humankind in general*

In spite of this disjunction, however, the covenant with Abraham marked by circumcision is explicitly linked to the earlier spoken declaration that man should be fruitful and multiply—first to Adam and Eve, and later to Noah and his family. Whereas the former instances of being fruitful and multiplying, however, are spoken in the imperative voice here it is clear that <u>Yahweh himself is the subject of the verbs, "...that I may...multiply you</u> *God makes it happen* greatly," (17:2) and "I will make you exceedingly fruitful..." (17:16).[210] Does the Lord here assume the responsibility to fulfill what he had previously tasked man—Adam, then Noah—to fulfill by command? Or, if one takes the earlier commandment to be fruitful and multiply (Gen. 1:28) as a divine imperative (this is how Luther takes it, which will be examined later in this book) the earlier command functioned more like the <u>"let there be"</u> *creates fertility* imperatives in Genesis 1—God's command creates the reality it dictates. In this sense, the shift in the "fruitful and multiply" declaration is not a shift from command to promise so much as it is <u>a shift from declaration to covenant.</u> What God declared for the sake of creation—linked to man's responsibility as God's image bearers in creation—he now commits himself

---

[209] Contrary to the individualism that characterizes discussion regarding the body in the contemporary world—we feel that our bodies are our own to do with whatever we personally wish—in the <u>Hebraic context the body becomes the most effectual connection between an individual and the covenant</u> *— unpack* community. The body cannot be spoken of, then, purely in individualistic terms. It is no mistake, then, that the New Testament likewise draws upon the human body as a metaphor for how the church ought to operate with respect to its many members and the body of Christ's unified essence and purpose, *i.e.* Romans 12:4-5; 1 Cor. 12:12-27; Eph. 3:6. *neither can our own — we are born by others — not self-generating*

[210] "I will make you fruitful," or "I will cause you to be fruitful" is reflected by the hiphil, וְהִפְרֵתִי, emphasizing both Yahweh's activity and Abraham's passivity in the fulfillment of this promise.

89

to and reveals his intentions in design via a covenantal bond for the sake of mankind's redemption. The Lord of creation is the Lord of redemption. Still further, in order to redeem creation God will employ a means already established in His natural order—procreation. As involved as God was in speaking creation into existence he is covenantally committed to his words of promise to redeem his fallen creatures.

It is clear, however, that circumcision alone did not make one a full recipient of the covenant promises by the mere act of submitting to the rite, *ex opere operato*. Circumcision was an outward sign corresponding to the inward reality of faith in the covenant promise. This is upheld throughout the many Old Testament passages which speak of a circumcision of the heart (Lev. 26:31; Deut. 10:16; 30:6; Jer. 4:4; 9:26; Ezek. 44:7). The same principle is delineated in the New Testament by St. Paul in Romans 2:29.

According to Robertson, Circumcision possessed both a "God-ward as well as a man-ward dimension."[211] Circumcision is both a rite of cleansing which signifies that one is in right relationship with God, but it also marks one's inclusion in the covenant community. There are, accordingly, both vertical and horizontal concerns reflected in the covenant sign of circumcision. Another way of expressing the two-fold relationship indicated by the rite of circumcision is that it reflects both ownership and membership. It implies *belonging*—one belongs to God (ownership) and one belongs to the covenantal community (membership).

If man is to be fully human the whole person—encompassing dimensions of בָּשָׂר, רוּחַ and נֶפֶשׁ should be properly oriented both unto God and unto man's created existence in the world. In short, man is not defined primarily in terms of possessing a "body," "soul" and "spirit," but finds his essential humanity primarily in terms of his orientation of the entirety of his being. The essence of man in the Old Testament is *relational* rather than partitive. This is not to suggest that man is essentially material any more than it is to suggest that man is essentially a soul or spirit. The essence of man cannot divide these various dimensions of humanity primarily *because* each dimension plays a pivotal role in how the human creature relates to God and the world.

---

[211] Robertson, *The Christ of the Covenants,* 152.

The Body in the New Testament

In Chapter 1, above, it has already been asserted that the philosophical categories of body and soul (or body, soul and spirit) as advanced in the monism–dualism debate are not biblically founded. That said, assuming the terms of that debate, this can lead to a number of conclusions when approaching the New Testament where words that seem to correlate with these different "parts" of the human creature are sometimes evoked. While this section will argue that the New Testament affirms a view of the human creature in continuity with the Old Testament it nonetheless must be granted that the language of the New Testament seems to suggest a two-fold or even three-fold view of the human being by distinguishing body and spirit (or, as could be argued—body, soul and spirit) more explicitly than Old Testament texts might suggest.

One cannot evade the admonishment Jesus offers his hearers in Matthew 10:28: "do not fear those who kill the body (σῶμα) but cannot kill the soul (ψυχή). Rather fear him who can destroy both body and soul in hell." As Gibbs points out, this is the sole use of ψυχή, within Matthew's Gospel where the term does not refer to the entire person, or to one's whole "life" or "being."[212] That said, contrary to common misconception, the view that the body and soul were separated at death was in fact a fairly common Jewish theme which Jesus here seems to affirm.[213] Even if ψυχή, is understood to encompass the entirety of the person rather than only a "soul" separate from the body, Jesus' words above nonetheless indicate that there is an entirety of the person who survives beyond death. Such a translation might be, "do not fear those who can kill the body but cannot kill you entirely. Rather fear him who can destroy both body along with your entire being in hell." Regardless of the precise meaning of ψυχή, here or elsewhere it is clear that

[handwritten marginal note: and is psyche also parallel to breath?]

---

[212] "In Matthew every other use of the Greek term ψυχή refers to the entire 'person' or to one's whole 'life' or 'being.' See it in 2:20; 6:23 (twice); 10:39 (twice); 11:29, 12:18; 16:25 (twice), 26 (twice); 20:28; 22:37; 26:38. The use here in 10:28 is unique in Matthew, owing to the way that Jesus distinguishes between 'soul' (ψυχή) and 'body' (σῶμα) when discussing physical death which severs one from the other." Jeffrey A. Gibbs, "Matthew 1:1-11:1," *Concordia Commentary*. (St. Louis: Concordia Publishing House, 2006), 530, fn. 9.

[213] "Jesus may here recall the Jewish martyr tradition, which exhorted its followers not to fear those who think they kill because eternal suffering awaits the soul that disobeys God's command (4 Macc 13:14-15)." Craig S. Keener, *A Commentary on the Gospel of Matthew* (Grand Rapids: Eerdmans, 2010), 325.

Jesus affirms that the destruction of the body does not eradicate the entire human creature. *or does not eradicate the breath*

In fact, both σῶμα and ψυχή, frequently denote the entire human person in New Testament use. Schwartz argues that σῶμα is "the most comprehensive term with which Paul denotes a human being."[214] Schwartz's recent assertion echoes Bultmann, whose identity of σῶμα with the entirety of the human person has already been cited.[215] Bultmann continues, however, to say that "*man, his person as a whole*, can be denoted by *soma*. ... Man is called soma in respect to his being able to make himself the object of his own action or to experience himself as the subject to whom something happens. He can be called *soma, that is, as having a relationship to himself* – as being able in a certain sense to distinguish himself from himself."[216] Bultmann's line of thinking proceeds along what Di Vito identified in the Enlightenment as a tendency amongst Christian theologians to move away from an examination of the body relative to the soul, but to instead focus on the relationship of the body to the "self."[217] Barr has suggested that the emphasis in modern exegesis to elevate the body and dismiss the soul likely reflects modern antipathy to Hellenistic dualism. For Barr, there has been a determined effort to set the "Hebrew mind" in opposition to the "Greek mind," attempting to anachronistically make the Hebrews appear as moderns (thus, adding an ancient credibility to the modern project).[218] That said, as has already been shown in the Old Testament analysis above, even if the Hebrews share with moderns a more "material" definition of the human being than the Ancient Greeks, there are significant departures in Hebrew thought completely foreign to modern thinking. The lack of any developed concept of the "inner self," for example, and the close connection of bodily terms to emotions in Hebrew thinking is difficult to grasp in a post–Freudian world where the

---

[214] Hans Schwarz, *The Human Being: A Theological Anthropolgy.* (Grand Rapids: William B. Eerdmans Publishing Co., 2013), 14.

[215] See p. 15.

[216] Bultmann, *Theology of the New Testament,* 1:195-96, emphasis original.

[217] Di Vito, "Old Testament Anthropology and the Construction of Personal Identity," 219.

[218] Barr, *Garden of Eden,* 2, 6-37.

"inner self" is taken for granted as the source of behavior and the seat of the true person.

If ψυχή, like σῶμα often stands in by synecdoche for the totality of the person, and even if ψυχή, can denote something distinct from the body as a component of the human person, it nonetheless remains to be asked whether a human ψυχή, exists at all *apart from* the body. 20th Century German New Testament scholar, Hans Conzelmann, went so far as to assert that "the soul belongs to man's earthly existence. It does not exist without physical life. It is not, say, freed from death, then to live in untrammeled purity. Death is its end."[219] Hans Schwarz rightly calls Conzelmann's position here an "overstatement." Granting that Paul places ψυχή, on the side of "flesh" when he contrasts ψυχικὸς man from the "spiritually discerned" man (πνευματικῶς ἀνακρίνεται) (1 Cor. 2:14ff), "this does not mean that there is a void after death...Any existence after death, just as our existence here and now, is dependent on God and will be an embodied existence."[220] Schwarz, too, might be committing an overstatement by demanding that man's post-mortem existence in the intermediate state must be an "embodied existence," though his point that man's existence beyond the grave is wholly dependent upon God is a crucial one. Debates regarding the constitution of man in the intermediate state are necessarily tentative. Scripture does not address the relationship of man to his body during the intermediate state. What does ring true is that man can continue to exist according to God's sovereign preservation of human identity regardless of how one might or might not attempt to understand the nature of man's existence in the intermediate state. What is equally true is that the intermediate state should never be thought of as more than intermediate. The New Testament unequivocally testifies to the fact that man's consummative existence *is an embodied existence* pivoting upon the affirmation of the resurrection of the body.

---

[219] Hans Conzelmann, *Theology of the New Testament,* trans. John Bowden (New York: Harper & Row, 1969), 179.

[220] Schwarz, *The Human Being*, 15.

The Resurrected Body

In many respects, the New Testament affirmation of the resurrection of the body—beginning with Jesus' resurrection as the first fruits of our own—is the clearest expression of what a Biblical theology of the body entails. Though not yet realized the ultimate and eternal existence of the human being, after the consummation of the age, will be a resurrected life. As important as it is to understand man's original condition, within the context of God's original creation of man, to define the nature of the human being it is equally important to understand the bodily existence of man that is yet to come. Despite man's present condition, sin pervading the entirety of man including the body, the Bible both begins and consummates its depiction of human existence in terms of a sinless bodily existence. As such, the New Testament—particularly in Paul's expression—sets forth both the Adamic and Christ-defined conceptions of human bodily existence to contrast man's bodily experience from creation, through the fall, until the resurrection. How man orients himself, here and now, either toward the fall or toward redemption, becomes definitive for how this present life is lived. There is either a recollectic or proleptic way of experiencing man's present condition and life that orients one's life either toward Adam's fall into sin or Christ's resurrection from the grave. The New Testament offers no "third" alternative. Life will be lived and experienced either according to fallen Adam or resurrected Christ—whether one understands their life in those terms or not. Accordingly, the resurrection of the body is more than an afterthought or an eventual hope for the Christian life. It is, rather, pivotal for understanding the Christian life from baptismal font to grave and beyond.

According to N.T. Wright the concept of "resurrection" was never used in the ancient world to imply a generic life-after-death existence but was *always*, even amongst those who denied its possibility, reserved for a post-mortem recovery of, or refashioning of the body.

> ...the word resurrection in its Greek, Latin, or other equivalents was never used to mean life after death. Resurrection was used to denote new bodily life after whatever sort of life after death there might be. When the ancients spoke of resurrection, whether to deny it (as all pagans did) or to affirm it (as some

Jews did), they were referring to a two-step narrative in which resurrection, meaning new bodily life, would be preceded by an interim period of bodily death. Resurrection wasn't, then, a dramatic or vivid way of talking about the state people went into immediately after death. It denoted something that might happen (though almost everyone thought it wouldn't) sometime after that.[221]

Schnelle has argued that "for Paul there is no human identity apart from bodily existence, and so he also thinks of the resurrection reality and the postmortal existence in bodily terms."[222] *Schnelle*

While it is true that Paul conceives of the human creature primarily in bodily terms, Schnelle might be overstating his case. While none of the categories of body, soul or spirit in the Greek New Testament cohere perfectly with philosophical proposals about the makeup of the human creature, it is clear nonetheless that something soul-like must exist that *why?* allows the human being to exist apart from the body even if such an existence is unideal or temporary. For example, when Paul recounted for the *but he* Corinthians that he had been caught up into paradise, unable to recall *never thought he* whether he was in his body or out of it (2 Cor. 12:2-4) he was assuming—or *was dead* was at least aware of the possibility—that his soul (or some form of his consciousness) could continue to exist apart from the body. At the same time, however, Paul clearly affirms in a manner that seems almost self-evident from his perspective that the eternal and future life of the human is a bodily one. In 1 Corinthians 15:35-44 this is abundantly clear. Two paired questions, "How are the dead raised?" and "With what kind of body (σῶμα) do they come?" evoke a lengthy explanation through which Paul makes clear that there is substantial continuity between what is "sown" (the corpse) and what is raised (the resurrected body). *both are creatures... both contingent*

At the same time however, Paul sets what is sown a "natural body" (σῶμα ψυχικόν) in contrast to the raised "spiritual body" (σῶμα πνευματκόν).[223]

---

[221] Wright, *Surprised by Hope*, 36.

[222] Udo Schnelle, *Theology of the New Testament,* trans. M. Eugene Boring (Grand Rapids: Baker, 2009), 284.

[223] 1 Corinthians 15:44.

For Paul, the existence of the former presupposes the existence of the later. The adjective ψυχικός here, is rendered as "natural" in the ESV. This is the only adjectival rendering of ψυχή, in the New Testament. While "natural body" as commonly translated misses the connection to ψυχή, it is not altogether inappropriate. A more literal rendering might be a "soulish body," but this translation must submit to the qualifications and cautions that a translation of ψυχή, as "soul" entails. Accordingly, "soulish body" would likely be even more confusing to modern readers who are likely to understand "soul" in the Greco-philosophical sense. While ψυχή, and πνεῦμα are sometimes interchangeable in both Pauline use and the New Testament more generally, here a "soulish" and "spiritual" body are clearly distinguished in some sense. To understand this distinction, however, Paul's evocation of Genesis 2:7 in the following verse (1 Cor. 15:45) offers some insight. If the first Adam became a living being (ψυχή ζῶσαν) and the last Adam, who is Christ, became a "life-giving spirit" (πνεῦμα ζῳοποιοῦν) the contrast between a "soulish body" and a "spiritual body" is not a distinction in essence but in orientation toward one prototype or another—Adam or Christ. Keener's insight here is helpful:

> In verse 45 Paul cites Genesis 2:7, where God made Adam a soul, a natural man; but many Diaspora Jews thought that Genesis 1:26-27 referred to a different, ideal man, the pure form and model for humanity, and Paul may play on this tradition here. The two kinds of body belong to the contrast between humanity's legacy in Adam and believers' destiny in Christ.[224]

According to the Flesh...According to the Spirit

Within the context of man's fallen condition Paul refers to the human body under such unflattering terms as "the body of sin" (τὸ σῶμα τῆς ἁμαρτίας)[225] and "this body of death" (σώματος τοῦ θανάτου τούτου).[226] The word σάρξ, however, is the most frequent word choice when it comes to addressing

---

[224] Craig S. Keener, *The IVP Bible Background Commentary: New Testament.* 2nd ed. (Downers Grove, IL: IVP Academic, 2014) 495.

[225] Romans 6:6.

[226] Romans 7:24.

the sinful condition of man within his earthly and bodily condition. The KJV frequently renders σάρξ as "carnal" placing the "carnal mind" in opposition to God himself (Rom. 8:7). The Corinthians are rebuked as being "carnal" due to their division based on the personality of their Christian leaders, some claiming loyalty to Paul but others to Apollos (1 Cor. 3:4). Elsewhere, the sinful component of σάρξ is not as evident. In Romans 15:27, in a discussion regarding how the Gentile Christians were openly sharing of the material goods and wealth with the church in Jerusalem, Paul says that because the Gentiles partake with them the same "spiritual things" (τοῖς πνευματικοῖς) they ought also to minister to the Jewish Christians in "carnal things" or, as the ESV renders it, "in material blessings" (ἐν τοῖς σαρκικοῖς). A similar use of σάρξ occurs when Paul speaks of reaping "carnal things," *i.e.* being provided for materially as payment, for his service to the Corinthians in the Gospel, having provided to them "spiritual things" (τὰ πνυματικὰ) (1 Cor. 9:11).

Rendered in the accusative, however, in apposition to the preposition kata. (typically κατὰ σάρκα) the word takes on a more technical meaning contrasted explicitly with the clause "according to the spirit," or κατὰ πνεῦμα. Paul sets these two orientations of the human being against each other in both Romans 8:4ff. and Galatians 4:29. These two contexts and uses are very different, however, and should be compared and contrasted so that the essential meaning of the clause, κατὰ σάρκα, can be more adequately deciphered. The Galatians use will be considered first because it helps to elucidate the meaning Paul intends in Romans. In Galatians the distinction is introduced in order to contrast Jacob and Esau. It is the child of the covenant, Jacob, who is κατὰ πνεῦμα. Jacob is persecuted by Esau who is κατὰ σάρκα. Here, the distinction effectively separates the son who belonged to the covenantal promise from his twin brother who did not. That the same distinction occurs in Romans 8, in relative proximity to another evocation of the distinction between Jacob and Easu in Romans 9:13, is no mistake. Paul is engaged in a similar discussion—he who lives κατὰ πνεῦμα lives in accordance with the covenant promises, like Jacob. It is to live as one of the elect. To live κατὰ σάρκα, therefore, is to live after the pattern of Esau. It is to live apart from the covenant. It is to live as the reprobate.

This interpretation is bolstered by Paul's uses of similar language in other epistles. In 2 Corinthians 5:16–17 a reborn Christian should no longer

so be careful to not literalize the metaphor of kata —, or kata —

be considered according to the flesh (κατὰ σάρκα) because being in Christ "he is a new creature." This condition or orientation as a new creature/creation effectively stands in for what Paul means by κατὰ πνεῦμα elsewhere. In other words, what is at stake here is not the constitutive nature of man's *exactly!* existence—whether man is essentially flesh or spirit—but the direction toward which man places his hope. To live κατὰ σάρκα is to live with one's faith adhering to only those promises that flesh can give—it is temporal, is passes away, it is prone toward corruption and sin. If, however, one lives κατὰ πνεῦμα or as a "new creature" he lives according to the promise that comes only by Christ in the Spirit. To live κατὰ πνεῦμα is to live covenantally. It means living in faith according to the promises that come only through Christ in the workings of the Holy Spirit. To live κατὰ πνεῦμα is not, therefore, to live according to a spiritual existence *per se*—but to live precisely according to the Holy Spirit. It is not that σάρξ is essentially evil or sinful. Rather, to live "carnally" is to live in a limited way according to the few promises earthly life alone can give.

KEY James D. G. Dunn has proposed—drawing upon the insights of D. E. H. Whitely—that the New Testament presents an *aspectual* relationship of body and soul to the human person as opposed to the secular Greek *partitive* concept of body and soul.[227] This is a theme that this study has shown has been evident throughout Scripture, in various contexts. The aspectual dimension of what constitutes the fullness of the human creature in the New Testament comes to bear significantly with respect to the eschatological resurrection of the body. A dualistic understanding of the resurrection tends *precisely / not / the gospel* to view it as a re-clothing of a "naked" soul with a reconstituted body. In other words, for many dualists the human creature remains in-tact through death, even without a body. An aspectual understanding of the resurrection, conversely, suggests a reconstitution of the *whole person* to a fuller

resurrection — renewed, restored, clean heart (B.5)

Hebrew is whole

[227] ". . . in simplified terms, while Greek thought tended to regard the human being as made up of distinct parts, Hebraic thought saw the human being more as a whole person existing on different dimensions. As we might say, it was more characteristically Greek to conceive of the human person "partitively," whereas it was more characteristically Hebrew to conceive of the human person "aspectively." That is to say, we speak of a school having a gym (the gym is part of the school); but we say I am a Scot (my Scottishness is an aspect of my whole being)." James D. G. Dunn, *The Theology of the Apostle Paul* (Grand Rapids, MI: Eerdmans, 1998), 54. Dunn attributes the aspective/partitive account to D. E. H. Whitely, *The Theology of St Paul* (Oxford: Blackwell, 1964).

what does that really mean?

expression of human life, or a fully-realized creaturehood. In a state of death, however the human creature continues to exist during the intermediate state, it is not in the fullness of what it means to be a human being as originally designed in the infinite imagination of the Creator.

A Temple of the Holy Spirit

any existence is contingent on God's will to maintain

The notion of the Christian's body operating as a "temple of the Holy Spirit" or as "God's temple" occurs throughout many of Paul's epistles. *architecture — provided for meeting of deity* Perhaps the most frequently cited example occurs in 1 Corinthians 6:19 when Paul exhorts the Corinthians to refrain from sexual immorality. After all, "do you not know that your body is a temple of the Holy Spirit within you, whom you have from God? You are not your own..." (1 Cor. 6:19, ESV). *exactly* That said, Paul does not use this notion exclusively with respect to sexuality. 1 Corinthians 3:17 seems to suggest that God will exact justice against those who persecute Christians in his own time: "If anyone destroys God's temple, God will destroy him. For God's temple is holy, and you are that temple." (ESV). The same notion is evoked to address the issue of marriage between believers and unbelievers (2 Cor. 6:14-16).

2 Corinthians 5:4 seems to speak of the body as an earthly tent (σκῆνος), suggesting that our existence in this tent leaves us burdened. It seems clear that Paul is referring to the body, here, as "tent." *as does John 1 — incarnation, and O.T.* Indeed, in the inter-testamental book Paul was surely familiar with, Wisdom 9:15 (RSV), it was declared, "for a perishable body weighs down the soul, and this earthly tent *garment = fleshly being* burdens the thoughtful mind." While one might attempt to evoke Paul's rarely evoked secondary vocation as a tent maker to understand this passage, a more likely reference here is to the Old Testament tabernacle. The KJV, in fact, translates σκῆνος as tabernacle here. This is connected to the notion of the body as a "temple" of the Holy Spirit because the temple was where God dwelled among His people. The tabernacle, furthermore, was transitory and impermanent. That said, the more permanent temple was built in continuity with the tabernacle. To put it plainly, to speak of the body as a "tent" is not to degrade the body, but to suggest a greater fulfillment or consummation of bodily existence that is yet to come. The fact that Jesus refers to his own body as "temple" (John 2:21) bolsters this perspective.

(who also "tent"s Jesus/Word)

The Body of the Christian and the Body of Christ

Paul employs σῶμα Χριστοῦ or "body of Christ" as a frequent descriptor of the church. Employing discourse analysis in his recent doctoral dissertation Sunny Y. Chen argued that one of Paul's most important applications of σῶμα Χριστοῦ is "to elucidate the social and corporate identity" of the community, particularly in his letters to Corinth.[228] While a significant exegesis of this connection could be pursued it would be beyond the necessary scope of this book to do so. Nonetheless, passages such as 1 Corinthians 10-11 evoking the division of the body, connected to the body of Christ, on account of divisions in the church emphasizes that the church bears continuity with Christ corporally.

social corpus

Conclusion

If the Old Testament affirms an aspectual or relational essence of the body in relevance to the totality of the human person the same can be said of the New Testament. In some ways, the body as the locus of how the human creature participates in relationship—both with God and with one's neighbor and the world—is even more clearly portrayed in the New Testament than in the Old. While it is clear that the human person survives beyond the death of the body, the intermediate state is not defined as bodiless *per se* but as transitory from one body to the next, or from the "soulish/natural body" to the "spiritual body" to employ Paul's terms. Paul directs his Christian audience to ponder the nature of the new Adam, our resurrected Lord, rather than the old Adam (our fallen forefather) if one is to understand what it means to be fully human, that is, a full participant in the Creator's vision for mankind. Just as it is not the grave—or the creedal affirmation of Jesus' descent into hell—that defines the essence of our Lord it is not the grave but the cross and resurrection that defines how the human creature should understand his bodily existence both here and in the evermore.

but not clear how

---

[228] Sunny Y. Chen. The Social and Corporate Dimensions of Paul's Anthropological Terms in the Light of Discourse Analysis. PhD. Diss. MCD University of Divinity, 2014. 105.

CHAPTER 3:
THE BODY IN THE
BEGINNING

THE DISTINCTION BETWEEN CREATOR AND CREATURE could be said to be among the most fundamental of Christian distinctions, particularly regarding human identity. As quoted in the opening words of the introduction above, as well as in the title of this book, Luther's exclamation, "I am God's creature!" expresses what it means to be human. To understand man as "God's creature" implies that the creation of man "in the beginning" is key to understanding the significance of man's creaturely identity. For Luther, this creaturely identity is understood primarily in terms of two distinct relationships: before God (*coram Deo*) and before the world (*coram mundo*). It is this distinction, most commonly termed the two kinds of righteousness, which Luther identified as "our theology" in his famous *Galatians Lectures*, 1535. While the two kinds of righteousness never emerges in Luther or the Lutheran confessions as its own distinct article, it permeates each of Luther's teachings running through each as a sort of "nervous system" allowing every article of the faith to function properly within the greater *corpus doctrinae*, or body of doctrine. Accordingly, it should be expected that Luther's understanding of the same would thoroughly permeate his handling of the creation narrative in the opening chapters of Genesis.

This chapter will examine how the two kinds of righteousness relates to the body in the creation narrative of Genesis. While the body never emerges as a particular article or as the subject of any particular treatise in Luther's works, his concern for defining what it means to be human frequently engages bodily themes. John Paul II began his *Theology of the Body* by returning to the "beginning" as accounted in Genesis. Because the late pontiff's work on the subject looms so large in contemporary theologies of the body, his insights here will first be summarized for the sake of bringing Luther's perspective on the matter into current discussion. As briefly discussed in the previous introductory chapter, John Paul II's work demonstrates a theology of the human body that is essentially relational – specifically spousal – in character. Luther's distinction between the two kinds of righteousness similarly emerges in Luther's understanding of the human creature, including his reflections regarding the body, as he returns to "the beginning."

The themes that develop from Luther's two kinds of righteousness within his exposition of the creation narrative of Genesis itself will be elucidated by other writings, particularly those writings wherein the Wittenberg reformer grounds his distinction between the two kinds of righteousness in creation. After having demonstrated Luther's concern for the body within the framework of the two kinds of righteousness as affirmed in Genesis the following chapters will proceed to consider the topic as it relates to man after his fall into sin and further as it relates to the restored creaturely identity of man in Christ. Finally, Luther's concept of the total man – *totus homo* – in relationship to God will serve to illuminate God's design in light of issues of particular consequence in today's world.

John Paul II's Return to "The Beginning"

If one were to identify a *sedes doctrinae* for John Paul II's theology of the body it would have to be the creation narrative of Genesis 1 and 2. The pope begins his lectures on the theology of the body by appealing to this text. His reason for appealing to "the beginning" is simple – Jesus directs him there. In Matthew 19 and Mark 10 Jesus is questioned by the Pharisees regarding the dissolubility of marriage. In response to the Pharisees' challenge, wherein they appeal to a provisional allowance for divorce by Moses, Jesus cites the creation of man and woman "in the beginning" as the basis for his position. What Moses had allowed was due to the hardness of man's heart. In a fallen world, infected to the core by sin, sometimes *no, to curb violence*

allowances have to be made on account of sin in an effort to <u>approximate</u> -
righteousness. Sin has so corrupted God's creation that sometimes no course
of action can be chosen where sin can be wholly avoided. In such
predicaments provisional approximations of righteousness may be the best
course of action. Such allowances, however, do not supersede the original
design – or natural law – of God's creation. An allowance, such as the one to
divorce one's wife which Moses permitted, may have been a "necessary evil"
but it is still an "evil" no less. Divorce, no less than death, was not a part of
God's original design for man and woman. The provision Moses allowed does
not justify the sin of divorce. No law, provisional or otherwise, changes what
God's design had been from the beginning. Seeking "loop holes" in the
Mosaic law will not get the sinner "off the hook."[229] The Pharisees are
looking to the law, and a provisional one at that, for justification. Jesus,
instead, directs his challengers to a portion of scripture he presumes they
should have known – Genesis 1 and 2.[230]

On the surface it might appear that Jesus is presenting an impossible
challenge. How can fallen man even imagine a return to the Edenic state?
What good does it do to ponder the state of innocence when man has fallen
so far from it? God's original design seems to be a long-lost dream that could
never again be realized. Far from confusing the matter this conundrum
reveals, for John Paul II, the very significance of Christ's return to "the
beginning."

> Christ's words, which appeal to the "beginning," allow us to
> find an essential continuity in man and a link between these two
> different states or dimensions of the human being [original
> innocence and that of original sin]. The state of sin is part of

---

What do you do with "bondage to sin" — this is

[229] It should be acknowledged that there are cases when a <u>single party</u> in a divorce is not necessarily *legal re-* guilty of sin—i.e. cases of marital unfaithfulness, abuse, or abandonment. The issue here, however, is not *not re-* individual guilt *per se* but a more fundamental notion of sin as anything that is contrary to God's natural *holiness* law from the beginning. While there may be instances when <u>one of the parties of a divorce did not sin,</u> personally, the very fact that divorce occurs reminds us of our fallen nature, and recognizes our need for Christ to restore his broken and fallen world.

not over vs the relationship

[230] "Have you not read that he who created them from the beginning made them male and female, and said, 'Therefore a man shall leave his father and his mother and hold fast to his wife, and the two shall *vs !?* become one flesh'? So they are no longer two but one flesh. What therefore God has joined together, let *the* not man separate." Matthew 19:3-6 (ESV)

black white.

"historical man," of the human beings about whom we read in Matthew 19, that is of Christ's interlocutors then, as well as of every other potential or actual interlocutor at all times of history and thus, of course, also of man today. Yet, in every man without exception, this state–the "historical" state–plunges its roots deeply into his theological "prehistory," which is the state of original innocence...Thus, historical man is rooted, so to speak, in his revealed theological prehistory; and for this reason, every point of his historical sinfulness must be explained (both in the case of the soul and of the body) with reference to original innocence...When Christ, according to Matthew 19, appeals to the "beginning," he does not point only to the state of original innocence as a lost horizon of human existence in history. To the words that he speaks with his own lips, we have the right to attribute at the same time the whole eloquence of the mystery of redemption.[231]

As the second Adam, Christ is in a unique position to reconnect man to his "prehistorical" roots. Only Christ can really direct one back to the "beginning" and carry one through one's present sinful situation into a hope that will be consummated in His redemption that restores the original condition of man.[232] Thus, for John Paul II, the return to the "beginning" is not mere nostalgia for an age long-gone by. The fact that Jesus himself directs his challengers there, through his very words, carries with it not only an affirmation of natural law but also the hope of a new creation of which he himself is the first-fruits. One can only look back to the "beginning" with hope when he returns to the beginning with his sight also fixed forward on the promise of redemption in Jesus as re-creator. Accordingly, John Paul II

---

[231] *TOB* 142-143

[232] "What is at issue here is not only the mystery of Christ. In him, it is the mystery of man that is revealed from the beginning. There is probably no other text on the origins of man so simple and yet so complete as that contained in the first three chapters of the Book of Genesis. Here not only do we find an account of the creation of man as male and female, but his particular vocation in the universe is made abundantly clear...The Church preserves within herself the memory of man's history from the beginning: the memory of creation, his vocation, his elevation, and his fall. Within this essential framework the whole of human history, the history of Redemption, is written." John Paul II, *Memory and Identity: Conversations at the Dawn of a Millennium* (New York: Rizzoli, 2005), 151.

returns to the Genesis text in a manner that one can only do living on this side of the cross–with redemption always in view. The complexities of sin after the fall present no substantive challenge to the essential theology of the body.

Analyzing the first two chapters of Genesis, then, John Paul II identifies what he terms the "original experiences" of man in the beginning. He sees no conflict between the creation account of Genesis 1 and that of Genesis 2. The difference between them is simply a matter of perspective. The first chapter elucidates the creation narrative on a grander perspective from the viewpoint of the triune God. The second chapter reveals the creation experience of the first man and woman from man's own perspective.[233] It is primarily, though not exclusively, from Genesis 2 where John Paul II discerns these "original experiences." It is worth noting that the use of the term "original" does not merely indicate long-lost experiences by man felt long ago at the beginning of human history, but they are "original experiences" because they lie at the basis of every other experience in the life of a human being. As Anderson and Granados point out, John Paul II's use of the word "original" "has the same double meaning as the Greek word arché, which signifies both a temporal beginning and the foundations of a building."[234] These original experiences are never wholly lost even though they are corrupted and difficult to discern on account of sin. These experiences essentially define what it means to truly be human.

The Meaning of Original Solitude

Focusing on Genesis 2, John Paul II elaborates upon the unique condition in which newly created man finds himself. God forms man from the ground, breathes life into him, yet still recognizes that "it is not good that man should be alone" (Gen. 2:18). In spite of being surrounded by every "good" thing God had already made, including every kind of plant and

---

[233] "After we've listened to the creative voice of God in the first account, we perceive man's answering voice in the second. The second creation narrative enables us to rediscover the inner experience through which we are to respond to the Creator's call." Carl Anderson and Jose Granados, *Called to Love: Approaching John Paul II's Theology of the Body* (New York: The Crown Publishing Group, 2009), 22.

[234] Ibid., 24.

animal, man was alone. Adam experienced what John Paul II calls "original solitude."

As God parades before Adam every creature, "to see what he would call them" (Gen. 2:19) Adam engages what John Paul II calls a test, or examination, that helps man gain "the consciousness of his own superiority" over the other animals of creation.[235] Through this exercise, man comes to "realize his special uniqueness" and dignity as a creature designed specifically in the image and likeness of God. As John Paul II writes in *Roman Triptych*, man is "alone in his wonderment, among many beings incapable of wonder."[236] This wonderment prompts man to seek his own identity through self-discovery and in so doing expresses his original solitude in unique relationship with his creator. The second side of the coin, though, through discovering his special relationship with God is that man begins to recognize that he is alone. No other creature is suitable as his help-mate. What God himself articulated, man feels and experiences at his very core: it is not good that he should be alone.

The significance of the unity between man and woman will be discussed in the next section. Let it suffice, at this point, to clarify that the creation of woman is not so much a remedy for "original solitude" as it is the necessary corollary man must embrace as a creature made in God's own image and likeness. Original solitude is not a problem, *per se*, but simply describes one component of human identity. Man's original solitude is not something that needs to be fixed. In solitude, alone, however man is unable to fully realize his humanity. In solitude man experiences a relationship with his creator that no other creature can enjoy. In order for man's unique relationship with his creator to be reflected outwardly in his life, though, it is necessary that man also embraces another so that he would fully realize his identity in God's image of love. The animals God parades before man will not suffice because these animals share no communion with man in his solitude. What John Paul II later terms the "spousal" or "nuptial" definition of the body, most clearly affirmed in the communion of man and woman in one flesh, is not a move beyond original solitude but is rather the context

---

[235] *TOB* 148.

[236] John Paul II, *Roman Triptych. Meditations* (Boston: Pauline Books and Media, 2006), 8.

wherein original solitude is experienced and embraced by man and woman together. *was too strained.*

How, then, does man's experience of original solitude relate specifically to the body? John Paul II affirms that it is precisely as man emerges in the visible world as a "body among bodies" that he is able to come to grips with his own solitude. *where does Adam state he is alone?*

He is pronounced alone, and when he sees

> The body, by which man shares in the visible created world, *that he* makes him at the same time aware of being "alone." Otherwise *says* he would not have been able to arrive at this conviction, which *"This at last, is flesh of* in fact he reached (as we read in Gen 2:20), if his body had not *my flesh.* helped him to understand it, making the matter evident to him... *First song in* The premise of this self-distinction on man's part is the fact *the sacred* that only he is able to "cultivate the earth" (see Gen 2:5) and to *texts.* "subdue it" (Gen 1:28). One can say that from the very beginning *—no—* the awareness of "superiority" inscribed in the definition of *God led him* humanity has originated in a typically human praxis or *to see it,* behavior...Man is a subject not only by his self-consciousness *and to* and by self-determination, but also based on his own body. *The* *not indulge* *structure of this body is such that it permits him to be the other of* *in* *genuinely human activity.* In this activity, the body expresses the *bestiality —* person.[237] *removed from self – too deceiving?*

Whereas the subject of human vocation is typically associated with the relationship man has with other creatures and the earth, John Paul II sees also here how the "original" human vocation sets man apart from the other living creatures thus revealing to man his unique relationship with God. *and every other* Accordingly, there is a link between genuinely human activity in the world *creature is also* and man's position before God. This is not to say, though, that man's *pronounced* original work establishes his relationship with God. It does, on the other *Good.* hand, reflect man's unique purpose in the world which in turn makes him aware of his connection to the Divine. Acting out his dominion over creation through his body man comes to understand his unique dual-relationship and *to be in dialogue to listen (obey) God*

---

[237] *TOB,* 152-154.

[handwritten note at top: God did not say you did not do/make the snake. God said you did not listen/trust me]

dual-response-ability before God and before the world. One might say that through this awareness man becomes response-able. As the recipient of God's selfless and loving act of creation man is able, with a unique awareness of this, to respond by exercising his dominion as a selfless and loving being on behalf of God for the entire world. *[handwritten: NO.]*

The Meaning of Original Unity

[handwritten: BY WORSHIPPING & LISTENING TO GOD]

The words of Genesis 2:18, where God declares that it is "not good" that man should "be alone" reveals not only the original solitude of man but also serves as a prelude to the account of the creation of woman. As John Paul II puts it, "together with this account, the meaning of original solitude enters and becomes a part of the meaning of original unity."[238] Whatever is "not good" about man's solitude is "broken" as the first man "reawakens from his sleep [as male and female."[239] For John Paul II, masculinity and femininity emerge as two different "incarnations" of the image of God in man. As such, original solitude is substantially prior to original unity and persists equally in both genders. The definitive creation of man results in an "ontological dimension of unity and duality."[240] Together, in unity, man and woman share a common humanity. On the basis of this shared humanity, there is a new duality *[handwritten: really, maybe]* constituting masculinity and femininity.

While many may read the account of Eve's creation as the story of how a male human being named "Adam" got himself a wife, John Paul II underscores that the very meaning of the name "Adam" signifies a connection to the earth. Anderson and Granados summarize John Paul II's point well:

> The picture changes somewhat when we learn that the name "Adam" is actually a play on the Hebrew word for earth: *hā'adāmāh*. For as John Paul II points out, it's only after the woman is created that the Bible first uses the Hebrew word for man in the sense of "male": 'iš. When Eve appears on the scene, a new vocabulary emerges along with her: The text shifts from

---

[238] *TOB, 156.*

[239] Ibid., 160.

[240] Ibid., 161.

hā'adāmāh which emphasizes man's connection to the earth, to '*iš*, which it then immediately pairs with the word for "woman": *iššā*. Note the ingenious wordplay: The woman is called *iššā* because she has been taken from man, '*iš*. It's as if Adam, hitherto a stand-in for "man" in the generic sense, had suddenly ~~woken up~~ *awakened* to the fact that he is a *male*, whose existence makes sense only because he has a *female* counterpart (and we have to imagine Eve going through a similar experience in her turn).[241]

[handwritten margin note: no, this does not hold the concept of "humankind" which covers enormous diversity]

When Adam awakens from his "torpor" and discovers woman for the first time his very first words recognize "the somatic structure" that man and woman share. John Paul II calls this "the homogeneity of the whole being of both."[242] As man awakens and discovers woman his very first words addressing woman as "flesh from my flesh" and "bone from my bones" (Gen. 2:23) recognize a bodily unity that substantially defines a common humanity persisting in both genders. Woman was, after all, made "with the rib" that God had taken from man. It is only through man's familiarity with his own body that he can recognize the similitude he and woman share. It is only through man's familiarity with his own body, likewise, that he can discover "the difference" that distinguishes male from female.[243] Kenneth Schmitz has summarized the significance of this moment well:

[handwritten margin note: so idealized]

[handwritten margin note: which is?]

> By any standard, the revelation is momentous, for it discloses that man as male comes to a new self-awareness and self-realization only with the coming into being of man as female. And since the self-awareness and self-realization come about

---

[241] Anderson and Granados, *Called to Love*, 45.

[242] *TOB, 160.*

[243] "Let us recall the passage of Genesis 2:23...In the light of this text we understand that the knowledge of man passes through masculinity and femininity, which are, as it were, two 'incarnations' of the same metaphysical solitude before God and the world–*two reciprocally completing ways of 'being a body' and at the same time of being human*–as two complementary dimensions of self-knowledge and self-determination and, at the same time, *two complementary ways of being conscious of the meaning of the body*. Thus, as Genesis 2:23 already shows, femininity in some way finds itself before masculinity, while masculinity confirms itself through femininity." *TOB, 166.*

[handwritten margin note: This is ancient Greek - Platonic Creation — where all people are males / just some better at it than others...]

within the distinctive solitude of humanity and with the emergence of another human being within that solitude, the process of self-recognition occurs in the woman as well. A new reciprocity is born within humanity–it is the internal reciprocity of solitudes–and with this inner reciprocity, humanity now acquires its essential completeness.[244]

This "essential completeness" through masculinity and femininity overcame original solitude while affirming what constitutes the human person in solitude. Original solitude, rather than a barrier toward relationship with others in the world, becomes a pathway toward the communion of persons experienced most intimately between man and woman in nuptial unity. While Genesis 1 speaks of man created in the "image of God," Genesis 2 points to the communion of persons. Man became the "image and likeness" of God, not only through his own humanity, but also through the communion he shares with his spouse.[245] John Paul II sees in the communion a reflection and image of the communion of persons in the Triune God.[246] The mystery that unites all three persons of the Trinity in one Godhead is similar to the mystery that unites man and woman as distinct persons in "one flesh."

This union is experienced especially in the conjugal act as the two become "one flesh." The body allows the unity of persons when they submit their communion to the blessing of fertility. As such, every time man and

---

[244] Kenneth L. Schmitz, *At the Center of the Human Drama: The Philosophical Anthropology of Karol Wojtyla/Pope John Paul II* (Washington DC: The Catholic University of America Press, 1993), 102.

[245] "The meaning of the original unity of man, whom God has created 'male and female,' is grasped (particularly in the light of Genesis 2:23) by knowing man in the whole endowment of his being, that is, in the whole wealth of that mystery of creation standing at the basis of theological anthropology. This knowledge, that is, the search for the human identity of the one who, at the beginning, is 'alone,' must always pass through duality, through 'communion.'" *TOB,* 166.

[246] "The function of the image is that of mirroring the one who is the model, of reproducing its own prototype. Man becomes an image of God not so much in the moment of solitude as in the moment of communion. He is, in fact, 'from the beginning' not only an image in which the solitude of the one Person, who rules the world, mirrors itself, but also and essentially the image of an inscrutable divine communion of Persons. In this way, the second account could also prepare for understanding the trinitarian concept of the 'image of God,' even if 'image' appears only in the first account. This is obviously not without significance for the theology of the body, but constitutes perhaps the deepest theological aspect of everything one can say about man." *TOB,* 163-164.

[handwritten: So if one does not become a sexually active being, one cannot grasp the mystery?]

woman engage in the conjugal act as "one flesh" they rediscover the mystery
of creation together. Sex allows each person to surpass the limits of their
own bodily solitude and assumes the solitude of the body of the second "self"
as one's own. This union results in children, thus participating in God's act
of creation. The purity of this union is first experienced through "original
nakedness."

[handwritten: —so does meditation, the "flow" experience of artists & athletes etc...]

The Meaning of Original Nakedness

The concept of "original nakedness" emerges from the concluding
verse of Genesis 2: "And the man and his wife were both naked and were not
ashamed" (Gen. 2:25). All of the above is realized as a bodily, somatic
experience particularly by man and woman's experience of original
nakedness. Put another way, "original nakedness is the ability to read the
language of the human body as a simultaneous expression of original
solitude and original unity."[247]

[handwritten: no, he is judging the category of lust vs recognition of love]

The unashamed state of man and woman in their nakedness might
seem, at first, to be a relatively inconsequential point. On the contrary,
though, it is precisely in the bodily experience of "nakedness" that the first
subjective realization of the contrast between the original innocence of man
and his post-fall sinful state becomes immediately evident. While this will
be more fully explored in the next chapter, it is certainly noteworthy at this
point to recognize that the change man and woman experience between their
Edenic and fallen state is one that is realized primarily with respect to their
bodies. Nakedness, according to the pope, signifies the original good of God's
vision, of the "pure" value of humanity as male and female, of the body and
of sex.[248] The body "manifests man and, in manifesting him, acts as in
intermediary *[handwritten: man]* that allows man and woman from the beginning, to
'communicate' with each other according to that *communio personarum*
willed for them in particular by the Creator."[249]

---

[247] Anderson and Granados, *Called to Love,* 92.

[248] "'Nakedness' signifies the original good of the divine vision. It signifies the whole simplicity
and fullness of this vision, which shows the 'pure' value of man as male and female, the 'pure' value of
the body and of its sex" *TOB, 177.* See also *TOB, 167-174.* Yet, this "original nakedness" turns to what
the former pope calls "original shame." After the fall, man is naked, likewise, to the wrath of God.

[249] *TOB,* 176.

The Spousal/Nuptial Meaning of the Body

All of the above original experiences together reveal what John Paul II calls the "spousal meaning" of the body. Though his analysis of the "beginning" in Genesis the pope grounds his anthropology in the theological context of the image of God in the "hermeneutics of the gift."[250] The concept of "gift" is the consummative meaning of original solitude–unity–nakedness. It is the heart of the mystery of creation and the theology of the body. Creation itself is a fundamental expression of a gift that comes into being out of nothingness (*creatio ex nihilo*). God has no need of creation, as if something were lacking in his own essence. Creation itself is a testimony to God as a selfless giver. Every creature, by its very existence, bears the sign of the original and fundamental gift. There is a giver, a receiver of the gift, and a relationship between the two. Man is created in the image of his gracious giver. As God entrusts the world to man, the entire world becomes a gift to man as well. Man can recognize, in his solitude, the gift God has given him but he is not able to substantially give anything back to God who lacks nothing. Man longs for someone with whom he can exist in a relationship of mutual giving. Man can only fully realize his essence by existing "with someone" and "for someone." The communion of persons, referred to above, means existing in a relationship of mutual gift, or reciprocating donation of self. Thus, through his unity with woman man's original solitude is fulfilled. The radical gift of God's act in creation becomes paradigmatic for their entire relationship as each expresses their thanks to God through their gift of self to the other. If the original couple's communion with God were to be fractured, their communion with each other would also be shattered. Both man's and woman's donation of self to the other, and the reciprocal reception of the other's gift, is only comprehended by the creator's original gift of life to man. Their marriage in turn, becomes the clearest demonstration of God's ongoing love for the couple. If their communion together were shattered, man would again be unable to fully realize his communion with his creator.

---

[250] Ibid., 190.

Thus, John Paul II is willing to call the body a primordial sacrament, "understood as a sign that efficaciously transmits in the visible world the invisible mystery hidden in God from eternity."[251] This mystery consists of truth and love, the "mystery of divine life, in which man really participates."[252] Marriage is not merely a civil institution, but is fundamentally a "sacrament" for John Paul II because it is a visible sign of God's ongoing grace as creator. It does *more* than bestow grace. When properly embraced, marriage is the consummative expression of God's grace experienced in the flesh. The body is essentially "spousal" or "nuptial" in meaning because the body itself is the visible, or sacramental, element that communicates both God's relationship with mankind in solitude and also fulfills that solitude through spousal unity in reciprocal gift of one's body to another. The human body is created to express love through the gift and to affirm the other through existential self-giving "for the other's sake." This acceptance of one for the other affirms the other. Accordingly, there is no *eisegesis* shame between man and woman in their nakedness. Vulnerability in their nakedness is not absent, but neither is it feared as each fully embraces the gift of the other. Each body is gift to the other, and fully affirmed by the other who receives and affirms the body of one's spouse as his or her own. This substantiates man's original happiness. *wow — he is trying to make it all under one umbrella*

Luther's "Two Kinds of Righteousness" in Creation

Martin Luther both inaugurated and concluded his career at the University of Wittenberg lecturing on the book of Genesis, grounding some of his most pivotal theological categories in the first article of the Creed. One could say that Luther both began and ended "in the beginning." This is true not only of Luther's historical chronology, but also is fundamentally true of his theology as a whole. While popular summaries of Luther's theology often assert that the second article of the creed was upheld as most central to his thought, Luther himself affirms that "I believe in God, the Father almighty, creator of heaven and earth" is the most lofty of all Christian articles. For Luther, any who confess that God is both almighty and creator, "dies to

---

[251] Ibid., 203.

[252] Ibid.

everything else...and confesses from the heart, that he has no capability on the basis of his own powers."[253] Recognizing the impact of the reformer's first article theology on his entire theological system is not difficult to imagine. Kolb argues that for Luther, God exists as, "the Creator, who had come to rescue his human creatures from the mystery of evil and restore them to their full enjoyment in the gift of humanity."[254]

Even if one were to grant that the second article, more often than not, emerges most prominently in Luther's works he clearly understands that salvation implies a fall, which in turn implies something from which man originally fell. There was an original state in which man was created that God himself once called "good." This original state of man Luther sometimes terms "original righteousness."[255] The work of Christ in redemption is not an altogether new work of God, but is a consummative work that brings God's original act of creation into teleological completion. While the state of man, restored in Christ, is not identical to man's original righteousness in creation it is nonetheless true that one cannot fully appreciate the consummation of Christ's restorative work in the human creature apart from the original condition of man prior to the fall.

Creation and redemption are inseparably linked in Luther's thought. God does not begin as a creator who later assumes the title of "redeemer" as plan B. On the contrary, the creator is the redeemer and the redeemer is the creator from the beginning. Redemption is, in the final estimation, proper

---

[253] Preface to the Genesis sermons, *WA* 24:18,26-33. Translated in Robert Kolb, "God and His Human Creatures in Luther's Sermons on Genesis: The Reformer's Early Use of His Distinction of Two Kinds of Righteousness," *Concordia Journal* 33, no. 2 (2007): 170.

[254] Robert Kolb, *Martin Luther: Confessor of the Faith* (Oxford: Oxford University Press, 2009), 198.

[255] For example, "If we follow Moses, we should take original righteousness to mean that man was righteous, truthful, and upright not only in body but especially in soul, that he knew God, that he obeyed God with the utmost joy, and that he understood the worlds of God even without prompting...It is part of this original righteousness that Adam loved God and His works with an outstanding and very pure attachment; that he lived among the creatures of God in peace, without fear of death, and without fear of sickness; and that he had a very obedient body, without evil inclinations and the hideous lust which we now experience. In this way a very beautiful and very accurate picture of original righteousness can be inferred from the deprivation which we now feel in our own nature...Original sin is the loss of original righteousness, or the deprivation of it, just as blindness is the deprivation of sight." *Lectures on Genesis, LW* 1:113-114.

to God's role as creator. As God once called all of creation out of nothing with his Word, breathing his Holy Spirit into man's nostrils, he calls the new man in faith out of nothing from man's sinful state and breathes his Spirit into man once again. While it has sometimes been said that theology is the "art of making distinctions" one cannot get Luther's theology right unless he understand that all theological distinctions also have connections. The connection between creation and redemption is an essential component of Luther's theology of the human creature.

In the Beginning

"In the beginning, God created the heavens and the earth."[256] From the beginning the subject and object of the creation narrative are immediately defined. God created and the object of his creation is the heaven and the earth. Every "let there be" that God speaks both furthers the distinction between the creator and his creation and also defines the relationship between the creator and all he calls into being. The foundation for what Luther would elsewhere term the "two kinds of righteousness" is already affirmed in this fundamental distinction from the beginning. "The simplest meaning" of this first verse in Genesis, in Luther's words is as follows: "Everything that is, was created by God."[257] From this fact emerges a distinction between creator and creature, between activity and passivity. In the act of creation God performs all the activity. The creature, on the other hand, is the passive recipient of God's creative action. The creature's passivity, however, is more fundamental to the identity of "creature" than one would normally associate with a single instance or action. Because the creature owes its very existence to the creator's action, passivity is a fundamental and essential component of creaturely identity. When Luther refers to the two kinds of righteousness in terms of "passive righteousness" (*coram Deo*) and "active righteousness" (*coram mundo*) he affirms a distinction that harkens back to the very beginning of creation itself. When Luther formulates his distinction between the two kinds of righteousness in his 1535 Galatians commentary, he returns to this fundamental distinction

---

[256] Genesis 1:1 (ESV).

[257] *Lectures on Genesis (1535/38), LW* 1:7.

between creator and creature as an indictment of both monastic orders and the papacy itself.

> ...all hypocrites and idolaters try to do the works that properly pertain to the Deity and belong completely and solely to Christ. They do not actually say with their mouths: "I am God; I am Christ." Yet in fact they arrogate to themselves the divinity of Christ and His function...Thus the monks have taught, and they have persuaded the whole world of this, that they are able to justify not only themselves with their hypocritical sanctity but also other to whom they communicate it, even though it is the proper function of Christ alone to justify the sinner. Thus the pope, by extending his divinity over the whole world, has denied and completely suppressed the work of Christ and His divinity. It is useful for these things to be taught and considered carefully, for they help one to judge about all Christian doctrine and all human life...All these things have their source in the refusal of this accursed hypocrisy to be justified by a divine blessing and formed by God the Creator. It refuses to be merely passive matter but wants actively to accomplish the things that it should patiently permit God to accomplish in it and should accept from him. And so it makes itself the creator and the justifier through its own works...Thus every hypocrite is the material and the worker at the same time...the material, because he is a sinner; and the worker, because he puts on a cowl or selects some other work through which he hopes to merit grace and to save both himself and others. Thus he is creature and creator at the same time...For this is the abomination standing in the holy place (Matt. 24:15), which denies God and establishes a creature in the place of the Creator.[258]

The groundwork for what would later form the dual relationship man would have between the creator and the creation is Luther's affirmation of

---

[258] *Lectures on Galatians* (1535), LW 26:257-259.

the medieval distinction between creator and creature, *creare* and *creatura*. Cortright discusses this distinction, expressed particularly in the writings of Thomas Aquinas,[259] as follows:

> As a concept, creation in medieval theology generally had two different thrusts. The first emphasized the work or deed of God *nature of God* in making all things–*creare*. The second emphasized the result or product of God's creating power–*creatura*. The first is bound up in the nature of God: God is the creating God; the second– what God has made–is distinct from God.[260]

For Luther, though, this distinction becomes more than a Thomistic affirmation of God as "first cause" in creation. It becomes, in Luther's eventual development, foundational for human identity. While this dynamic is essential to human identity, though, it cannot be considered essential to God's identity. God does not need to create in order to be God. God exists in his fullness infinitely prior to creation. For Luther, God is always both hidden (*Deus absconditus*)[261] and revealed (*Deus revelatus*). In his infinite majesty, God's existence prior to creation is unknowable to man. Luther notes a number of questions often posed that, in the very fact that they are asked, fail to comprehend the infinite character of God's nature. Consider Augustine's answer to a popular question amongst the speculative theologians of his day: "What was God doing before the beginning of the world?" Augustine's answer, "God was making hell ready for those who pried into meddlesome questions," satisfies Luther. *also depicted in Job*

---

[259] See, for example, *ST Ia*, 44 (*Treatise on Creation*) where Aquinas examines "The procession of creatures from God, and of the first cause of all things." *be careful of politique ...*

[260] Cortright, *Poor Maggot Sack That I Am*, 56.

[261] The term *Deus absconditus* originates from the Vulgate's rendering of Isaiah 45:14. Luther picks up on this phrase as a source of comfort. "These are the words of the prophet, who had already predicted these words of consolation. Now he is snatched into a trance of the Word of God, as if to say, 'Dear God, how strangely you deal with us!' It is a matter beyond comprehension to which reason cannot attain. Is this not a wonderful deliverance, that restoration is promised to Jerusalem, the temple, etc.? There the flesh sees nothing and concludes: Nothing produces nothing. Nevertheless, we see that in this Nothing all things will come to pass through the Word of consolation. Thus we observe God and His incomprehensible plans. So today we see in the Word the progress of the church of God against the force and the schemes of all tyrants. Since faith is the conviction of things not seen, the opposite must appear to be the case." *LW* 17:131-132.

Indeed, the modesty of Augustine pleases me. With perfect frankness he says that in the case of questions of this kind he hauls in the sails of his acumen, because even if we should engage in endless speculation and debate, these matters nevertheless remain outside our comprehension...Let us, therefore, rid ourselves of such ideas and realize that God was incomprehensible in His essential rest before the creation of the world, but that now, after the creation, He is within, without, and above all creatures; that is, He is still incomprehensible. Nothing else can be said, because our mind cannot grasp what lies outside time. God also does not manifest Himself except through His works and the Word, because the meaning of these is understood in some measure. Whatever else belongs essentially to the Divinity cannot be grasped and understood, such as being outside time, before the world, etc.[262]

It is only through the Creator–creature dynamic that man has access to God as he chooses to reveal himself to man. Luther's *Deus absconditus* is not the *Deus incognito* (the unknown God) of the Dionysian mystical tradition.[263] God's revelation in creation is not given in order to "tease" man toward closer communion with the unknown God. No degree of finite revelation in nature can ever comprehend the infinite majesty of God. Man is to cling to God not by using God's revelatory means as a spring board upward into divine majesty, but to cherish God's word given man as a creature. God's act of creation, while not definitive for God's essence, defines the terms of the relationship between God and man.

Creation as a Trinitarian Act

It should be noted that for Luther creation is a Trinitarian act. The Trinity is evident, for Luther, already by the second verse of Genesis: "And the Spirit of the Lord hovered over the waters."

---

[262] *Lectures on Genesis (1535/38), LW* 1:10-11.

[263] See Luther's critique of Dionysian mysticism in *The Babylonian Captivity of the Church, LW* 36:109.

so honest ☺!

Some explain that "the Spirit of the Lord" simply means "wind." But it is more to my liking that we understand Spirit to mean the Holy Spirit. Wind is a creature which at that time did not yet exist, since so far those masses of heaven and earth lay mixed together. Indeed, it is the great consensus of the church that the mystery of the Trinity is set forth here. The Father creates heaven and earth out of nothing through the Son, whom Moses calls the Word. Over these the Holy Spirit broods. As the hen broods her eggs, keeping them warm in order to hatch her chicks, and as it were, to bring them to life through heat, so Scripture says that the Holy Spirit brooded, as it were, on the waters to bring to life those substances where were to be quickened and adorned. For it is the office of the Holy Spirit to make alive.[264] *Sometimes Luther so gets it... less is more.*

As certainly as all three persons are involved in the creation event in general, the entire Trinity participates in the creation of man as well. Luther describes the creation of man as the "most beautiful work of God."[265] The beauty of this act is set apart from all of God's other acts of creation by the grammar of the text itself. In Genesis 1:26 God speaks, "Let us make man in our image, after our likeness." Whereas God spoke previously, "Let there be an expanse," "Let the waters swarm," "Let the earth bring forth," and the like, in the creation of man God involves himself more intimately. According to Luther, "Let us make," indicates forethought and deliberation that is different than anything God does previously.

> He says: "Let us make." Therefore he includes an obvious deliberation and plan; he did nothing similar in the case of the earlier creatures. There, without any deliberation and counsel, He said: "Let the sea be put in motion," "Let the earth produce,"

---

[264] *Lectures on Genesis (1535/38), LW* 1:9.

[265] *Lectures on Genesis (1535/38), LW* 1:55.

> etc. But here, when wants to create man, God summons Himself to a council and announces some sort of deliberation.[266]

Whereas many modern commentators see in the words “Let us make” a plurality of majesty as opposed to an affirmation of what they would deem “later” developments in Trinitarian thought, Luther has no qualms understanding this text as a reference to all three persons of the Godhead.[267] The council to which God calls himself is a council between Father, Son and Holy Spirit. This is not surprising as Luther had also spotted Father, Son and Holy Spirit each operating concurrently in the first few verses of Genesis. For Luther, understanding this text in a Trinitarian fashion is not an anachronistic imposition of later theology on a more primitive time, but indicates that the Holy Trinity is himself as primitive as he is modern. Similarly, Luther rejects the exposition of this text (which he attributes to the Jews) that suggests the plurality of “Let us make” refers to the angels. First, the angels are not creators. Second, man is not made in the image of angels but in the image of God alone.

The significance of the Trinitarian involvement in the creation of man harkens forward toward what John Paul II later terms “original solitude,” as outlined previously. There is, Luther grants, great similitude between man and the beasts. Like man, the beasts also tend toward community as they both “dwell” and “eat” together. Like man, the beasts also receive nourishment from the same materials of the earth. “If you take into account their way of life, their food, and their support, the similarity is great.”[268] John Paul II made the same observation.[269] While man is certainly a creature he is nonetheless a unique creature incomparable to any other in creation.

---

[266] *Lectures on Genesis (1535/38), LW* 1:56.

[267] “...the word ‘Let Us make’ is aimed at making sure the mystery of our faith, by which we believe that from eternity there is one God and that there are three separate Persons in one Godhead: the Father, the Son, and the Holy Spirit.” Ibid., 57.

[268] Ibid., 56.

[269] “The awareness of solitude could have been shattered precisely because of the body itself. Braising himself on the experience of his own body, the man could have reached the conclusion that he is substantially similar to the other living beings (*anamalia)*. By contrast, as we read, he did not arrive at this conclusion, but in fact reached the conviction that he was ‘alone.’” *TOB,* 152.

Man, being uniquely created by the special plan and providence of God as the Holy Trinity summons a deliberative counsel, "is a creature far superior to the rest of the living beings that live a physical life, especially since as yet his nature had not become depraved."[270]

Creatio ex nihilo

Luther's reflections on *creatio ex nihilo* further define the difference between the Creator and his creatures, particularly the creature of man. God does not mold borrowed material into his design. This distinguishes God as creator from all creatures. In spite of all human ingenuity, especially pronounced in today's technological era, man cannot create ex nihilo. At most, man can creatively engage created matter and unleash its latent potential.

Embracing the concept of *creatio ex nihilo* Luther both affirms a long tradition of the doctrine and also departs from it in terms of emphasis and purpose. *Creatio ex nihilo* is not a biblical expression *per se*.[271] It certainly is not found within the Genesis narrative where the concept is often grounded. Cortright has outlined the history of *creatio ex nihilo* as having its origins in the anti-Gnostic fathers.[272] Augustine further developed the doctrine, though his use of it was largely a metaphysical argument employed to affirm God as the highest, or best, of all beings in existence.[273] While Luther often embraced Augustine, his use of *creatio ex nihilo* was accented very differently.

---

[270] *Lectures on Genesis (1535/38), LW* 1:56.

[271] The Latin *Vulgate*, however, does use a similar expression in 2 Maccabees 7:28: *"Peto, nate, ut aspicias ad caelum et terram, et ad omnia quae in eis sunt: et intellegas, quia ex nihilo fecit illa Deus, et hominum genus."*

[272] "In their writings they maintained that the world was not–as the Gnostics believed–the work of an evil demiurge, but the *ex nihilo* creation of the good, freely-loving God. Early Christian theology rejected Gnostic dualism, but...it also dallied with the notion of the eternity of *materia* under the influence of Greek philosophy. After Irenaeus [d. *ca.* 202], however, the viewpoint that the world was made by God alone *ex nihilo* triumphed." Cortright, *Poor Maggot Sack That I Am,* 60.

[273] Augustine writes in his *Confessions,* XII:7: "There was nothing beyond you from which you might make them, O God, one Trinity and trinal Unity. Therefore, you created heaven and earth out of nothing, a great thing and a little thing. For you are almighty and good, to make all things good, the great heaven and the little earth. You were, and there was naught else out of which you made heaven and earth: two beings, one near to you, the other near to nothingness, one to which you alone would be superior, the other to which nothing would be inferior." Saint Augustine, *The Confessions of Saint Augustine* (New York: Doubleday, 1960), 308-309.

"plan"

Luther explicitly rejected Augustine's allegorical understanding of the Genesis creation narrative in favor of a literal interpretation of the text.[274] What is to be discerned from the text was not a philosophical category; it is not a sort of "negative" principle against Platonic ideas about a material creation.[275] For Augustine, *creatio ex nihilo* demonstrates God's power as Creator over that of the creation. While this is technically true for Luther, Luther's main thrust is not God's superiority over the material world *per se*, but that God creates because creating ex nihilo follows from his nature as a loving God. *Creatio ex nihilo* demonstrates that God acts in total freedom, with no duty toward preexistent material, thus it is an expression of God's will and love for what he creates.[276] In short, Luther "augments the medieval concept of *creatura*, including, of course the human body: more than being merely that which has been made, the creation is that which has been commanded or willed into being by the sovereign will and love of God."[277]

because that is a given

Single Nature!

Creation as Present Reality

(esse) — that is the revelation —

As indicated previously, Luther identifies the Word in creation with the "word made flesh," the second person of the Trinity. Luther's Trinitarian theology, his concept of *creatio ex nihilo*, and his theology of the Word are intimately linked in Luther's theology of creation. For Luther, John 1:1[278] elucidates the fuller significance of Genesis 1:3.[279]

---

[274] *Lectures on Genesis (1535/38), LW* 1:3-4.

[275] See Roland J. Teske, S.J., "Genesis Accounts of Creation," in *Augustine Through the Ages,* ed. A.D. Fitzgerald, OSA (Grand Rapids, MI: Eedrmans, 1999) 379-381. See also Colin E. Gunton, "The End of Causality?" in *The Doctrine of Creation: Essays in Dogmatics, History and Philosophy,* ed. Colin E. Gunton (Edinburgh: T&T Clark, 1997), 71.

[276] Juntunen's conclusion is the same: "For Luther God is in his essence a pure, giving love whose motive is not to get good for himself, but to give good to that which lacks in itself, God's love is creative; it never finds its object as something preexistent. Rather, it turns to that which is nothing and is in itself needy in order to create it and make it existent and good through loving it." Juntunen, "Luther and Metaphysics," 131. The same conclusion is determined by Heinrich Bornkamm, *Luther's World of Thought,* trans. Martin H. Bertram (St. Louis: Concordia, 1956), 180-184.

[277] Cortright, *Poor Maggot Sack That I Am,* 59.

[278] "In the beginning was the Word, and the Word was with God, and the Word was God." (John 1:1 ESV)

[279] "And God said, 'Let there be light,' and there was light." (Genesis 1:3 ESV)

[John] is in proper agreement with Moses. He says: "Before the creation of the world there was not a single one of the creatures, but God nevertheless had the Word." What is this Word, or what did He do? Listen to Moses. The light, he says, was not yet in existence; but out of its state of being nothing the darkness was turned into the most outstanding creature, light. Through what? Through the Word. Therefore in the beginning and before every creature there is the Word, and it is such a powerful Word that it makes all things out of nothing.[280]

dabar YHWH —*acting* word, *teleological* word

For Luther, the word of God in creation, by which he creates ex nihilo, does not fade into oblivion after the heaven and earth are made. The very same words God spoke "in the beginning" persist into the present. As Johannes Schwanke has persuasively demonstrated, Luther's conception of primordial history is always a history of the present. — they are opened into Time

the world decay John Paul II's idea
Luther is reluctant to interpret primordial biblical history as the beginning of things, the *initium*, but rather insists that its meaning be understood in terms of a *principium.* He does not — YES! allow himself to be distracted by any isolated, past original history, by any "beginning of things," but instead, in the lectures on Genesis, he sees himself radically placed into the creative event of primordial history. It is not Adam who is ultimately relevant here, but Luther.[281]

In other words, God's office as "creator" is not to be forgotten once one thinks of God in terms of "redeemer" or "sanctifier." Creation is, in fact, the *principium* of God's action that extends beyond the original act of creation into every present moment. Redemption and sanctification belong to this same *principium* and cannot be rightly confessed apart from one's confession of God as "make of heaven and earth." No less than Adam and Eve does every human being owe one's origin to a continual act of God as creator. In *Creation and Law* Gustaf Wingren demonstrates Luther's

---

[280] *Lectures on Genesis (1535/38)*, LW 1:17.

[281] Schwanke, "Luther on Creation," Kindle Loc. 903.

— as in the Psalms + Isaiah — Should God not be creating, all that is collapses into nothingness.

affirmation of continual creation from the Small Catechism linking God's original act of creation to every subsequent generation of human life:

> Creation means at the one time both the creation of the world, the creation of heaven and earth, and my personal creation, that is, my birth. This was Luther's great understanding of both the first and second articles of the Creed: "...He has created me...given me body and soul...He is my Lord." He interprets the third article in a similar way. There is no doubt at all that there are good New Testament grounds for Luther's interpretation of the second and third articles concerning Christ and the Spirit, but we must emphasize that the Old Testament itself also thinks of the work of Creation as continuing in the present time, and, as it were, personalized, in such a way that birth is seen to be the same act of formation as the work of Creation itself, though more intimately related to myself, and coming to an end in my own life, with all that this life implies.[282]

Luther affirms that the creation of each and every human creature is "no less miraculous than that the first man was created from a clod, and the female from a rib of the man."[283] Why should Adam and Eve's creation seem so incredible while the birth of every human creature does not seem so miraculous? It is only because, as Luther attributes the insight to Augustine, that "miracles become commonplace through their continuous recurrence."[284] Like many take the wonderful rising of the sun as a daily phenomenon for granted, so too the normal course of childbirth is seen as commonplace. If God had chosen to continually propagate the human race by forming each person from the clay, "by now, this, too, would have ceased to hold the position of a miracle for us; we would marvel at the method of

---

[282] Gustaf Wingren, *Creation and Law* (Edinburgh: Oliver and Boyd, 1961), 26.

[283] *Lectures on Genesis (1535/38), LW* 1:126.

[284] Ibid.

124

o, Luther, if only you understood the evolution too

procreation through the semen of a man."[285] In short, Luther exhorts his audience to have gratitude for God's continual work of creation from which we owe our very existence. "Should we not wonder at His works, delight in them, and proclaim them always and everywhere?"[286]

The technical term *creatio continua* has been used to describe Luther's view of creation as a continual, present reality. This is not entirely inappropriate, but the term has emerged in the 20th Century in a different manner than Luther's theology would be accurately described. Some caution and clarification regarding the term is in order. Some theologians have been critical of the concept of *creatio continua* differentiating the act of creation "in the beginning" from God's ongoing act of preserving what was already made. Bonhoeffer, most notably, has explicitly rejected the concept of *creatio continua*.

well, he was in a Nazi ethos where anthropology was highly biased.

not just preserving — behold, I am doing a new Thing...

There is an essential difference between *creatio continua* (continual creation) and preservation. In the concept of continual creation the world is wrested forever from the void. But this idea, by the concept of a discontinuous continuity, deprives the creatorhood of God of its absolute freedom and uniqueness. It is just the fact that we cannot anticipate God's action that this idea does not respect. But at the same time the concept of continual creation ignores the reality of the fallen world, which is not ever newly created but creation preserved.[287]

Bonhoeffer's concern, though, should not dissuade one from Luther's opinion. Bonhoeffer is addressing the concept of *creatio continua* as it had been used amongst the emerging process philosophies of his day which constantly saw the world in the process of "becoming" anew.[288] The primary

process theology

---

[285] Ibid., 127.

[286] Ibid.

[287] Bonhoeffer, *Creation and Fall*, 26.

[288] "'Creativity' is the universal of universals characterizing ultimate matter of fact...it is that ultimate principle by which the man, which are of the universe disjunctively, become the one actual occasion which is the universe conjunctively. It lies in the nature of things that many enter into a complex unity." Alfred North Whitehead, *Process and Reality: An Essay in Cosmology* (New York: MacMillan-

yep...

difference between Luther's understanding of creation as "present reality" and the *creatio continua* of process theologians is that for Luther it is the same Word of God spoken "in the beginning" that keeps life in motion. Life is "preserved" precisely because the creative Word of God has not departed from creation entirely. It is "continual creation" because it is the same Word that persists in all that has life. Bonhoeffer is, in fact, in agreement with this aspect of Luther's understanding of the continual creative Word of God in creation.[289]

One might draw similar parallels between Luther's view of *creatio continua* and his view of the Lord's Table in terms of communion with Christ's death and resurrection. Rejecting the Roman Catholic doctrine of the sacrifice of the mass, Luther viewed the Sacrament not as a re-sacrifice of Christ that the church offers to God, but a real participation in the death and resurrection of Christ through eating and drinking in a sort of timeless act as God's people receive the Lord's body and blood. Similarly, Luther's view of *creatio continua* is not an ongoing repetition of God's initial creative Word, but creation continually participating in God's word as it was spoken in the beginning. This is different than the process theology Bonhoeffer was concerned to address that saw continual creation as an act God continually repeats in time. The word of God persists in creation, and if the word were to ever be taken from creation it would simply cease to be and fall back into nothing–*nihil*. In this sense, sin, understood as a rejection of God's word has an affinity with nihilism. Death is the result of sin not because sin is some sort of poisonous substance that kills, but it is the result of sin because it involves a rejection of the only source of life–the word of God. Sin, in its most fundamental sense, is a denial of one's creaturely identity.

Free Press, 1978) 21f.

[289] "One could think that God had now surrendered the work of preservation to his creatures themselves, that the world and nature provided for themselves, and that the fixity of the law and the fruitfulness of the living together constituted the powers of the preservation of the world. The clock is wound up and now runs by itself. But the Bible clearly knows that in the created world nothing runs 'by itself.' The law and life-creating life are, as the work of God, created out of nothing and stand only in the void; that is, only in the freedom of the Word of God. If God withdrew his Word from his work it would sink back into nothingness." Bonhoeffer, *Creation and Fall*, 26.

The "new creation" is not in the process of "becoming," as if the Word were a bit of yeast that takes time to spread and have its effect. God's Word of new creation does not gradually progress until the ratio of new to old favors the new. The original creation is both 100 percent fallen in Adam and also 100 percent redeemed in Christ. Accordingly, Luther's theology of creation is intimately linked to his theology of redemption: "Paul regards the conversion of the wicked – something which is also brought about by the Word – as a new work of creation."[290] As the trained art expert can spot the work of any good artist based on the character, technique, and method employed by the artist, so too does a good theologian spot the same character, technique and method employed by God in both creation and redemption. Redemption is not a wholly new work of God, as if God were dealing with man differently according to various dispensations. Redemption is the work of the Creator restoring his original masterpiece and, in fact, ushering his original work into its ultimate consummative end.

The Creation of Man

While the prelapsarian understanding of Luther's two kinds of righteousness takes on a different character apart from sin,[291] as an essential description of human identity, these two relationships persist from the moment man was first formed from the dust of the ground: "...then the LORD God formed the man of dust from the ground and breathed into his nostrils the breath of life, and the man became a living creature."[292] This verse shows from the beginning man's creaturely origins in terms of relationship *coram mundo*, having been formed from the dust of the ground,

---

[290] *Lectures on Genesis (1535/38), LW* 1:17.

[291] Luther makes the argument that Scriptures pertaining to the law after the fall cannot be universally applied to man prior to the fall. Luther addresses what he believes to be a faulty syllogism: "No Law has been given for the just; Adam was just; therefore no Law has been given to him, but only a sort of exhortation." First, Luther deals with the context of 1 Tim. 1:9-10, "The Law has not been given for the just person, but for murderers, adulterers, etc." affirming that Paul is speaking only about the "Law which was given after sin, and not about this Law which the Lord gave when Adam was still guiltless and righteous." Luther, then, deconstructs the false syllogism: "...there is in this reasoning the fallacy of composition and division, because a truncated Scripture text is introduced. There is also the fallacy of equivocation. The first consists in this, that the Law before sin is one thing and the Law after sin is something else; the second consists in this, that 'righteous' does not have the same meaning after sin and before sin." *Lectures on Genesis (1535/38), LW* 1:108-110.

[292] Genesis 2:7 (ESV)

127

and *coram Deo*, having received through his nostrils God's breath of life. Man's initial existence is immediately understood in a dual-relationship with the rest of the creation and also with the Creator. In a dynamic interplay between these two relationships man became a "living creature." If one is to consider what it means to truly be human, to be God's creature, the two kinds or righteousness must be considered.

One would be amiss, however, to drive a wedge between the body and soul, as if the body alone had its origins in the dust of the ground while the soul owed its existence to the breath of God. Man did not spontaneously fashion himself from the dust, but his body was formed from the dust by God's intervening action. Elsewhere, Scripture describes man's creation from dust as the act of a potter forming clay.[293] This image implies both manual and creative intervention on God's part upon the medium of his finest sculpture–the human frame. Yahweh shapes man with his own hands. The significance of this act cannot be overemphasized. Bonhoeffer discerns two significant insights from this fact:

First, the bodily nearness of the Creator to the creature, that it is really he who makes me–man–with his own hands; his concern, his thought for me, his design for me, his nearness to me. And secondly, there is his authority, the absolute superiority in which he shapes and creates me, in which I am his creature; the fatherliness in which he creates me and in which I worship him. That is God himself, to whom the whole Bible testifies.[294]

The significance of this "bodily nearness," as Bonhoeffer terms it, between God and man in creation is reflected in redemption as well. As previously discussed, for Luther God's roles as creator and redeemer involve closely related acts. While some distinction can be made between "creation" and "redemption," both acts on God's part bear the same signature. God is doing a similar kind of thing when the Word assumes human flesh to redeem creation as when the Word first spoke creation into existence. As the Word

---

[293] For example, Isaiah 29:16, 64:8 and Romans 9:21.

[294] Bonhoeffer, *Creation and Fall*, 50.

128

first spoke life into existence, and the breath of God entered man's nostrils making him a living creature, so also the Word made flesh redeems man and the Spirit enters man's ears through the means of grace redeeming, or re-creating, man as God's creature in proper relationship to his Creator. As such, a full-bodied theology of redemption cannot be wholly comprehended apart from a full-bodied theology of creation. Accordingly, Bonhoeffer's above insight regarding the creation of man is wholly consistent with Luther's theology of creation in general as "present reality." *I don't think so — at least not as you argue it —*

Moreover, the image of the potter and his clay helps to distinguish the relationship man has with his creator from the relationship man has with the rest of creation. This "second point" from Bonhoeffer's reflections above is more explicitly embraced by Luther. Lecturing on Genesis 2:7 Luther also imports the metaphor of the potter and his clay while discussing the creature/Creator distinction in terms of the freedom of choice, or will.

> ...we are vessels of God, formed by God Himself...He Himself is our Potter, but we His clay, as Is. 64:8 says. And this holds good not only for our origin but throughout our whole life; until our death and in the grave we remain the clay of this Potter. Moreover, this helps us to learn something about the properties of the free will...In a certain way we indeed have a free will in those things that are beneath us. By divine commission we have been appointed lords of the fish of the sea, of the birds of the heavens, and of the beasts of the field. These we kill when it pleases us; we enjoy the foods and other useful products they supply. But in those matters that pertain to God and are above us no human being has a free will; he is indeed like clay in the hand of the potter, in a state of merely passive potentiality, not active potentiality. For there we do not choose, we do not do anything; but we are chosen, we are equipped, we are born again, we accept, as Isaiah says: "Thou are the potter; we, Thy clay."[295]

---

[295] *Lectures on Genesis (1535/38), LW* 1:84-85.

That is your / now, prove it. Thesis

Man's dust-formed body cannot, therefore, be exclusively understood in terms of its relationship to creation apart from its relationship to the creator. Being fully human necessitates both relationships. These two relationships, however, ought to be carefully distinguished in terms of activity and passivity. It is not that man is created merely with two *different* relationships, but that man is created with two fundamentally different *kinds* of relationship. These relationships can be termed different kinds of righteousness because righteousness is, in its final estimation, an account of living according to one's proper identity. Righteousness is right living, or living rightly. Because being properly human is predicated upon these fundamentally different kinds of relationship, one can speak similarly of different kinds of righteousness. One way that Luther distinguishes the two kinds of righteousness is, as discussed previously, according to the terms "passive righteousness" and "active righteousness."[296] Luther's above comments about the human will, even in man's Edenic state, are revealing. It is not simply because sin has entered the world that righteousness *coram Deo* must be received passively. This is affirmed explicitly in Luther's theology of *creatio ex nihilo* previously discussed. Even in the state of innocence Luther describes the human will as passive before God. The relationship between man and his Creator is wholly initiated and maintained by the Creator alone from the beginning. Only the Creator is ever truly free, with complete liberty, in his act of creation. Passivity, with regard to God, is an essential component of human creaturely identity.

as created human

Man may attempt to imitate the creator through ingenuity. One might describe man's ingenuity and "creativity" as *imitatio Dei*, but it is always *imitatio* and never *creatio* in the truest sense. While man's inventions,

---

[296] "We set forth two worlds, as it were, one of them heavenly and the other earthly. Into these we place these two kinds of righteousness, which are distinct and separated from each other. The righteousness of the Law is earthly and deals with earthly things; by it we perform good works. But as the earth does not bring forth fruit unless it has first been watered and made fruitful from above–for the earth cannot judge, renew, and rule the heavens, but the heavens judge, renew, rule, and fructify the earth, so that it may do what the Lord has commanded–so also by the righteousness of the Law we do nothing even when we do much; we do not fulfill the Law even when we fulfill it. Without any merit or work of our own, we must be justified by Christian righteousness, which has nothing to do with the righteousness of the Law or with earthly and active righteousness. But this righteousness is heavenly and passive. We do not have it of ourselves; we receive it from heaven. We do not perform it; we accept it by faith, through which we ascend beyond all laws and works." *Galatians Lectures, 1531-1535, LW* 26:8.

technologies, and artistic expressions may demand "creativity" these actions can never be termed "creation" strictly speaking. Invention is not the same thing as creation because man can never create with absolute freedom *ex nihilo*.[297] *art always imitates nature*

Just as man's connection to the dust of the ground cannot fully be comprehended in terms of a singular relationship, either to the world or God, the breath of God upon man cannot be understood completely apart from both concurrent relationships. The specificity of the breath of God entering into the nostrils of man, resulting in man's creaturely life, affirms from the beginning that the breath, or spirit, of God is immediately concerned with the body. The text does not say that God breathed life into man generically, or into a metaphorical "heart" of sorts, but directly into his nostrils. This corporeal description of the original encounter between man as creature and his creator indicates that the body is the locus whereby the relationship between God and man is both initiated and continued.[298] The very nostrils through which the breath of God entered, thus giving man life, are a part of the body God Himself formed with his hands from the dust. The creation of man is both a bodily and spiritual encounter between creature and Creator.

It is worth noting here that the origins of the human dichotomy of body and soul are first evident here. The body is formed first into the human frame, with God's great care, as a potter forms his clay into a masterpiece. The body precedes life itself. When God breathes his Spirit (רוח) into man's nostrils man becomes an animated body. What is commonly called the "soul" is first evident here, and the "soul" knows no home but the body in

remember John!

---

[297] See George Steiner, *Grammars of Creation* (New Haven and London: Yale University Press, 2001), 130-131. The distinction between "creation" and "invention" is a central theme to contemporary philosopher George Steiner. For Steiner creation is distinguished from invention primarily in terms of the absolute freedom and liberty with which one truly creates. For Steiner, though, "creation" is defined "as that which is enacted freedom and includes and expresses in its incarnation the presence of what is absent from it or of what could be radically other." In other words, a "created act" always declares alongside its existence "the fact that it could not have been otherwise."

[298] This emphasis on the bodily encounter between man and God from the beginning will have significant importance for Luther's sacramental theology as well. The sacraments should be deemed no less an encounter between man and the Divine than God's encounter with man was in the beginning when he breathed his Spirit into man's nostrils. Again, creation and redemption are similar acts of God. As such, Luther's theology of creation is very important for understanding the sacraments, both with respect to their status as "means of grace" and also the corporeal manner by which God operates through these means in man. This point will be addressed further in chapter four.

131

which God breathed it as life. While Luther speaks of man often doing certain tasks "according to the body" or "according to the soul," every action performed by body or soul necessitates the participation of the entire person. Seeing a parallel in man's anthropology to the unity and distinction of the divine and human natures in Christ, Luther addresses the *totus homo*, or the total man, consisting both of body and soul in his 1537 sermons on the Gospel of St. John:

> ...body and soul present two distinct entities in a natural and sound person; yet the two constitute but one person, and we ascribe the functions, activities, and offices of each to the whole person. We say of every human being that he eats, drinks, digests, sleeps, wakes, walks, stands, works, etc., although the soul participates in none of these activities, but only the body. And yet this is said of the entire person, who has a body and a soul. For it is one person, by reason not only of the body but of both the body and the soul. Again, we say that man thinks, deliberates, and learns. According to his reason or soul, he can become a teacher or master, a judge, councilor, or ruler. Neither the body nor any one of its members gives him this competence. And yet we say: "He has a clever head; he is sensible, learned, eloquent, artistic." Thus it is said of a woman that a mother carries, bears, and suckles a child, although it is not her soul but only her body that makes her a mother. And still we ascribe this to the entire woman. Or if someone strikes a person on the head, we say: "He has struck Hans or Greta." Or if a member of the body is injured or wounded, we think of the whole person as being wounded.[299]

In other words, the body cannot be exorcised from the definition of the human creature. On the contrary, the body with the soul defines the human creature. What one does according to the body, or the soul, involves the participation of the entire human creature. Another way to put it is that the

---

[299] *Sermons on the Gospel of St. John: Chapters 14-16, LW* 24:106.

human creature does not have a body and a soul, but that the human creature *is* a body and soul. A faithful soul does not exonerate the person from the actions of a disobedient body any more than bodily discipline alone can save the soul. What one does according to the body has an impact on the entire person who stands in relationship both with God, *coram Deo*, and everything else in creation, *coram mundo.*

The Creation of Woman

Like John Paul II, Luther reflects on The Lord's observation that it is not good that man should be alone (Gen. 2:18). Whereas John Paul II focuses his discussion on the meaning of "alone," or man's original solitude, Luther's primary concern is with the word "good." Luther distinguishes between the "personal good" of Adam in his state of innocence and the "common good" of the human species.[300] Man was made "good." It is not as if there is something in the constitution of man himself that is lacking or that God left incomplete. That said, unlike the animals, man is not yet able to procreate. When God says "it is not good" he is referring, for Luther, to the "common good" of the human species. "Adam as the most beautiful creature is well provided for so far as his own person is concerned but still lacks something, namely, the gift of the increase and the blessing–because he is alone."[301]

As discussed earlier Luther identifies in the first person plural of Genesis 1:26, "let us make," an affirmation of the Trinity called together in a special council for the creation of man. Luther saw, here, a certain degree of forethought and deliberation in the creation of man that set man apart from all other creatures. There is, as was pointed out, much similarity with what John Paul II called "original solitude." For Luther, all that was said above regarding the creation of man applies to woman as well.

> Now also the household is set up. For God makes a husband of lonely Adam and joins him to a wife, who was needed to bring about the increase of the human race. Just as we pointed out above in connection with the creation of man that Adam was

---

[300] *Lectures on Genesis (1535/38), LW* 1:115-116.

[301] Ibid., 116.

133

created in accordance with a well-considered counsel, so here, too, we perceive that Eve is being created according to a definite plan. Thus here once more Moses points out that man is a unique creature and that he is suited to be a partaker of divinity and of immortality...Eve was created according to a unique counsel that it might be clear that she has a share in immortality, a life better than that of the remaining animals, which live only their animal life, without hope of eternal life.[302]

The "solitude" that John Paul II speaks of when man is contrasted against the animals is also definitive for the woman. This is true both for John Paul II and for Martin Luther. Like man, the great difference between woman and the animals reveals to her that she has a special relationship with her creator that includes, also, a participation in divinity and eternal life. Luther identifies a sort of original equality between man and woman in terms of their bodily and intellectual capacities:

...if the woman had not been deceived by the serpent and had not sinned she would have been the equal of Adam in all respects. For the punishment, that she is now subjected to the man, was imposed on her after sin and because of sin, just as the other hardships and dangers were: travail, pain, and countless other vexations. Therefore Eve was not like the woman of today; her state was far better and more excellent, and she was in no respect inferior to Adam, whether you count the qualities of the body or those of the mind.[303]

One should not read into Luther's affirmation of equality, though, modern notions that might presume that equality means that man and woman were identical. For Luther, while man and woman were equal in respect to righteousness and even with regard to bodily and intellectual capability, man and woman were still created differently and in a relationship of mutual dependence. Man's need for woman is expressed in

---

[302] *Lectures on Genesis (1535/38), LW* 1:115, 117.

[303] Ibid., 115.

Luther's 1527 Genesis sermons concerning the word to be "fruitful and multiply" (Gen. 1:28):

"help mek"

Woman was created in order to be a helper for the man, not for pleasure, but that he might fulfill the saying "be fruitful and multiply." Therefore, for this reason they are created: to be fruitful. This also, again, condemns papistic celibacy, for this word works in us powerfully. God alone is able to change us, for we are his formation. To those whom he gives that great and rare gift of chastity, they alone are able to live in chastity. To the others who remain the blessing of the Lord and the work of God cannot be warded away, and this word "be fruitful" cannot be abolished. It must be diligently observed.[304] *─ but in all things,, other parts of Scripture decry the senseless multiplication of kids*

Accordingly, man depends upon woman in order that he might be faithful to God's word that he multiply. Righteousness, properly speaking, leaves man in a certain dependence upon woman who alone is able to serve as man's "helper" for procreation. As "helper," though, Luther's discussion tends to speak of woman's part in procreation in a passive manner. It is most common for Luther to speak of the man who procreates, with the aid of woman's body. Some of this is due to Luther's misconceptions regarding the anatomy of the human reproductive system common in the medieval era.[305] Too much should not be read into this manner of speaking, though, as it largely emerges from the context of the discussion of woman as "helper" in Genesis. Luther does, in fact, speak of a contribution of a "drop of blood" from both parents. This is not considered an act of man and woman alone, however. This action remains as much the Creator's miracle as it was when man was formed from the dust of the ground and woman from man's rib.[306]

---

[304] *Sermons on Genesis, 1527, WA* 24:78-79. *The, the house eroticism of Our Lord...* *above*

[305] In medieval thinking woman were considered as imperfect versions of men whose genitals were turned inside out. According to a surgeon of Luther's era, Abrose Paré [1510-1590], "women could turn into men if, owing to an accident, their internal organs were suddenly pushed outward," quoted in Caroline Walker Bynum, *Fragmentation and Redemption: Essays on Gender and the Human body in Medieval Religion* (New York: Zone Books, 1991), 220. For a more detailed discussion of this matter in Luther's own thinking see Cortright, *Poor Maggot Sack that I Am,* 108-110.

[306] If we believe that God is the efficient and final cause, should we not wonder at His works,

As much as man depends upon woman for the sake of procreation, woman also depends upon man for the support of her body and life. As John Paul II saw in the interplay of the Hebrew words "'*iš*" and "*iššā*" a new awareness of the body as distinctly male and female, Luther recognizes from these words a relationship of dependence particularly of the woman upon the man. Giving woman her name, *iššā*, Luther recognizes that man holds authority over her.[307]

As already affirmed, for Luther the equality of man and woman does not imply that they relate to one another in an identical manner. Male and female are not interchangeable. Even if they wished to, male and female cannot simply swap roles. The equality of man and woman in righteousness is, in fact, only realized in their dependence upon one another.[308] If one were to push the original equality of man and woman to the point of losing the distinctiveness of both one would essentially abandon the essential goodness of the human creature and the body. It would also confound the definition of righteousness itself. Righteousness is, again, understood as "living rightly"

---

delight in them, and proclaim them always and everywhere? But how many are there who really do this from the heart? We hear that God took a clod and made a human being; we wonder at this, and because of our wonder we regard it as a fairy tale. But that He now takes a drop from the blood of the father and creates a human being, this we do not wonder at, because it happens every day, while the other thing was done only once; yet each of the two is brought about through the same skill and the same power and by the same Author. For He who formed man from a clod now creates men from the blood of their parents." *Lectures on Genesis (1535/38), LW* 1:127.

[307] "Now see how Adam gives her a name and calls her woman, because, he says, she has been taken from a man. In Hebrew the word is actually *ish*: a man among men, for among other animals the word used is *sohar*. From his own name he names her *isha*; she takes her name from and for him, and it remains [the practice] up until now that a woman is called after the man...So she has to take her name from him, and he gives it to her and maintains authority over her" *Sermons on Genesis, 1527, WA* 24:80. Translated by Susan C. Karant-Nunn and Merry E Wiesner-Hanks, *Luther on Women: A Sourcebook* (New York: Cambridge University Press, 2003), 18.

[308] The Commission on Theology and Church Relations of the Lutheran Church–Missouri Synod (CTCR) has reflected on the significance of this dependence, "Man and woman, therefore, belong to and are dependent upon one another. First, the man was created. Later, the woman was made from the man's side as a companion for him. The woman subsequently gives birth to a man. A man leaves his father and his mother and "holds fast" to his wife, caring for her. Paradoxically, their difference gives birth to their interdependence. As the apostle Paul so eloquently stated centuries later: "Nevertheless, in the Lord woman is not independent of man nor man of woman; for as woman was made from man, so man is now born of woman. And all things are from God" (1 Cor 11:11-12; see also 1 Cor 11:7-10)." *The Creator's Tapestry: Scriptural Perspectives on Man-Woman Relationships in Marriage and the Church* (Saint Louis: December, 2009), 15.

according to God's design. Modern notions that would tend toward erasing the distinctions between man as male and female in the name of equality would, for Luther, actually be a gross inequality. Gender is not equalized by ignoring the distinctions between male and female but by embracing those very distinctions and differences. As such, modern attempts to equalize man *human beings ?* by erasing the differences between man as male and man as female would violate the definition of the human creature. Thus, when Luther speaks of the equality between man and woman in the beginning one should be careful not to impose modern notions on his words. The equality Luther speaks of is far more fundamental. For Luther, male and female are equals in terms of righteousness *precisely in their respective masculinity and femininity. or - ? equal in their difference as in*

The body reveals both what is similar between male and female as *the* creatures made in the image of God with dominion over creation, and also *as in* the difference between male and female. God causes man to fall into a deep *the Trinity.* sleep. Luther discerns from the Hebrew text a specific sort of sleep that occurs by those who are so overcome by tiredness that they "fall asleep unawares and nod their heads."[309] This underscores, once again, the passivity of man as God once again enters into creative action. While woman is taken from the rib of man, man has no active part to play in the creation of woman. Thus, when he awakes man cannot claim woman as his own creation. She can only be received as a gift given him by God the creator.

This point is further developed when, as Adam awakens, God brings woman and presents her to him. "Adam," Luther emphasizes, "does not snatch Eve of his own will after she has been created, but he waits for God to bring her to him."[310] As the woman is brought before man, as one body *in the creature parade.* before the other, Adam immediately recognizes their bodily unity even though he had been in a "deep sleep" when God created her from his rib. When Adam exclaims that woman is "bone from my bones" and "flesh from my flesh" he speaks as one "filled with the Holy Spirit" recognizing that "the effecting cause of the wife and of marriage is God."[311] The equality between man and woman that persists through their diversity is recognized *no, consummation*

---

[309] *Lectures on Genesis (1535/38), LW* 1:129.

[310] Ibid., 134.

[311] Ibid.

most immediately and fundamentally in the bodily relationship between man and woman. The principle of headship does not violate the equality of man and woman in Luther's thought any more than the headship of God the Father indicates inequality between the Father and the Son or the Spirit. This is, as was already indicated above in Luther's earlier Genesis sermons, maintained in his later Genesis lectures when man gives his new helpmate the name woman:

> And now, just as through the Holy Spirit Adam had an understanding of past events which he had not seen, and glorified God and praised Him for the creation of his mate, so now he prophesies regarding the future when he says that she must be called "Woman."... Moreover, this designation carries with it a wonderful and pleasing description of marriage, in which, as the jurist also says, the wife shines by reason of her husband's rays. Whatever the husband has, this the wife has and possesses it in its entirety. Their partnership involves not only their means but children, food, bed, and dwelling; their purposes, too, are the same. The result is that the husband differs from the wife in no other respect than in sex; otherwise the woman is altogether a man. Whatever the man has in the home and is, this the woman has and is; she differs only in sex and in something that Paul mentions 1 Tim. 2:13, namely, that she is a woman by origin, because the woman came from the man and not the man from the woman.[312]

Luther's earlier lectures on 1 Timothy (1528) further elucidate his point: "Adam was first, etc. Therefore the greater authority lies in the man rather than in the woman."[313] This is, however, an authority that persists within a shared dominion that man and woman are given together over the rest of creation. Headship, in this Edenic context, is an expression of equality rather than subjection (which will occur after the fall into sin). "There [in

---

[312] Ibid., 137.

[313] *Lectures on 1 Timothy, LW* 28:277.

paradise] the management [of the household] would have been equally divided, just as Adam prophesies here that Eve must be called 'she-man,' or 'virago' because she performs similar activities in the home."[314] Each one, Adam and Eve, becomes a gift to the other in their mutual call to exercise dominion over the creation. Functioning properly as man and woman, in Edenic bliss, their different roles are unified in a common purpose and calling as lords over creation itself.

In no way is the vast difference between man in his later fallen state seen more clearly than in the expression of man and woman in their unashamed nakedness with which Genesis 2 concludes. Luther's reflections here are not unlike John Paul II's. Luther recognizes a connection between man and woman's unashamed nakedness and their coherence with the will of God. That man and woman can celebrate their nakedness, like other traits discussed earlier, reveals a glory in their bodies that was "something most beautiful and the unique prerogative of the human race over all the other animals."[315] Man can celebrate his own body, and delight in the body of his spouse without sin. This only occurs because man's will still accords with God's who unites man and woman as "one flesh." Without sin in the world lust is not kindled by nakedness, thus the naked body is commended and man and woman are free to delight in one another. The stark contrast between man and woman in their original nakedness and the shame that occurs in their nakedness after their fall into sin will be addressed in the next chapter.

The Original Vocation of the Human Creature

For Luther, horizontal righteousness (or righteousness *coram mundo*) is expressed *iuxta vocationem*, that is, according to one's vocation. For Luther, no vocation or calling is supreme to another before God. One can only live life in righteousness before the world and in relationship to others when he or she remains faithful to the specific calling God has placed upon him or

---

[314] *Lectures on Genesis (1535/38), LW* 1:138.

[315] Ibid., 141. Luther also writes earlier, "Therefore what would have been our greatest glory at that time is now extreme shame. It would have been something glorious for man that, though all the animals needed hair, feathers, and scales to cover up their ugliness, he alone was created with such prestige and beautify of body that he could walk about with a hairless and naked skin." Ibid., 140.

Walter Deller contends that "human kind in community" bears the imago

her. Man and woman both share, as bearers of God's image, the responsibility of dominion over the earth. Wingren understands man's dominion as an extension of God's lordship over creation: "When man, even in his sinfulness, 'has dominion' over Creation, it is not, properly speaking, man who 'has dominion,' but God, who in man is continuing to create."[316] God's prelapsarian word to "be fruitful and multiply" and also to "subdue" the earth reflects a goodness in God's original design that persists, albeit in corruption, in spite of man's sin. What might be called the "original vocation" of man is part and parcel of man's essential identity as a creature. Man and woman, though, exercise this dominion in a manner that is both mutually dependent and at the same time is particular to each gender. There is, inherent in gender already, a distinct calling that differentiates man and woman from the beginning. In order to "subdue" the earth, multiplication is necessary. For the human creature to properly represent God's dominion over the earth both genders must exercise their proper roles.[317]

It is worth noting that when God says "be fruitful and multiply" (Gen. 1:28) Luther understands these words as creative words of God, not as a commandment to be obeyed. By saying "be fruitful and multiply" man and woman actually become "fruitful" creatures who multiply. For Luther these words are performative, not imperative. These words are a component of God's on-going work of creation manifested particularly through marriage and the sexual union between man and woman. Being "fruitful" is as unavoidable to human identity as one's gender. Luther emphasized this point in his 1522 sermon on The Estate of Marriage.

> For this word which God speaks, "Be fruitful and multiply," is not a command. It is more than a command, namely, a divine ordinance [werck] which it is not our prerogative to hinder or ignore...just as God does not command anyone to be a man or a

---

[316] Wingren, *Creation and Law,* 103.

[317] According to Wingren, this is virtually inescapable even in sin. "The one thing neither men nor woman can do is withdraw from the given relationship to the other sex which is established by their very manhood and womanhood. The two sexes are always related to one another and must choose what this relationship shall be; but neither can choose in the way that God did when he made male and female and determined the pattern of the sexes." Ibid., 104.

140

woman but creates them the way they have to be, so he does not command them to multiply but creates them so that they have to multiply...to produce seed and to multiply is a matter of God's ordinance [geschöpffe], not your power.[318]

It has already been established how man's original vocation to "cultivate the earth" (Gen. 2:5) and to "subdue it" (Gen 1:28) reveals for John Paul II an awareness of man's body that sets him apart from all other living creatures. While other creatures depend upon the earth for their survival, they are unable to master the earth so that it would bring forth the fruit they desire. This awareness is what John Paul II terms "original solitude."

Luther reflects, though, more on the nature of man's work in creation in his comments on Genesis 2:15.[319] This verse indicates, for Luther, that man was never intended to remain sedentary or idle. The human creature is designed for work. God assigned to Adam a twofold duty, "to work or cultivate this garden and, furthermore, to watch and guard it."[320] This work, however, would not have been at all painful or unpleasant prior to man's fall into sin. If Adam had remained in a state of innocence, "he would have tilled the earth and planted little lots of aromatic herbs, not only without inconvenience but, as it were, in play and with the greatest delight."[321] The bearing and rearing of children, as woman's correlative original vocation, would have likewise been a much easier experience. Luther speculates that children born prior to the fall would, perhaps, not have needed their mother's milk as long, they might have stood and walked on their feet immediately "as we see in the case of chicks," and "would have sought their own food without any effort on the part of their parents."[322]

---

[318] *The Estate of Marriage (1522), LW* 45:18-19.

[319] "The LORD God took the man and put him in the garden of Eden to work it and keep it." Genesis 2:15 (ESV)

[320] *Lectures on Genesis (1535/38), LW* 1:102. ← ecology!

[321] Ibid.

[322] Ibid.

Regardless of the particulars that Luther speculates may have been the case, the common theme is that man's original vocation in the beginning was to be a joy without any frustration or toil. Work was not at all a distasteful thing, but was rather one of man's greatest pleasures. While much of that original experience has been lost as it has been complicated by sin, the fact that these duties belong to man's design in creation still can be observed. "Even now in this wretched state of nature we observe that for someone who has a delightful garden sowing, planting, or digging are not a hardship but are done with zeal and a certain pleasure. How much more perfect this would have been in that garden in the state of innocence!"[323] Even while work now involves a certain degree of frustration and toil, man cannot wholly escape it. While more will be discussed regarding the fallenness of man from his original vocation in the next chapter, from today's perspective one can only attempt to understand this original duty of man by contrast from man's broken experience in the fallen world. Attempts to artificially eradicate work from human existence are not only unrealistic, but involve a certain denial of man's creaturely identity. Luther addresses this as a critique of medieval monasticism: "But it is appropriate here also to point out that man was created not for leisure but for work, even in the state of innocence. Therefore the idle sort of life, such as that of monks and nuns, deserves to be condemned."[324]

For Luther the fall of man is a matter both of his spirit and his body. Where man falls spiritually, the body falls as well. Man's disobedience to God has bodily consequences. "For just as through sin man fell in his spirit, so also in his body he fell into punishment."[325] It follows, conversely, that prior to the fall man's delight in bodily activity was connected to the communion sinless man shared with God. Departing from communion with God in disobedience it follows that the earth would also frustrate man in his attempts to cultivate the soil. Only in full dependence upon his creator is man able to engage his original vocation in joy, receiving the fruits of the earth as God's gift rather than as a product of his own works.

---

[323] Ibid.

[324] Ibid., 103

[325] Ibid.

Not only the earth rebels against man's dominion after sin by accompanying his efforts to cultivate the soil with thorns and thistles, but man's very body resists his own dominion and afflicts him with ailments *cravings* and injury. This will be more fully explored in the next chapter with regard to Luther's critique of monastic bodily disciplines, but let it suffice for these purposes to establish the intimate connection between the body and man's creaturely identity that persists from the beginning. The beginnings of justification by grace through faith are already lurking in these early chapters describing man's history. Original man received all things by faith. Trusting that God would provide all man needs for his body and life his working of the ground was no trouble, but a pleasurable experience rendered in thanks for the fruits the earth willingly would yield. Only when man takes what had not been given him in disobedience as he eats the forbidden fruit does man plunge into a life of faithlessness and thanklessness that frustrates his efforts in relationship to both God and the rest of creation.

At this point an important point regarding Luther's view of original vocation must be emphasized. While tilling the ground receives considerable attention here, as occasioned by the Genesis narrative, Luther also sees the origins of his doctrine of the "three orders" or "three estates" (*Dreiständelehre*) from the very beginning. According to Oswald Bayer, Luther's 1535 exposition of Genesis 2:16-17 is "the most trenchant summary of his mature view" on the doctrine, the substance of which can be traced back as early as 1520.[326] Here, and elsewhere, Luther speaks of three fundamental "orders" (*Stände*) divided into that of the household (*oeconomiam*), the government (*politiam*) and the church (*ecclesiam*).[327]

In Genesis 2:16-17 God commands man that he may eat of every tree of paradise except from the tree of the knowledge of good and evil. As already affirmed, Luther saw the tree of the knowledge of good and evil as man's

---

[326] Oswald Bayer, "Nature and Institution: Luther's Doctrine of the Three Orders," *Lutheran Quarterly*, 12 (1998), 127.

[327] Arguably, the most common *locus* identified in Luther's works for the doctrine is in his 1528 *Confession Concerning Christ's Supper*. "But the holy orders and true religious institutions established by God are these three: the office of priest, the estate of marriage, the civil government." *LW* 37:364ff. Luther further employs the distinction in 1542-43 as a hermeneutical key for biblical interpretation as recorded by Heydenreich in his *Table Talk*, *LW* 54:445.

occasion for worship. Luther sees the establishment of the churchly estate (*ecclesiam*) here as the first of the three orders of creation. "Here we have the establishment of the church before there was any government of the home and of the state; for Eve was not yet created."[328] The second estate of household government (*oeconomiam*) emerges alongside Eve's creation. That the churchly estate precedes the government of the home is significant.

> ...after the establishment of the church the government of the home is also assigned to Adam in Paradise. But the church was established first because God wants to show by this sign, as it were, that man was created for another purpose than the rest of the living beings. Because the church is established by the Word of God, it is certain that man was created for an immortal and spiritual life, to which he would have been carried off or translated without death after living in Eden and on the rest of the earth without inconvenience as long as he wished. There would not have been in him that detestable lust which is now in men, but there would have been the innocent and pure love of sex toward sex. Procreation would have taken place without any depravity, as an act of obedience.[329]

The word of God regarding the tree of the knowledge of good and evil, Luther affirms would have been "like a Bible for him" and the sermon text he would have used as he preached to Eve and their children as they all gathered before the tree each Sabbath day.[330] Apart from sin there would be no civil government as the third estate is established only "as a remedy required by our corrupted nature."[331]

That Luther identifies two of the three "estates" prior to sin is certainly significant. This distinction cannot be relegated, in terms of Lutheran or Reformed ethics, to the sole purview of the law's first use. There

---

[328] *Lectures on Genesis (1535/38), LW* 1:103.

[329] Ibid., 104.

[330] Ibid., 105.

[331] Ibid., 104.

can be no "curb" of sin before sin enters the picture. The only estate that originally functioned to "curb" sin is that of the civil government. Accordingly, Luther's doctrine of the three estates can only be apprehended properly when first considered according to the first article of the Creed and the creation of man. The significance of Luther's doctrine of the three orders, or estates, for a theology of the body will become more evident in the next chapter.

The Human Being as Tabernacle: Luther's Theological Anthropology

If a theology of the body is concerned to elucidate the place of the body in the relationship between man and God, a theological anthropology is preeminently concerned with the relationship of the body to the other constituent parts of man. While this book's primary emphasis is Luther's theology of the body, and not his theological anthropology *per se*, how one views the body with respect to humanity's constitution nonetheless has a significant impact on a theology of the body. As such, drawing a neat line between Luther's theology of the body and his theological anthropology with respect to the body is not always possible. That said, lest this book leave the reader with the mistaken notion that Luther elevated the body to too high a place in man's constitution while neglecting the soul or spirit, a few comments on Luther's theological anthropology are appropriate.

Reflecting on Mary's exclamation, "My soul magnifies God, the Lord," after hearing she would bear the Christ, Luther presents his trichotomy of body, soul and spirit. In *The Magnificat* (1521) Luther moves from Mary's exclamation to 1 Thessalonians 5:23: "Now may the God of peace himself sanctify you completely, and may your whole spirit and soul and body be kept blameless at the coming of our Lord Jesus Christ" (ESV). Proceeding in order, Luther begins to explain that the spirit "is the highest, deepest, and noblest part of man...It is, in brief, the dwelling place of faith and the Word of God."[332] Interestingly, Luther says that the soul and spirit are the same in terms of their essential nature. Functionally, however, the soul performs "a different role, namely giving life to the body and working through the body."[333] It's the body, however, that brings the whole person to bear on the

---

[332] *The Magnificat (1521), LW* 21:303.

[333] Ibid.

the medieval mystification of, disship/action

world. The body's purpose is to "carry out and apply that which the soul knows and the spirit believes." Luther's favorite analogy for depicting the constituent components of man—body, soul and spirit—was the Old Testament tabernacle, or temple. Continuing his commentary on the Magnificat, Luther writes,

> In the tabernacle fashioned by Moses there were three separate compartments. The first was called the holy of holies: here was God's dwelling place, and in it there was no light. The second was called the holy place; here stood a candlestick with seven arms and seven lamps. The third was called the outer court; this lay under the open sky and in the full light of the sun. In this tabernacle we have a figure of the Christian man. His spirit is the holy of holies, where God dwells in the darkness of faith, where no light is; for he believes that which he neither sees nor feels nor comprehends. His soul is the holy place, with its seven lamps, that is, all manner of reason, discrimination, knowledge, and understanding of visible and bodily things. His body is the forecourt, open to all, so that men may see his works and manner of life.[334]

all the light that is not seen... where the night is as bright as day...

so it is not soma sensing (as Fouts suggests early on)

Perhaps the most important insight derived from Luther's analogy of the human being to the tabernacle, at least in terms of the body, is that the proper function of the body is to live man's spiritual life in the world, visibly, where one can engage others. The body is designed to work in concert with man's totality, just as the outer-court of the tabernacle was to connect the Israelite worshippers to God's presence within.

coram deo / we have no other "way" to grasp God.

You are still separating Luther's wholeness.

Summary

There is clearly a great deal of similarity between John Paul II's use of the "beginning" as a foundation for his theology of the body and Luther's reflections on the creation narrative in Genesis. Luther's affirmation of the uniqueness of man amongst the other creatures coheres with John Paul II's

---

[334] Ibid., 304.

description of "original solitude." There is a unique relationship that man has with God from the beginning that no other creature can enjoy. Appropriating John Paul II's insights on "original solitude" into Luther's understanding of righteousness *coram Deo* is helpful. As God's creature, man stands particularly in his body in a concrete and unique relationship with his creator that is marked essentially by passivity. An awareness of man's uniqueness, or solitude, from the beginning is an essential part of this insight.

The link between the human creature's passivity *coram Deo* and his activity *coram mundo* is further aided by John Paul II's spousal, or nuptial, definition of the body. Activity in the world, as much as passivity before God, is essential to human identity. Man's activity in the world is only understood properly as a reflection of God's selfless act of giving which establishes his relationship with man. John Paul II's "hermeneutics of the gift" sees a paradigmatic relationship between God and man in solitude that is "broken" (in a positive sense) allowing man and woman to live in relationship of reciprocating donation of self to the other. Luther's insight on man's passive reception of woman as she is "brought" to him as gift echoes this theme. John Paul II's insight helps to further define how man and woman as gift to one another is played out in God's design for marriage. John Paul II's insights bring to the table significant considerations regarding human sexuality that couples well with Luther's distinction between the two kinds of righteousness regarding questions of human sexuality that are continually emerging in the contemporary world.

Thwarting anthropological dualities that would commonly separate body from soul, both Luther and John Paul II essentially define the human being in terms of relationship, rather than in terms of his constituent parts. Body and soul, both for the former pope and the 16th Century reformer, cohere in the total person in a unique relationship with God and also as man extends his relationship with God into his relationships in the world. Whereas John Paul II's insights on the body do not frequently extend beyond questions of human sexuality, Luther's two kinds of righteousness allows these insights to extend further into other matters of concern for the body as man stands in relationship to the rest of creation, his neighbor, and even his own flesh. In short, Luther derives his anthropology from God's creation of man directly, which coheres likewise in the nuptial union. From Luther's perspective, what is "not good" when man is alone is not a matter of man's essence. God created man without flaw from the ground. What is "not good" is man's functional role, or vocation of dominion, which could not be wholly fulfilled in solitude. John Paul II errs in defining an essential flaw in man's nature that is only rectified in spousal union. Thus, he confuses the horizontal for the vertical, righteousness *coram mundo* with righteousness *coram Deo*. That said, John Paul II is not wrong that there is a revelatory character to the spousal significance of the body. Man not only recognizes, but is finally able to actually fulfill his responsibility in the world as God's representative when he is united to woman in the flesh. The body serves as the locus whereby man's righteousness before God is able to be expressed in his responsibility as a creature. The marriage between man and woman codifies the unique relationship that man has with his creator and allows him to express God's love through his bodily love for another creature. The celebration of man's original nakedness in the beginning means that all of the above can only be understood properly as a theology of the body. In the end, the body emerges as necessary for a proper understanding of what makes a person fully human according to God's design from the beginning.

148

CHAPTER 4:
THE BODY OF SIN

HAVING EXAMINED A THEOLOGY OF THE HUMAN BODY from the "beginning" it becomes readily apparent how far from original righteousness man has fallen. As one encounters the narrative of man and woman "in the beginning," it is immediately evident even before arriving at Genesis 3 that a proverbial shoe is about to drop. Daily life and common experience will lead one to either dismiss the Genesis account of man's beginnings as a fantastical fairy tale or to conclude that man and woman in creation have fallen far from their original design. It is no surprise that the veracity of this narrative has so frequently been a point of conflict in popular discourse. An encounter with the "beginning," as the natural law of God's blueprint for man is exposed, leaves contemporary man with no recourse but to either reject the premise entirely, or to repent. If he chooses the former, man ends up living a fairy tale himself.

It is a fairy tale that man and woman chose "in the beginning" when they succumbed to the temptation to be "like God" themselves. When man chose to deny his identity in God's "image" and "likeness," in favor of an attempt to become a law unto himself, he ultimately denied that he is a creature. He attempted to usurp the role of creator. Of course, man's mutiny could never succeed. Attempts to live a fairy tale never turn out well in the real world where one's fiction never accords with genuine experience. One may imagine himself a sort of knight in shining armor, but real life soon shows him that his armor tarnishes and continually polishing it is an arduous process that never ends. The armor he falsely trusts is no better than tinfoil. In other words, no matter how much a man may wish to deny it, he is God's creature. Denial of one's identity, attempting to live discordantly from God's natural design, never goes well because the essence of God's original blueprint remains at the foundation of human identity. Whether he encounters it in the pages of Genesis or not, man in rebellion always lives in tension with his "beginning." The more he attempts to deny it and implement his fairy tale existence, the more he is driven back into conflict with his own creaturehood. No matter how much it offends fallen man's sensibilities, his "beginning" remains as a beacon, continually calling the human creature back to repentance.

Man experiences his sinful condition, or fallen state, most immediately in the body. Just as the body is where man finds himself, in the beginning, in a dual-relationship with the Creator and the rest of creation it is in his relationship with his own body that man first becomes aware that neither of these relationships is as they should be. The body, both in the beginning and in the fall, is revelatory. Whereas the body once revealed to man his unique creaturely identity, in sin the body continually reminds man that he is a sinner in need of a bodily savior.

This chapter will begin by examining man's first experience of sin from the beginning: the temptation, the fall and the experience of shame in his nakedness. John Paul II's insights on "original shame" will be discussed alongside Luther's reflections on the same. The immediate consequence of a breakdown between the sexes as a result of sin will be given considerable attention. Luther was convinced of man's depravity in sin as much from his own experience as he was from scripture itself. Luther's evolving perspective on sex and marriage, having once been a chaste monk who later took a wife, will be considered. Perhaps most fundamental to his thought on the body, will be his theology of vocation. Of particular relevance here will be Luther's experience and critique of monastic disciplines. Following a similar pattern in sin which disrupted the relationship between man and woman, man's frequently strained relationship with the earth itself will be evaluated. Luther knew little modesty when it came to his own bodily struggles and ailments. Accordingly, Luther's comments regarding his own body will be examined as well as his overall perspective on disease, the medicinal arts, and even death. Luther's rhetorical use of the body will also be engaged.

While Luther's own life experiences, which most frequently occasioned his insights on bodily life, provide the context for this discussion Luther nearly always reflected on his bodily experience in the light of Scripture. His writings on apropos biblical texts will be given consideration as appropriate.

The Fall

Genesis 2 concludes with an affirmation of man and woman's unashamed nakedness. The opening verse of Genesis 3 introduces the serpent and his temptation. Something about the nature of the temptation, and how the fall occurred, must be addressed before addressing the particular effects of sin on the human body. Whereas the Genesis text never explicitly identifies the serpent, Luther understands the serpent to be a vessel possessed by Satan. The devil does not appear in his natural form, but chooses the "serpent" as a creature man and woman would have been familiar with. One may presume, as with all the creatures, the serpent is one whom man himself had previously given its name. Being naturally endowed with a "gift of cleverness" Satan chooses the serpent as a vessel well suited for his temptation.[335]

Satan reaches man, though, by way of the woman. Thus, Luther believes Satan strategically targets man where he is weakest. Luther asserts that it is precisely due to her dependence on man, and a sort of natural disadvantage that can be discerned even between the genders in the animals, that Eve became the target of Satan's temptation as opposed to Adam.[336] This is not a "disadvantage" that makes woman any less dignified before God,

---

[335] *Lectures on Genesis (1535/38), LW* 1:145.

[336] Luther suggests that woman was, due to natural weakness, somewhat more vulnerable to temptation than man. This is pointed out as the reason why Satan targets woman with his temptation rather than man: "Satan's cleverness is perceived also in this, that he attacks the weak part of the human nature, Eve the woman, not Adam the man. Although both were created equally righteous, nevertheless Adam had some advantage over Eve. Just as in all the rest of nature the strength of the male surpasses that of the other sex, so also in the perfect nature the male somewhat excelled the female. Because Satan sees that Adam is the more excellent, he does not dare assail him; for he fears that if he had tempted Adam first, the victory would have been Adam's. He would have crushed the serpent with his foot and would have said: 'Shut up! The Lord's command was different.' Satan, therefore, directs his attack on Eve as the weaker part and puts her valor to the test, for he sees that she is so dependent on her husband that she thinks she cannot sin." *LW* 1:151. Luther affirmed the same in his 1527 sermon on Genesis, "[Satan] takes hold of a man where he is the weakest, namely through the feminine person, that is Eve and not Adam." *Sermons on Genesis, 1527, WA* 24:76-81.

[handwritten margin notes: "but we cannot use this as anthropology - our anthropology must take into account both - creation accounts"; "so, if Adam had protected Eve from the snake..."; "and Paul does not say through the first Eve but first Adam (the first Adam / the first human)"; "is this in the text? no"]

151

nor is it one that makes her "inferior" to man essentially. As noted in the previous chapter, Luther insists that prior to the fall man and woman are equal in all respects. Man is the head of woman, thus, bearing a more immediate responsibility with regard to God's creative word and his command regarding the tree of the knowledge of good and evil. Vocationally speaking, the male is charged with the responsibility to hold the Edenic couple in concord with God's word.

The serpent approaches the woman as an imitator of God.[337] In order to deceive her he must, in some way, adorn his lies with the skin of truth. He does this by questioning God's word and adding a bit of his own. The object the serpent uses to lure man to his false word is the tree of the knowledge of good and evil. The Lord had commanded, "Do not eat from the tree of the knowledge of good and evil." This is the word of God that Satan attacks. The tree, and the prohibition God had given man regarding eating from it, is both "Gospel and Law; it was [man's] worship, it was his service and the obedience he could offer God in this state of innocence."[338] To tempt man and woman by this tree struck at the core of their human identity before God. The serpent's temptation was an attack on the very worship they offered to God, their obedience and relationship with their creator.

For Luther, the "chief temptation" was "to listen to another word and to depart from the one which God had previously spoken."[339] The first chapter of Genesis presents God as one who speaks. The serpent likewise "speaks" according to the Genesis account. As Luther puts it, "with a word it attacks the Word."[340] While it is unnecessary to explore Luther's exegesis of the serpent's temptation for these purposes, let it suffice to say that Luther identifies within the serpent's alluring words a temptation that reaches man at every component of his being, body and soul.

---

[337] "In the first place, Satan imitates God. Just as God had preached to Adam, so he himself also preaches to Eve. What the proverb says is true: 'Every evil begins in the name of the Lord.'" Therefore just as from the true Word of God salvation results, so also from the corrupt Word of God damnations results." *Lectures on Genesis (1535/38), LW* 1:147.

[338] Ibid., 146.

[339] Ibid., 147.

[340] Ibid., 146.

Satan spoke in order to lead them away from what God had said; and after he had taken away the Word, he made corrupt the perfect will which man previously had, so that he became a rebel. He corrupted the intellect also, so that it doubted the will of God. The eventual result is a rebellious hand, extended against the will of God, to pick the fruit. Next the mouth and the teeth became rebellious. In short, all evils result from unbelief or doubt of the Word and of God. For what can be worse than to disobey God and to obey Satan?[341]

Recalling that it was by the word that God first called creation into existence, and thus established the distinguishing relationship between creator and creature, the temptation to heed a different word than God had spoken to Adam and Eve is more than a temptation to disobey a single command. It is ultimately an attack on man's fundamental identity as a human creature of God. Man's identity as "creature" is compromised as he heeds a word contrary to God's which spoke all creation into being. Instead of placing his faith in God's word, and worshipping the Lord at the tree, man doubts God and places faith in the serpent's false word. Thus, the primary sin is not eating the forbidden fruit *per se*. The tree of the knowledge of good and evil is there because, as a corporeal creature man's act of faith and worship must involve a corporeal object. This is why the tree, for Luther, localizes man's worship of God. To depart from God's word in exchange for the serpent's would fundamentally deny man's creaturely identity and fracture the relationship man had with his creator. Man's first sin is one of misplaced faith and worship. By consequence, the effects of sin permeate every component of the human creature including the hand, mouth, teeth, stomach and entire body. In Luther's view, the total man (*totus homo*) partook in man's disobedience.

Original Shame

The first recognizable impact of sin in the world is one that is recognized chiefly with respect to the body. Man and woman recognize their bodily nakedness and are ashamed. They quickly scurry to find something

---

[341] Ibid., 147-148.

with which they could cover their genitals. It is noteworthy that shame precedes any explicit experience of juridical guilt due to the Edenic couple's transgression. Before God even encounters them, they already experience in their very flesh the shame that accompanies sin.

Their unashamed nakedness prior to sin had been an expression of their embodied righteousness as God's creatures. Original nakedness was the couple's actual experience of what John Paul II calls "original innocence" and Martin Luther terms "original righteousness." After succumbing to the tempter's scheme, man and woman recognize their nakedness as shameful and search for a covering. The first evidence that man and woman had fallen from their original righteousness is a decidedly bodily experience. Recalling what John Paul II termed the "spousal" or "nuptial" meaning of the body, identifying the body as the "sacramental" element communicating both God's relationship with mankind in solitude and also fulfilling that solitude through nuptial unity, is significant. In the reciprocal gift of each body to the other, man and woman were able to stand together in solitude before God. This unity between spouses makes the body "sacramental" for John Paul II because it connects man and woman "in one flesh" with their creator. Original nakedness was their experience of this reality. The experience of shame in the body after the fall, then, is more than a statement about the body itself. Their bodily experience of shame bears witness to the fact that the fullness of their spousal unity was broken, thus corrupting and fracturing their relationship with God. By covering their genitals, man and woman hide themselves from each other. The part of their bodies primarily responsible for man and woman's fulfillment of God's word to fruitfully multiply becomes a source of shame.[342] When God encounters man and woman again, they hide also from God.[343] Such flight from God Luther sees

---

[342] "Adam and Eve not only were ashamed because of their nakedness, which previously was the most honorable and the unique adornment of man, but they also made girdles for themselves for the purpose of covering, as though it were something most shameful, that part of the body which by its nature was most honorable and noble. What in all nature is nobler than the work of procreation? This work was assigned by God neither to the eyes nor to the mouth, which we regard as the more honorable parts of the body, but to that part which sin has taught us to call the pudendum and to cover, lest it be seen. Moreover, although in the innocent nature the entire work of procreation would have been most holy and most pure, after sin the leprosy of lust has made its way into this part of the body." Ibid., 167-168.

[343] "...after their conscience has been convicted by the Law and the feel their disgrace before God

[handwritten: gt Luther]

[handwritten: Our instinct is to dis-connect / healing comes from re-connecting]

as evidence of sin's stupidity. "It happens naturally in the case of every sin that we stupidly try to escape God's wrath and yet cannot escape it. It is the utmost stupidity for us to imagine that our cure lies in flight from God rather than in our return to God, and yet our sinful nature cannot return to God."[344] Sin had corrupted every relationship man and woman previously knew. Shame, particularly with respect to their bodies, is how they immediately experience their new sinful reality.

For John Paul II the first effect of the fall is the detachment of spousal love from its source in the love of the original giver. At the very core of their relationship, Adam and Eve are seized by an anxious fear of God.[345] This fear, or shame, is not related only to the body. "In reality, what shows itself through 'nakedness' is man deprived of participation in the Gift, man alienated from the Love that was the source of the original gift, the source of the fullness of good intended for the creature."[346] Recall that it was *[handwritten: not exactly]* considered necessary in the beginning that man be united to woman in order to fully participate the image of God in love. The separation of man from the source of love, on account of the original sin, would create shame in all his relationships. As such, "nakedness" is not the basis for their shame. Their shame in "nakedness" is symptomatic of a deeper wound that touches to the heart of creaturely identity.

To put it differently, employing Luther's paradigmatic distinctions, shame is the manifestation of sin in both kinds of righteousness. Righteousness *coram mundo* is fractured first in the relationship between *[handwritten: before the world.]* man and woman. Then, in the curse, the relationship man has with the earth itself is fractured as well. *Coram Deo* man's original righteousness is lost as

[handwritten: before God]

[handwritten: —or in their own belovedness — key — the unworthiness]

and themselves, Adam and Eve lose their confidence in God and are so filled with fear and terror that when they hear a breath or a wind, they immediately think God is approaching to punish them; and they hide." Ibid., 170. "This brings about what is worst: that Adam and Eve avoid their Creator and take refuge under the protection of the fig trees, both to cover themselves and to hide in the midst of the trees. What can be termed more horrible than to flee from God and to desire to be hidden from Him?" Ibid., 172.

[344] Ibid., 173-174.

[345] "Shame touches in that moment the deepest level and seems to shake the very foundations of their existence...The need to hide shows that, *in the depth of shame they feel before each other* as the immediate fruit of the tree of the knowledge of good and evil, *a sense of fear before God has matured: a fear previously unknown." TOB*, 238.

[346] Ibid., 239.

man seeks to be a god unto himself, heeding the tempter's word rather than the creator's, and denies his true creaturely identity. In every instance, man's fall from original righteousness is a decidedly bodily experience.

The Impact of Sin on Human Sexuality

As discussed earlier, John Paul II understood human sexuality with respect to the "hermeneutics of gift." The sexual dimension of the human creature is, for the pope, essential to human identity. According to Michel Séguin, John Paul II's entire philosophical and theological conception of the human person "boils down to the statement that the person is a 'being-gift.'"[347] Sister Mary Timothy Prokes further elucidates how this identification of the human person as "being-gift," or as she puts it "person-gift," is expressed primarily through human sexuality:

> Let us begin with a 'working definition': sexuality is our human capacity as whole persons to enter into love-giving, life-giving union in and through the body in ways that are appropriate...First of all, our sexuality is totally human. It is not an animalistic drive identical to that found in subhuman species. Human sexuality is person-al, involving the giving and receiving of person-gift...Sexuality enables us bodily to be person-gift. This derives from each human person's being created in the image and likeness of God, the Trinity of Persons who are in constant perichoretic union through total Self-gift to the other Persons, and through total receptivity to the Self-gift of the other Persons. It is Jesus' revelation concerning divine inner life that gives a context for understanding human sexuality in its foundational sense as revelatory self-gift.[348]

While Luther never develops this theme to the same extent, his thoughts regarding the mutual dependence of man and woman upon one another for the sake of adhering to God's ordinance to "be fruitful and

---

[347] Michel Séguin, "The Biblical Foundations of the Thought of John Paul II on Human Sexuality," *Communio,* 20, 2 (Summer, 1993), 276-277.

[348] Mary Timothy Prokes, *Toward a Theology of the Body* (Grand Rapids, MI: Eerdmans, 1996), 95-97

multiply" has similar implications regarding human sexuality. As discussed in the previous chapter, Luther viewed God's words to "be fruitful and multiply" not as a command, but as a "work" of God (*wercke*) and act of on-going creation (*geschöpffe*). According to his 1522 sermon The Estate of Marriage, the human urge to procreate is as undeniable as one's biological gender. Just as one cannot will himself to be male or female, but is one gender or the other according to design, one cannot deny his essential procreative prowess.[349] As such, sexual sin is essentially a denial of one's creaturely identity and follows from one's attempted resistance to God's word to "be fruitful and multiply."

> ...just as God does not command anyone to be a man or a woman but creates them the way they have to be, so he does not command them to multiply but creates them so that they have to multiply. And wherever men try to resist this, it remains irresistible nonetheless and goes its way through fornication,

[margin notes: core to modern arguments; bingo — crooked being; not commanded in each instance but a biological resistance]

---

[349] Contemporary questions regarding "gender identity" could form an extensive excursus from this point. The very notion that some sort of internal impulse, contrary to the biological evidence of particular genitals that identify one's sex, depends upon a sort of mind-body dualism that necessarily prioritizes the mind, or some sort of undetermined impulse, above the body. Contemporary debates regarding "transgender" bathroom access, for example, reflect the controversy that pitting internal impulses (be they identified with the mind, or some other hormonal factor) with the outward presence of particular reproductive organs presents. Even while some suggest that one might internally "identify" with a gender that is different than their bodily parts presents, the fact remains that the concern for bathroom privacy has everything to do with bodily parts, and nothing to do with one's internal impulses. While chromosomal disorders—something one might associate with a bodily reality—might account for a certain component of the "transgender population," these chromosomal abnormalities represent a small fraction of what is already an incredibly small fraction of the larger population. Even more, in the contemporary debate over "transgender" restrooms, the evocation of chromosomes is a red-herring. Advocates of equal bathroom access according to which ever gender one "identifies" with is the argument of the day and ultimately rests upon a mind-body dualism that conflicts with both theology, and neurology (see Ch. 1 of this book). It is this author's contention that liberal thinkers will have to reconcile their materialist concept of the human being—*i.e.* their rejection of a notion of "soul" or "mind" that is separate from the body—with their desire to affirm transgenderism as "natural" in spite of the clear biological evidence the body itself reveals by way of male or female genitalia. Something has to give. One will either have to affirm a sort of radical dualism that discards the body as an inaccurate representation of one's true person or identity (*i.e.* one identifies as "females" in the mind, and that must take priority then over the body which is a less reliable determinant of one's true gender identity) or by affirming their materialist concept of the human person will have to admit that transgenderism is a mental disorder. Even if one relies upon neuroscience to explain the phenomenon, however, there is still a disjunction between however the brain processes gender and gross anatomy. Ockham's razor suggests that it would be the brain rather than the genitals that are likely to blame in absence of any chromosomal evidence suggesting otherwise.

[margin notes: avoiding the actual evidence of biological confusions — who is being dualistic w/ body?!; and what of being predictable; Wow, would love to see you argue re: race... or sex differences.]

adultery, and secret sins, for this is a matter of nature and not of choice...For the Word of God which created you and said, "Be fruitful and multiply," abides and rules within you; you can by no means ignore it, or you will be bound to commit heinous sins without end.[350]

so biologically we are beyond determining our selves physically

and he would have looked at modern science very carefully

Accordingly, in Luther's view, sexuality is not something that can be suppressed without grave consequences. Celibacy is considered a rare gift and should be considered as an exception to the norm rather than the rule.[351] Sexual sin is fundamentally a misdirection of a God-given urge placed in man when God first spoke, "be fruitful and multiply." Sexuality is not essentially bad. Sexuality is a God-given inclination within man that is part and parcel of being human. Only in the fall, when one fails to receive one whom God would give him in "nuptial unity," does sexuality lead to sin. Sex is wrought with sin, though, not only when one unites himself with someone other than his spouse. Even married couples are not immune from sexual sin within the confines of their own union. Luther makes this point clear as he concludes his sermon, *The Estate of Marriage:*

heterosexual

---

[350] *The Estate of Marriage (1522), LW* 45:18-19.

Eunach is his metaphor to explain the lack of sexual urges

[351] In *The Estate of Marriage* Luther discerns from Matthew 19:12 three "categories of men" who are exempt from the natural need for man to marry. "There are eunuchs who have been so from birth, and there are eunuchs who have been made eunuchs by men, and there are eunuchs who have made themselves eunuchs for the sake of the kingdom of heaven." Apart from these groups, Luther says that no man should "presume to be without a spouse." The first category, "eunuchs who have been so from birth," are understood as the "impotent" who are as unable to bear children as a person born crippled or blind is not obligated to see or walk. The second category, those who have "been made eunuchs by men" are victims of an act of violence. These "castrates" Luther says are an "unhappy lot" for the desire to marry and reproduce is often still within them but they are unable to consummate their desire. The third category "consists of those spiritually rich and exalted persons, bridled by the grace of God, who are equipped for marriage by nature and physical capacity and nevertheless voluntarily remain celibate." This category describes a class of man who are exceptionally rare, "not one in a thousand, for they are a special miracle of God." Thus, celibacy should not be willfully chosen for any man apart from a call from God. Monastic vows, and the forbidding of clergy to marry, Luther believes, have compelled too many men out of a misguided desire for supreme righteousness to choose celibacy apart from nature or a call from God. "Beyond these three categories...the devil working against men has been smarter than God, and found more people whom he has withdrawn from the divine and natural ordinance, namely, those who are enmeshed in a spiderweb of human commands and vows and are then locked up behind a mass of iron bolts of bars. This is a fourth way of resisting nature so that, contrary to God's implanted ordinance and disposition, it does not produce seed and multiply...If men are really able to resist God's word and creation with iron bars and bolts, I should hope that we would also set up iron bars so thick and massive that women would turn into men or people into sticks and stones." Ibid., 19-22.

tells you how much lust he encountered in the monastery

great image of Church misguided boys

With all this extolling of married life, however, I have not meant
to ascribe to nature a condition of sinlessness. On the contrary, I
say that flesh and blood, corrupted through Adam, is conceived
and born in sin, as Psalm 51 [:5] says. Intercourse is never
without sin; but God excuses it by his grace because the estate
of marriage is his work, and he preserves in and through the sin
all that good which he has implanted and blessed in marriage.[352]

[handwritten margin note: ~ Bothold / for / Pelagian...]

For Luther, due to the fall, sexuality is inevitably fraught with sin even
within the context of marriage. Consider how man and woman, once they
fell, immediately were ashamed to be seen by the other and felt the urge to
cover their nakedness. Even within the Godly union between Adam and Eve
each spouse ceased, as sinners, to receive the other as "gift," reducing their
partner to an object to satisfy their selfish carnal desires. Even husbands and
wives do not receive each other as they ought, according to God's original
design. Nonetheless, consistent with Luther's *theologia crucis*, he maintains
that God accomplishes his good will in spite of, and even through the agency
of, the sinful acts of man. As God had spoken, "let there be light" in the
beginning and it became reality, God's word to "be fruitful and multiply"
persists as reality in spite of and even through man's sinful rebellion. Even
deviant sexual activity, either within or apart from a holy marriage, God may
bless with children in spite of man's sinful intentions. As such, the fruitful
product of the sexual union, a newborn child, is always God's good act
regardless of the circumstances by which that child was conceived.

[handwritten margin note: God uses it to the good — Joseph's word to his brothers]

[handwritten margin note: but we did not believe this in many decades...]

Excursus: Pornography

A personal and social morality formed by
pornography...detaches desire from the demands of love and
attaches it instead to the mute machinery of sex. This represents
no less than a total transformation of the way we envisage, and
live out, our human embodiment. Sex idolized is in fact sex
abolished and lost. Pornography's cult of the flesh, ironically

[handwritten margin note: or is it just gratification, the self to the self... not idol, but self-reference]

---

[352] Ibid., 49.s

pursued largely by virtual, non-fleshly means, is in fact the
desecration of the flesh. What may appear on the outside to be
appreciation for the body, is in fact hatred for the body.[353]

It is no secret that the emergence of the internet and ever-evolving
technologies to access it has resulted in an unprecedented proliferation of
pornography in today's society. A 2002 report from the American Academy
of Matrimonial Lawyers revealed that 56% of all divorces in the United States
involved one party having "an obsessive interest in pornographic
websites."[354] The proliferation of pornography in American society has
brought its use out of the darkness of secrecy and is increasingly being
perceived of as acceptable. What used to be used predominantly in secret
accompanied by a recognition of personal shame has become increasingly
commonplace and ethically neutral. According to a 2007 study among 813
students from six U.S. schools 66.5% of young men and 48.7% of young
women said viewing pornographic materials is an acceptable way to express
one's sexuality. According to the same study only 13.9% of young men said
they never view pornography.[355] The epidemic has plagued the clergy as well.
A 2002 survey of 1,351 pastors revealed that 54% of pastors admitted to
having viewed internet pornography within the previous year and 30% of
those admitted to doing so within the last month.[356]

As alarming as the above statistics may be, statistics as such do
nothing to address the core problem. According to Scrunton, "The growing
toleration of pornography, which will soon be regarded as an industry like
any other…is rapidly changing the way the human body is perceived…When

---

[353] Cooper, *Life in the Flesh,* 232-233.

[354] Jonathan Dedmon, "Is the Internet bad for your marriage? Online affairs, pornographic sites playing greater role in divorces." Press Release from The Dilenschneider Group, Inc., Nov. 14, 2002. http://www.prnewswire.com/news-releases/is-the-internet-bad-for-your-marriage-online-affairs-pornographic-sites-playing-greater-role-in-divorces-76826727.html (accessed Jan. 29, 2014).

[355] Jason S. Carroll, Laura M. Padilla-Walker, Larry J. Nelson, Chad D. Olson, Carolyn McNamara Barry, and Stephanie D. Madsen, "Generation XXX: Pornography acceptance and use among emerging adults." *Journal of Adolescent Research* 23 (2008): 6-30.

[356] Brenton Evans, "Till porn do us part," FireProofMyMarriage.com. http://www.fireproofmymarriage.com/dload.php?file=_images/_needhelp/InternetSafety.pdf (accessed Jan 29, 2014).

— like the commodification of all of nature ...

sex becomes a commodity, the most important sanctuary of human ideals become a market, and value is reduced to price. That is what has happened in the last few decades, and it is the root fact of post-modern culture."[357] It would be a grave negligence on the part of theologians to ignore the damaging impact pornography has caused in the church and the world. Merely labeling the use of pornography as "sinful lust" is less than sufficient and likely only increases the allure of the taboo amongst Christians. This excursus will contend that the use of pornography is more than a sinful act *per se*, but ultimately is a denial of human creaturely identity and a violation against one's own body, not to mention the bodies of others. While it is beyond our purposes here to propose a solution to the problem, it is the intent of this excursus to at least address the problem within the framework of a theology of the body that will, in turn, aid Christians to address the matter at a more fundamental level regarding human identity.

his thesis re pornea

It should be noted, as John Paul II points out, that not every visual depiction of the human body is pornographic in nature. John Paul II's discussion regarding the problem of pornography occurs within the context of his discussion of the ethos of the body in art and media. The human body is a perennial object of culture because the person is always the subject of culture.[358] Whether depicted in living art (theater, ballet, concerts, etc.), as a model (sculpture, painting, etc.) or as a reproduction of living man (photography or film) each medium, at varying degrees, involves a certain depersonalization of the body. By losing contact with the person behind the work of art the body becomes objectified.[359] This does not mean that the nude human figure is inappropriate as a subject for art, however. As Cooper points out, "Wojtyla will always be remembered as the pope who restored

---

[357] Roger Scruton, "Shameless and Loveless," *The Australian Family* 26:3 (2005): 40-42.

[358] "Before all else it should be observed that the human body is a perennial *object of culture in the widest sense of the term,* for the simply reason that man himself is the subject of culture and employs his humanity in his cultural and creative activity, thus also including his own body in this activity." *TOB,* 366.

[359] "Artistic objectification of the human body in its male and female nakedness for the sake of making of it first a model and then a subject of a work of art is *aLWays* a certain transfer outside of this configuration *of interpersonal gift* that belongs originally and specifically to the body. It constitutes in some way an uprooting of the human body from this configuration and a transfer of it to the dimension of artistic objectification specific to the work of art or to the reproduction typical for film and photographic technologies of our time." Ibid., 368. *!?*

interesting

Michelangelo's Sistine Chapel nudes to their pristine, unclothed condition."[360] It simply means that the value of such works of art falls on a continuum that is not merely aesthetic, but also moral. While all depictions of the human frame are apt to objectify the body to a certain degree, the moral value of the artistic expression is gauged by the degree to which the image of the body preserves or connects the consumer of the art to the personhood of the body.[361] While any particular work of art may involve a divorce of the body from the specific person who was the artist's subject, certain works of art nonetheless serve to emphasize the personal dimension of bodily personhood while others denigrate it.

For John Paul II the fundamental problem with pornography is not that it reveals too much, but that in a sense it reveals too little. Pornography exposes the body, for sure, but in the manner it is exposed as an object for another's use it actually obscures the nuptial significance of the body and the person's true beauty as a bearer of the divine image. In turn, the one who lustfully consumes pornographic images denigrates his own body as he allows himself to be dominated by the image of another's body apart from the donation and reception of another person. This "domination," as John Paul II terms it, is due to the fact that one's concupiscent lusts become evoked by a mere image without the accompanying donation of a total person which is granted in a genuinely human nuptial encounter.[362]

detached from an ethic of reception

---

[360] Cooper, *Life in the Flesh*, 232.

[361] "In the course of the various epochs from antiquity down–and especially in the great period of classical Greek art–there are works of art whose subject is the human body in its nakedness, the contemplation of which allows one to concentrate in some way on the whole truth of man, on the dignity and beauty–even 'suprasensual' beauty–of his masculinity and femininity. These works *bear within themselves in a hidden way, as it were, an element of sublimation* that leads the viewer through the body to the whole personal mystery of man." *TOB*, 376. *—depicted in longer, mythic narrative*

[362] "The whole problem of 'pornovision' and of 'pornography,' as it appears on the basis of what was said above, is *not the effect of a puritanical mentality* or of a *narrow moralism*, nor is it the product of a way of thinking burdened by Manichaeism. What is at issue is rather an *extremely important* and fundamental *sphere of values* to which man cannot remain indifferent because of the dignity of humanity, because of the personal character and eloquence of the human body. Through works of art and the activity of audiovisual media, this whole content and these values can be formed and deepened, but they can also be deformed and destroyed '*in in man's heart.*' We can see that we find ourselves continually within the orbit of the words Christ spoke in the Sermon on the Mount. The problems we are dealing with here should also be examined in the light of the words that speak about 'looking' born from concupiscence as 'adultery committed in the heart.'" Ibid., 373. *↳ so the English literary critical pre-occupation w/ the "male gaze" (one could also refer to the "white" gaze)*

162

Ultimately, pornography disrupts what John Paul II terms the "being-gift" by separating the human being, or person, from the nuptial nature of the body as gift.[363] According to Cooper, "although pornography makes human flesh its particular material focus, by using it to construct an imaginary situation into which the viewer virtually places himself it actually ends up alienating people from the real world of the flesh, in separating bodies from the persons to whom they belong."[364] Following Cooper's insight, the idea that one can "use" the image of another human body for self-gratification apart from violating the person behind the image is a fiction that depends upon a radically dualistic separation of the body from human personhood. The revelatory function of the body, as addressed earlier, reveals the very person to whom the body belongs. One cannot merely lust after another's body without, at the same time, directing their lusts at the person who is the body they are viewing. Even if the body depicted in a pornographic image is not an actual person, such as is the case in digitally produced or animated pornography, the image itself encourages a general objectification of the body divorced from human personhood. Accordingly, the pornography consumer in every instance violates his or her own unified body-and-soul humanity by objectifying the body apart from human personhood.

As such, the consumption of pornographic images disrupts human relationships in the "real world" as the tendency to lustfully objectify the body causes a rift in interpersonal relationships throughout one's entire life experience. The impact of pornography can be felt throughout one's entire communal life. While the impact is felt across all human interaction, the disruption pornography can cause in a marriage is particularly acute. Pornography can impact a marriage even when one's spouse is unaware that the other is indulging in pornography. The objectification of the human body through the consumption of pornography conditions the viewer toward a

---

[363] "The one as well as the other [pornovision or pornography] happens when one oversteps the limit of shame or of personal sensibility with regard to what is connected with the human body, with its nakedness, when in a work of art or by audiovisual media *one violates* the body's *right to intimacy in its masculinity and femininity* and–in the final analysis–when one violates that deep *order of the gift and of reciprocal self-giving*, which is inscribed in femininity and masculinity across the whole structure of being human." Ibid., 370.

[364] Cooper, *Life in the Flesh*, 229.

general objectification of other "bodies" as well as his own. This has particular consequences for a marriage as one begins to value or devalue their spouse's body apart from the nuptial meaning of the body in spousal union. Ceasing to see one's spouse in terms of gift, and one's own body in terms of gift for his or her spouse, will ultimately objectify the entire relationship. Pornography conditions the individual to perceive every human relationship, particularly marriage, in terms of how another individual can serve one's self. As such, when one spouse ceases to serve the other's felt-needs in either a physical or emotional way, the union itself is devalued and divorce often results.

The implications of this precede the marital relationship and have an impact on single young people, who the previously cited surveys show are viewing pornography at extraordinarily high frequency. It should be noted that the romantic ideal of "falling in love" as a prerequisite for marriage is nowhere found in scripture. Biblically speaking, love is not necessarily a prerequisite for marriage but is more essentially the result of being married. As offensive as it may be to contemporary culture, arranged marriages are found throughout Scripture and nowhere does scripture speak against this practice. Adam only expressed his love, exclaiming "flesh of my flesh," etc., after the Lord had given him Eve. By God's design, spousal love is engendered by nuptial union, it is not the basis for it. The same can be said regarding physical attraction. The notion that one begins to court or date a member of the opposite sex based on an initial physical attraction, followed by a nurtured romance, that may result in marriage turns the biblical pattern on its head. Throughout scripture marriage may happen due to any number of circumstances. Sometimes love or attraction may precede the marriage (*i.e.* Jacob and Rachel), but it is not necessarily the case. Marriage is the biblical foundation the leads to spousal love and physical attraction. Marriage is not the result of a physical attraction and a nurtured romance. In other words, the spousal union is the foundation for the enjoyment of one's spouse. Luther asserts that a husband ought to see his wife as the most attractive person on earth, not by comparison to any other body, but precisely because she is the one whom God has given him.[365] Attraction is

---

[365] "As I have pointed out more fully in my other discussions of marriage and married life, it would

164

the result of the gift, it is not what warrants the spousal gift. The enjoyment
of another human creature is not the foundation for marriage but the result
of it. *So, it is not based on "feelings" but on the gift of the other, accepted & cherished*

Pornography is particularly damaging for single people because it
conditions one toward the objectification of another's body and establishes
expectations that are neither realistic nor godly for one's eventual marriage.
In other words, the use of pornography by single people becomes a rehearsal
for objectification within a spousal union. It furthers the shameful condition
of post-Edenic man as one values other human creatures in terms of their
ability to be used for one's selfish interests.

In short, the use of pornography entrenches man in his experience of
original shame. How much one gets out of a relationship becomes the
condition upon which one will value their marriage rather than how much
one can give to their beloved. Further, what one gets from their spouse is no
longer received as gift, but is seized as if it were their due. Each spouse's
body becomes an object for personal gratification. In turn, each spouse
becomes exploited by the other. Pornography leads to so many divorces not
only because it is an objectification of the body, but because one has already
objectified their spouse as a result of the fall. When one's spouse's body
ceases to have the allure that one derives from their objectified pornographic
image, one ceases to value their spouse seeing him or her instead as an object
to seize, possess and exploit. In other words, pornography is destructive
because fallen man has already objectified their spousal union by losing sight
of the nuptial gift that defined the union of man and woman "in the
beginning." Pornography pours fuel upon the fire of original shame and

---

be a real art and a very strong safeguard against all this if everyone learned to look at his spouse correctly
according to God's Word, which is the dearest treasure and the loveliest ornament you can find in a man
or a woman. If he mirrored himself in this, then he would hold his wife in love and honor as a divine gift
and treasure. And if he saw another woman, even one more beautiful than his own wife, he would say: 'Is
she beautiful? As far as I am concerned, she is not very beautiful. And even if she were the most beautiful
woman on earth, in my wife at home I have a lovelier adornment, one that God has given me and has
adorned with His Word beyond the others, even though she may not have a beautiful body or may have
other failings. Though I may look over all the women in the world, I cannot find any about whom I can
boast with a joyful conscience as I can about mine: This is the one whom God has granted to me and put
into my arms.'" Martin Luther, *The Sermon on the Mount, LW* 21:87.

the Word adorns spouse.

furthers the destruction that man's original sin already engendered in the flesh.

It should be noted, though, that there is a significant difference between being "without shame" as Adam and Eve were prior to the fall and being "shameless." In *Love and Responsibility* Wojtyla affirms that Adam and Eve prior to sin felt "no shame," not because they were shameless, but because where love is mature "it is no longer necessary for a lover to conceal from his beloved or from himself a disposition to enjoy, since this has been absorbed by true love ruled by the will."[366] Conversely, for Wojtyla "shamelessness" can be manifest as either physical or emotional shamelessness. Physical shamelessness is "any mode or behavior on the part of a particular person in which the values of sex as such are given such prominence that they obscure the essential value of the person."[367] Emotional shamelessness consists in "the rejection of the healthy tendency to be ashamed of reactions and feelings which make another person merely an object of use because of the sexual values belonging to him or her."[368] Drawing upon Wojtyla's insights and the late pope's entire argument about pornography Cooper defines pornography as "simply shamelessness in art."[369]

Pornography is one manifestation of the commercialization of the human body in modern culture. Commercialization of the body is, in a sense, the inevitable consequence of the body's objectification for today's world. As one indulges in pornography he becomes accustomed to simply disposing of one image in exchange for another when one image ceases to satisfy his desires. It is not hard to imagine how this commercialization of the flesh translates into marital problems. Viewing the body of another human creature in a commercialized manner furthers the notion that if one becomes dissatisfied with his or her partner's body it may be returned or exchanged for another model. When one views his or her spouse's body not in terms of

---

[366] Wojtyla, *Love and Responsibility,* 174.

[367] Ibid., 187.

[368] Ibid., 188.

[369] Cooper, *Life in the Flesh,* 231-232.

nuptial gift, but as a commercial exchange of goods and services, one accepts the other's body only under certain conditions. *Trump . . .*

Understood within the terms of Luther's two kinds of righteousness, pornography furthers the destruction of one's relationships *coram mundo* as he persistently rebels against the passivity of gift reflected in his relationship with God, *coram Deo.* Through original shame Adam and Eve covered themselves from each other, experiencing shame *coram hominibus*, and drove them to hide themselves from God, experiencing shame *coram Deo*. Shame, unlike shamelessness, is experienced precisely because one recognizes and values the embodiment of the human person and realizes the violation sin has caused against it. Shamelessness, physical or emotional, is a denial of *KEY* embodied personhood at its very core. Through the shamelessness of consuming pornography one ultimately denies his or her creaturely identity and violates his own body and the bodies of others. In the previous chapter the body was described as the locus where man experiences his identity in dual-relationship vertically before God and horizontally before man and the world. Consuming pornography involves shameless denigration of the body, thus confounding one's experience of both kinds of righteousness. As such, the consumption of pornography involves more than the single sin of lust, but reflects the ultimate loss of "original righteousness" and fundamentally violates the identity of the human being as God's creature. It is not only a sin against God, but it is contrary to man's very humanity.

Luther on the "Image of God"

Generally discussions on the "image of God" would occur beneath a subheading of creation rather than the fall. In fact, Luther does address the image of God in his commentary on the first chapter of Genesis. That said, it is Luther's theology of sin that finally drives his interpretation and definition of the image of God. Ultimately, Luther relies upon man's postlapsarian experience to govern his interpretation of man's prelasparian reality. *we have no other way of "getting at it"*

When it comes to defining the image and likeness of God (Gen. 1:26) Luther often offers inconsistent interpretations, seeming unwilling to commit to any particular definition of the "image of God." Thus, when Luther affirms that the image of God is lost, after man's fall into sin, it is important to recognize which definition of the "image of God" Luther is operating with in context. Even within the Genesis lectures, for example, Luther offers and addresses a variety of definitions of the "image of God," suggesting at one point a preference for one understanding without necessarily committing himself to it in any dogmatic fashion.

Luther effectively rejects Augustine's view that the image of God should be associated with the memory, will and mind that distinguishes rational man from irrational beasts. The problem with this view, Luther writes, is that "if these powers are the image of God, it will also follow that Satan was created according to the image of God, since he surely has these natural endowments, such as memory and a very superior intellect and a most determine will, to a far higher degree than we have them."[370] Luther argues, instead, that the image of God must have been something so excellent that fallen man can no longer fully understand or express what it might have been.[371] That said, even while admitting a mystery behind what the image of God entails, he offers a general interpretation:

> Therefore my understanding of the image of God is this: that Adam had it in his being and that he not only knew God and believed that He was good, but that he also lived in a life that was wholly godly; that is, he was without the fear of death or any other danger, and was content with God's favor. In this form it reveals itself in the instance of Eve, who speaks with the serpent without any fear, as we do with a lamb or a dog. For this reason, too, if they should transgress this command, God announces the punishment: "On whatever day you eat from this tree, you will die by death," as though He said: "Adam and Eve, now you are living without fear; death you have not experienced, nor have you seen it. This is My image, by which you are living, just as God lives. But if you sin, you will lose this image, and you will die."[372]

---

[370] Ibid., 61.

[371] Ibid., 60.

[372] Ibid., 62-63.

Thus, Luther likens the image of God to a fearless state which, in the fear that man experiences immediately following his fall, testifies to the fact that this image was lost. His great concern is that those who maintain an element of the image of God within man after the fall ultimately "minimize original sin."[373] At the same time, however, Luther indicates "when we speak about that image, we are speaking about something unknown. Not only have we had no experience of it, but we continually experience the opposite and so we hear nothing except bare words."[374] In short, though, without committing to a definition of the image of God it is unclear how Luther can reasonably affirm that the image was lost. Luther appears to put the cart before the horse here—by presuming that the image of God is wholly lost he concludes that it must be something wholly unknowable to postlapsarian man.

When lecturing on Genesis 9:6, which evokes the concept of the image of God in which man was made as the basis for the prohibition of murder, Luther seems to both double down on his affirmation that the image of God is lost while, at the same time, suggesting that God's desire to restore his image within man ought to govern man's respect for one another:

> This is the outstanding reason why He does not want a human being killed...man is the noblest creature, not created like the rest of the animals but according to God's image. Even though man has lost this image through sin, as we stated above, his condition is nevertheless such that it can be restored through the Word and the Holy Spirit. God wants us to show respect for this image in one another; He does not want us to shed blood in a tyrannical manner.[375]

It appears here, however, that Luther is straining to maintain his insistence that the image of God is lost after man's fall in order to justify the basis for the biblical prohibition on murder which is derived from it. Luther

---

[373] Ibid.

[374] Ibid.

[375] *LW* 2:141.

never presents a clear exegetical basis for his insistence that the image of God is lost only implying, instead, that any notion that preserves the image of God after the fall might weaken the doctrine of original sin. This is inconsistent, however, with the insistence that sin is not a component of man's essence—a problem that the next generation of Lutherans had to address when the flaw in this perspective emerged in the Flacian controversy. Relying largely upon a misapplication of Luther's original intentions in the *Genesis Lectures*, and elsewhere, Matthias Flacius Illyricus ended up arguing that when man fell into sin he was "transformed" into the image of Satan, arguing as a result that sin became a component of human essence. While the *Formula of Concord* rejected the Flacian position, it ultimately likened original sin to the "lack of the original righteousness acquired in Paradise" and equates this original righteousness with the image of God.[376] The *Formula* continues, evoking Luther's Genesis Lectures in his commentary on Genesis 3 where Luther employs the word *accidens* to describe the nature of original sin in man—not to minimize original sin, but to distinguish the devil's handiwork from God's handiwork in man's being.[377] Ultimately, the Flacian controversy presented a dilemma that Luther's perspective on the loss of the image of God in man necessitated. While the resolution of the controversy in the *Formula of Concord* did not explicitly reject Luther's position, it effectively maintained by necessity a certain coherence of the image of God in man's essence by affirming that original sin belongs to the *accidens* of man, not man's essential nature.

Luther on the New Testament Distinction between Flesh and Spirit

In *De servo arbitrio*,[378] Luther decidedly refutes Erasmus' assertion that the New Testament dichotomy between "flesh" and "spirit" (*i.e.* John 3:6. Romans 3:23) rends the human will, reckoned to man's "spirit," immune to the bondage of sin. For Luther, when the New Testament whether it be John or Paul refers to "flesh" and "spirit," it is not distinguishing between the parts of man but, rather, describes the orientation of the total man.

---

[376] Kolb and Wengert, "The Solid Declaration of the Formula of Concord," in *The Book of Concord,* 533.

[377] Ibid., 542. *LW* 1:160-182.

[378] Lit. "*On Bound Choice*," commonly known as *The Bondage of the Will.*

170

According to Luther, when the New Testament writers say "man is flesh or spirit, it means the same as we mean when we say man is carnal or spiritual...Holy Scripture...calls man flesh, as if he were carnality itself, because he savors too much of the things of flesh and indeed of nothing but these; and it calls him spirit because he savors of, seeks, does, and endures nothing but the things of the spirit."[379] Thus, Luther refuses to accept any anthropology that allows one part of man or another to escape either the effects of sin, or to be saved in turn apart from the rest of man. This accords with what was observed regarding the New Testament use of carnality/spirituality, flesh and spirit indicated in Chapter 2. The entire man stands condemned on account of his sin even as the entire man stands redeemed on account of Christ through faith.

Luther on Common Grace and the Creator's Bodily Provision

When it comes to provisions for the flesh, however, God makes no differentiation between the elect and the reprobate. God provides for man's bodily needs equally, regardless of whether one is a Christian or an unbeliever. Naturally, Luther makes this point preaching on Jesus' words in Matthew 5:45, "...he makes his sun rise on the evil and on the good, and sends rain on the just and on the unjust." In *The Sermon on the Mount* (1532), Luther reflects, "...to the whole world, to His enemies as well as His friends, God gives body and life and everything it needs and uses, generously and freely every day."[380] Interestingly, Luther connects this notion to a fairly robust medieval ecology. He recognizes that all God gives he "produces, and preserves...through the sun," but adds that we must have rain, lest the sun dry up the world and "everything would dry up and wither away on account of the heat, and no food or grain could grow for man or beast." Evoking Aristotle's four categories of natural elements, Luther reflects that God consistently balances the "cold and warm, dry and moist."[381] Accordingly, God demonstrates bodily care for all creatures, believer and unbeliever alike, by maintaining a complex ecological balance in creation. On this basis, then,

---

[379] *WA* 18:728; *The Bondage of the Will*, *LW* 33:226-227.

[380] *The Sermon on the Mount*. *LW* 21:126.

[381] Ibid.

Luther follows the impetus of the argument first articulated by Jesus in Matthew 5:46ff. Having received every good thing from God that preserves and sustains us in the body, Christians must likewise show care and concern for one's neighbor, even if that neighbor be an enemy of the Christ as well as the Christian. Luther exhorts his hearers, "How you must reproach yourself, then, for your lack of love toward God, your failure to do any favors for your neighbor, and your refusal to show at least some regard for others, when He is continually doing you so much good by means of all the creatures?"[382] This, Luther emphasizes, was not a new teaching even when Christ first shocked his hearers with an exhortation to love one's enemies in this way. Luther cites Exodus 23:24, wherein Moses exhorts the Israelites to return their enemy's ox or ass if he should see it going astray.[383] That the Christian should love one's neighbor, even his enemies, and help him care for his body and provide for his needs, is closely related to Luther's doctrine of vocation. Through believers' various callings they become the masks of God, *larvae Dei*.[384] While God cares for creation immediately, he also calls people according to various vocations whereby He sees to it that the sustenance He has provided in creation itself is delivered and administered to all men. Thus, "the whole creation is a face or mask of God," and the Christian as God's image bearer becomes an extension of God's provision for the world.[385]

The Impact of Sin on Human Vocation

Luther's doctrine of the three "orders" or "estates" (*Dreiständelehre*) can be deciphered from the very beginnings of primordial man's existence.

---

[382] Luther continues, "Now, this is what He has to put up with daily from the whole world. Still He is so faithful that daily He sends the sunshine and His other superabundant blessings upon people who do not deserve even to have a blade of grass or a moment of sunshine, but to be showered with incessant hell-fire and to be pelted with thunderbolts and hailstones, spears and bullets. He really ought to be called a faithful Father for letting such desperate scoundrels have all those possessions, lands, servants, and good weather, for letting them act like the lords of all and the squires of His domain! Why, even the sun and the moon, together with all the creatures, have to serve them, letting themselves be misused in opposition to God by the whims and the wickedness of such people. Now, if we want to be sons of the Father, we ought to let this sublime example move us to live likewise. "Ibid.

[383] Ibid., 127.

[384] *Lectures on Galatians (1535), LW* 26:94.

[385] Ibid.

[handwritten margin note: Interesting — estates are divisions — would they not all come postlapsaria]

As discussed in the previous chapter, Adam was given the unique responsibility to govern the first two estates from the beginning: the household (*oeconomiam*) and the church (*ecclesiam*). The civil government (*politiam*), in turn, becomes an added necessity after the fall.

> And again, the situation of Adam, as the initiator of sin, was worse than ours, if we appraise it correctly. Where we work hard, each one in his own station, Adam was compelled to exert himself in the hard work of the household, of the state, and of the church all by himself. As long as he lived, he alone held all these positions among his descendants. He supported his family, ruled it, and trained it in godliness; he was father, king, and priest. And experience teaches how each one of these positions abounds in grief and dangers.[386]

[handwritten margin note: Flawed logic]

[handwritten margin note: so ? have no estate?]

That Luther sees dignity in human labor across the three estates is significant. When Luther's former teacher and colleague, Andreas Bodenstein Von Karlstadt, was expelled from Saxony in 1523 and took residence in Orlamünde he renounced his place amongst the "privileged" and took on farming as an "honest mortification of the flesh." In a polemical address to Luther in 1525 Karlstadt grounded his position on the fact that "God had commanded Adam to work the soil" and explicitly praised the work of peasants as "more honorable" than his previous work as a professor in Wittenberg.

> I thank God that his divine grace has graciously brought me to the frame of mind where I would gladly do [peasants'] work now without dread of what the whole world says. What do you think Luther? Are not blisters on your hands more honorable than golden rings?[387]

---

[386] *Lectures on Genesis (1535/38)*, *LW* 1:213-214.

[387] "*Wölte God das ich ein rechter Bawr, Ackersman oder handtwercksman were, das ich mein broth im gehorsam Gottes ess, das ist, im schweyss meines angesichts, Ich hab aber der armbe lewt arbeyt gessen, den ich gar nichts darfür thon hab, hab sy dartzu nicht zu recht hand gehabt, noch vermöcht*

173

It is Karlstadt's above argument that Luther has in mind when addressing man's vocation according to the "three estates" in his 1535 Genesis lectures. Like Karlstadt, Luther opposes the elevation of certain "privileged" vocations to a more dignified position before God than the work of peasants. Likewise, along with Karlstadt, Luther condemns idleness. To abandon one's calling, though, under the impression that working the fields is more spiritually dignified is equally condemnable. Luther addresses this lecturing on Genesis 3:19, "In the sweat of your face you will eat your bread."

> But here the question arises whether we all ought to be farmers or at least work with our hands, as some foolishly maintained when the Gospel was first proclaimed. They misused this passage, as well as others which command the work of the hands, to make young men give up their studies and follow occupations requiring manual labor. Thus their leader Carlstadt gave up his position, bought a country place, and dug and tended it himself. But surely, if it were right to abandon one's calling, it would be far easier and more pleasant for me to be in the garden, to dig with a hoe, and to turn the ground with a spade than it is to carry on the work which I am now doing. For work on the farm does not compare with this strenuous exertion of ours. Therefore we must utterly reject the opinion of those who maintain that only manual labor may be called work...the sweat of the brow is of many kinds: the first is that of the farmers or householders; the second is that of the officers of the state; and the third is that of the teachers in the church...It is, therefore, the utmost stupidity for the enthusiasts to insist on manual labor, which is useful for strengthening the body, when, by

---

handthaben [=schützen], Jedoch nichts destmynder ire arebeytt in mein hauss genommen, vermöcht ichs, ich wölt inen alles widergeben, das ich entpfangen. Gott hatt Adam ein gebott geben, das er arbeytten soll, und das gebott lauttet von der arbeyt des feldes...Und solch arbeyt ist ein redlich tödtung des fleysches...Das will ich aber Got dancken, das mich seyn götliche genad, auss gnaden, zu dem gemüet gebracht, das ich yetzt one schew, aller welt rede unnd wort, gern wolt arbeyten. Wie meynstu Luther ob uns blassen nicht eerlicher in den hended stünden, denn guldene rewffe?" Andreas Bodenstein Von Karlstadt, *Anzeig,* Hertzsch, ii, 95.21.96.5. Quoted and partially translated in Ronald J. Sider, *Andreas Bodenstein von Karlstadt: The Development of His Thought, 1517-1525* (Boston: Brill, 1997), 178-179.

contrast, these very great labors in the state and church wear out the body and drain off all vitality, as it were, from its innermost centers.[388]

Luther's affirmation of vocations that span the three "estates" is wholly consistent with his affirmation of man as *totus homo*. The entire man participates in any labor the person engages. While an activity may be thought of as primarily physical, or primarily intellectual, it is nonetheless the entirety of man who is involved in the labor. Thus, when one labors with his mind and pen writing against the enthusiasts (as Luther certainly did), the body becomes exhausted together with the mind. A farmer's labor in a field certainly must engage the mind as well lest the crops be planted or harvested in unideal conditions. Preaching, as can be testified by those who have been called to do so, can be physically exhausting. In Luther's day, before the invention of sound systems a great deal of lung capacity would inevitably be involved if the preacher's words were to be heard. Similarly, prior to the invention of air conditioning, preaching a sermon would certainly be a labor that drew sweat upon the brow. In short, while certain vocations may involve a greater or lesser degree of labor according to the body, or according to the mind, it is always the entire person (*totus homo*) who is engaged in the activity and it is the whole person in all his faculties that labors in toil.

That said, it should be remembered that the "sweat" upon the brow that accompanies labor according to Genesis 3:19 is a result of the fact that sin as labor now involves toil and pain. It is not the barometer by which the godliness of a particular vocation should be determined. Luther is critical of those who use the privilege of their position as an opportunity for idle or gluttonous living.[389] While Luther often indicts princes and popes under

---

[388] *Lectures on Genesis (1535/38), LW* 1:211-213.

[389] "But we may say this about the pope, the cardinals, and the whole pack of wicked men who use up great wealth, although they do no work and are concerned only with their bellies and their leisure. They are the ones to whom that familiar statement of Paul's applies (2 Thess. 3:10): 'He who does not work should not eat.' But to work in the church means to preach, administer the Sacraments, contend with the enthusiasts, remove offenses, edify the godly, etc. Of those who do this Christ says (Luke 10:7): 'The laborer is worthy of his hire.'" Ibid., 213.

these charges, his most thorough exposition of the problems of "idleness" emerges in his writings against monastic orders.

Luther on Monastic Disciplines

It is difficult to peruse Luther's more polemical works without engaging his critical view of monasticism. While Luther rarely treaded lightly when addressing his opponents, his frequent critiques of monasticism are particularly poignant. Luther criticizes monasticism from the first hand perspective of an Augustinian monk, or more precisely, a friar. Luther wore the monk's habit for nearly twenty years, between the age of twenty-two and forty-one, during some of the most important years of his life and those years that saw the beginning of the Reformation. While Luther's criticisms of monastic life are many and varied this section is concerned primarily with Luther's critique of monastic practices and disciplines, particularly derived from his theology of vocation.[390]

Luther was critical of monastic orders for a number of reasons. Luther's most complete treatment of the matter was *The Judgment of Martin Luther on Monastic Vows* (1521).[391] While Luther's language in the treatise seems polemical, it was not an attack on monasticism *per se*, but was written for the sake of the consciences of monks and nuns who, as a result of the Reformation, had already left or were thinking of leaving their monasteries

---

[390] It is worth noting that Luther also constructs a similar argument against the Anabaptists, for many of the same reasons. In a sermon on the final verses of John 6 and the first verses of John 7, after explaining that one must be willing to even give up good and Godly things under persecution, if the alternative is denying Christ, Luther emphasizes that one should never make the neglect of one's calling in life into a spiritual discipline. "...in the absence of an emergency everyone must remain in his town, place, and calling, and not forsake his family; all should remain together where they belong. But if the alternative ever confronts us—either to leave our calling and position or to deny Christ—then I declare: "Rather than deny Christ, I will sacrifice life, house, home, etc." I am directing these words against the Anabaptists, who inflict sufferings on themselves, who forsake all and then boast of being martyrs. They seek their own honor. But do not choose your own affliction. Neither you nor anyone else has been ordered to incur danger to life and limb voluntarily. For your help and sustenance God made so many creatures and devised so many means and ways. He has the fields cultivated to forestall famine. He gives so much wool to keep you from freezing. He provides so much wood and stone, such a variety of weather, all sorts of gifts, to enable you to attend to your bodily needs and preserve your health. Furthermore, God gave you your inheritance, wife and child, house and home, and everything in order that you and your wife might stay together. Consequently, your first duty is to provide for your body; that is God's will." *Sermons on the Gospel of St. John, LW* 23:203.

[391] *WA* 8:573-669; *LW* 44:243-400.

or convents.[392] The poignant critique of monastic vows founded herein should be seen within the context of a monk who had yet to completely shed the habit himself.[393] As harsh as his words were, they were written by a monk who had yet to totally lose hope that monasticism, as such, could be reformed. That said, it seems from the tone of this treatise that his hopes for reforming monasticism were fading quickly. The corruption of monasticism in its condition at the time were so deeply seeded that he could not fault one who chose to renounce his vow and leave the monastery or nunnery, and doing so may even be necessary according to conscience. Luther's arguments here ultimately led to the closing of monasteries throughout the German evangelical territories.[394] This treatise became the basis for the treatment of monastic vows in Article XXVII of the *Apology of the Augsburg Confession*.[395]

It is unnecessary for these purposes to outline Luther's entire argument here. Under five separate headings Luther deals with the burdens that monastic vows place on the conscience. The overarching theme is that many elements of monastic discipline are good, but the nature of the monastic vow takes what could be a salutary practice and misuses it as an attempt to earn special favor with God. One would be amiss, then, to suggest that Luther's critique of monastic orders, even in his other polemical works, rejects monastic discipline outright. On the contrary, Luther finds many benefits in monastic living, even from his own experience, which can be embraced by the common Christian. The abuse of monastic disciplines, by subjecting them to vows that bind consciences, does not negate their godly use for Luther. In other words, it is the matter of the "vow" that was most problematic, not the disciplined life. Such discipline requires no vow aside

---

[392] *LW* 44:247.

[393] Luther was a monk for nearly twenty years between July 17, 1505 when he first applied to the monastery and October 1524 when he renounced the monastic life formally and put away the monastic habit. See *LW* 23:348.

[394] For a fuller background of Luther's monastic life, and a summary of the tension with which Luther writes this treatise as a monk himself, see Dorothea Wendebourg, "Luther on Monasticism," *Lutheran Quarterly, XIX,* (2005), 126-135.

[395] The *Apology of the Augsburg Confession* explicitly identifies Luther's 1521 work as the foundation for Article XXVII. "Since, however, Luther dealt with this entire matter carefully and complete in a book, *On Monastic Vows*, we want to be interpreted here as reiterating that book." Kolb, Wengert and Arand, eds. *The Book of Concord: The Confessions of the Evangelical Lutheran Church,* 279.

from the vow of faith proceeding from a glad heart comprehended by the Gospel of Jesus Christ.

> Further, a man taking his vows in a Christian and godly way would of necessity think thus in the presence of God, "Look, O God, I vow to thee this kind of life, not because I think this is a way to attain righteousness and salvation or to make satisfaction for my sins. Such an attitude might turn away thy mercy from me. This would cause harm to my Lord Christ, since it would be to deny his merits and profane his blood, and to hold thy Son as a reproach. To him alone belongs the glory of being the Lamb of God who takes away the sin of the world. He washes and justifies all with his blood. I will not so blasphemously reject thy grace. My expectations and hopes I shall set in him alone, never at all trusting in myself or in any other creature, to say nothing of trusting in my vows and good works. *I do this because I must live in the flesh and cannot be idle. I take this way of life upon myself for the sake of disciplining my body to the service of my neighbor and meditating upon thy word. I do this just as another man may take up farming or a trade—every man a job—without any thought of merits or justification.* Justification exists first and foremost in faith. It will always be the most important and will always reign supreme, etc.[396]

The *Augsburg Confession* follows a similar line of thought. While not from Luther's pen directly, Luther's influence and contribution is undoubtedly felt here. In Article XXVI, *Concerning the Distinction of Foods*, it is affirmed that "all Christians should so train and restrain themselves with bodily discipline, or bodily exercises and labors, that neither over exertion nor idleness may lure them to sin." Again, it is reinforced that these labors do not merit forgiveness or grace, neither do they make satisfaction for sin. Nonetheless, such bodily exercises should "always be encouraged" (Latin text) and "maintained continually" (German text) by the Christian and not

---

[396] *The Judgment of Martin Luther on Monastic Vows (1521), LW* 44:294-295. Italics added.

relegated to particular feasts or occasions. A number of scriptural citations (Luke 21:34, Mark 9:29, 1 Corinthians 9:27) are given to support the conclusion that such punishments or mortifications of the body serve "not to merit forgiveness of sins through such discipline but to keep the body under control and fit for spiritual things and to carry out his responsibilities according to his calling."[397]

Clearly, Luther found great benefit in applying the disciplines of monastic living to the common Christian according to one's particular calling. Bodily discipline, whether it be through intentional exercise, fasting, or the like, has two primary functions for the sake of two primary ends. Bodily discipline functions both to keep the passions of the flesh in check and to preserve the health of the body. According to Luther's 1528 *Lectures on 1 Timothy*, "One must control his body to preserve his health and bridle his passions."[398] These two functions serve two parallel ends: to prevent gross sin and to allow one to serve his neighbor according to his vocation.

The concern in the *Augsburg Confession* that either "overexertion" or "idleness" could lead to sin offers a significant corrective to either neglecting bodily discipline or to taking it to an unhealthy extreme. Keeping sin at bay in the flesh means neither succumbing to gluttony and idleness nor to excessive disciplines that place the health of the body at risk. The flesh is disciplined best in moderation. Being that every person's body requires different degrees of discipline and rest, however, Luther insists in his 1528 *Lectures on 1 Timothy* that no universal prescription for bodily discipline can be made.

> Treat your body in such a way that it does not waste away. Both are sins—to go to excess in drinking and in fasting...Whenever a body has taken precautions for its lust, as when it eats bread, much strength and power come into the innermost parts of the body. It is different when it drinks wine. We cannot, therefore, establish a rule for so great a diversity of bodies. Here we have to consider the diversity of both the makeup of bodies and bodies

---

[397] Kolb, Wengert and Arand, eds. *The Book of Concord: The Confessions of the Evangelical Lutheran Church*, 78-81.

[398] *Lectures on 1 Timothy (1528), LW* 28:357.

themselves. This is what Paul means...He wants Timothy to train himself, but no farther than to preserve the health and welfare of his body. Gerson says this well. "Which one is to be thought of as pure, excess in eating or in fasting? Here we ought to compliment no one." It is hardly better, he says, to be excessive in spending than to sin in need. Why? When one's strength is exhausted and has nothing to prepare for food, it drains itself. This is quite dangerous—a situation to be feared...Everyone should test his own strength like a brave man. The man who burns much has much strength. He ought to wear himself out in a way different from that of a weak man. The man who eats rough bread is assailed differently from the way another is who eats eggs and meat. Therefore we must not behave like the monks...One must control his body by watching so that it does not become wanton. If the body is weak, one ought to give it meat and drink...To summarize this teaching: we must discipline the body, but we must do it wisely, not equally for all, because all men are not equal.[399]

As previously indicated, Luther's great concern is that one's body need be in good health in order to fulfill one's Christian vocation. Because one cannot serve and love his neighbor apart from the body, the body must be cared for. Loving one's neighbor, then, in fulfillment of the second great commandment of Christ, is not primarily a feeling one directs toward his neighbor but it is sacrificial action and service.

The body can suffer whenever moderation is not observed in either extreme. Too little food, as often was the case due to monastic fasts, could

---

[399] Ibid., 356-357. Similarly, Luther had previously written in his 1520 *Treatise on Good Works,* "I am quite prepared to allow everybody to fast on any day he likes and choose which food and how much of it he likes, provided he does not stop there but pays attention to his own body. One must discipline the flesh with fastings, watchings, and labor only insofar as it is proud and self-willed, no more. Not even if the pope, the church, bishop, father confessor, or anybody else commands it. For nobody ought to measure and regulate fasts, vigils, and tasks, matters of amount or kinds of food, or special days. These matters should be regulated by the ebb and flow of the pride and lust of the flesh. For it was solely to kill and subdue the pride and lust of the flesh that fastings, vigils, and penances were instituted. If it were not for this lust, eating would be as meritorious as fasting; sleeping as watching; idleness as labor; and one would be as good as the other without any distinction." *LW* 44:74.

make one just as ill as a gluttonous eater. Too much bodily work and not enough rest can also harm the body leaving one in no better position to serve his neighbor than one who is lazy or idle. By indulging either extreme the body is likely to suffer, complicating one's ability to fulfill his vocation and offering opportunity for sin to take hold in the flesh. As such, disciplining the body (as the *Augsburg Confession* affirms) cannot be relegated to monastic living nor to particular times and seasons. Because one's vocation is a component of one's creaturely identity, bodily discipline should be encouraged by all Christians according to their various bodily constitutions and situational demands lest one be unable to fulfill his or her God given calling. The problem with monastic disciplines is summarized, then, in that the monastics misdirect their disciplines by engaging in them for the sake of righteousness *coram Deo* rather than disciplining their bodies for the sake of neighbor. By reorienting Christian discipline according to righteousness *coram mundo* Luther is able to nuance such disciplines according to the distinctive locus of each Christian both with respect to their individual bodily needs and with respect to their daily vocations.

That said, there is a spiritual component to bodily discipline as well. For Luther, the body needs to be disciplined not only for the sake of serving one's neighbor, but also because an undisciplined body gives opportunity for sin in the flesh. As referred to previously, the *Augsburg Confession*'s concern for bodily discipline is that "neither over exertion nor idleness may lure them to sin." In *The Apology of the Augsburg Confession*, Article XV, it is similarly affirmed that while "reason" would make bodily discipline an act of worship that justifies, the purpose of such disciplines "is to restrain the flesh."[400] As much as a sinful "mind" can drive the body into performing sinful actions, the passions and lusts of the body can take the mind captive as well. Again, it is Luther's affirmation of the *totus homo* that makes it impossible for him to relegate the starting point of sin exclusively to the mind. Sinful inclination can begin in the thoughts or in the bodily passions but ultimately involves the entire person. Luther's distinction between actions "according to the Spirit" and those "according to the flesh" is not a mind/body dichotomy at all. When one lives "according to the Spirit" it is

---

[400] Kolb, Wengert and Arand, eds. *The Book of Concord: The Confessions of the Evangelical Lutheran Church*, 227.

the entire person who lives according to the Holy Spirit of God. To say that one lives "according to the flesh," it is to affirm that the entire person is living according to the sinful nature apart from the Holy Spirit. As such, a sinful thought is indulged according to the flesh even while a godly action is performed according to the Spirit. In either case, it is the entire person who is involved.

Excursus: Physical Fitness

While Luther affirmed the dignity of vocations that primarily involve intellectual labor, as well as physical labor, he nonetheless presumed that all vocations involved activity. Idleness, in any respect, is frequently warned against. Few in Luther's day could get away with an idle lifestyle, or a gluttonous one, without either being in a position of high prominence or taking a monastic vow. For Luther, idleness was often relegated to the wealthy, princes, pope and monks. Even the professor or the pastor, who rightly was supported by farmers and laborers of the city, had a close connection with those who toiled the soil and provided for his needs. As discussed previously, contra Karlstadt, Luther affirmed the dignity of human vocation in all three "orders" or "estates." He recognized, however, that often by necessity one must engage in physical activity if his vocational duties do not inherently involve it. Bodily discipline, then, is not something that should be relegated to the monasteries, and only then during certain appointed fasts, but should be engaged by all Christians at all times. Luther praised Emperor Maximilian who, though he "was so occupied with the affairs of state" was often compelled to "get away from his tasks and to hide in the forests, where he went hunting." While some thought his interest in hunting was a fault, "those who had a knowledge of his work and of his private life were of the opinion that he adopted it because of necessity rather than for pleasure."[401] In short, Luther recognized that not all bodily discipline needed in order to fulfill one's vocation necessarily is gained through the exercise of one's vocation alone. Supplemental bodily exercises or disciplines must sometimes be added in order to care for one's body properly.

---

[401] Ibid., 212.

but they understood (clothed, work / gluttony / knew somehow — biblical

There was no "fitness industry" in Luther's day. People did not have gym memberships or workout programs. Most people in the sixteenth century, regardless of their vocations, needed to exert themselves physically in the course of daily living. Even those whom Luther chastises as being "idle" would likely have been more active by necessity than many can get away with today. Nonetheless, Luther recognized the importance of supplemental Christian discipline for the sake of the body's health. God designed man's body from the dust of the ground and gave man the immediate responsibility to work the same ground from which he was fashioned—first as a pleasurable duty, and after sin in toil and pain. Man was not only given the responsibility to work the ground, but having been made from the ground there was an intimate connection between man's original responsibility and his bodily constitution. In short, God created man in order to work and be active.

The health benefits of ongoing moderate to intense physical activity, as well as the detriment to one's health caused by sedentary living has been well documented by the modern medical community.[402] That said, engaging in the sort of activity levels the body demands has become something that must be fit into a schedule rather than something that simply happens in the course of one's daily responsibilities. Physical activity, unless intentionally engaged, has become harder to come by in the prosperous Western world. Sedentary or idle living is no longer relegated to the well-to-do or the privileged class. The technological revolution, with all its benefits, has robbed the body of what used to be unavoidable activity. In an age dominated by industry and commerce it is no surprise that another industry, namely the fitness industry, would arise by necessity. Wendell Berry's reflections on the modern conundrum are fitting.

> It is plain that, under the rule of the industrial economy, humans, at least as individuals, are well advanced in a kind of obsolescence. Among those who have achieved even a modest success according to the industrial formula, the human body has

---

[402] For a comprehensive report, with additional studies cited, see "The Benefits of Physical Activity." Harvard School of Public Health. http://http://www.hsph.harvard.edu/nutritionsource/staying-active-full-story/ (accessed February 6, 2014)

been almost entirely replaced by machines and by a shrinking population of manual laborers. For enormous numbers of people now, the only physical activity that they cannot delegate to machines or menials, who will presumably do it more to their satisfaction, is sexual activity. For many, the only necessary physical labor is that of childbirth...In such a circumstance, the obsolescence of the body is inevitable, and this is implicitly acknowledged by the existence of the "physical fitness movement." Back in the era of the body, when women and men were physically useful as well as physically attractive to one another, physical fitness was simply a condition. Little conscious attention was given to it; it was a by-product of useful work. Now an obsessive attention has been fixed upon it. Physical fitness has become extremely mental; once free, it has become expensive, an industry—just as sexual attractiveness, once the result of physical vigor and useful work, has now become an industry. The history of "sexual liberation" has been a history of increasing bondage to corporations.[403]

Increasing technologies have resulted in, at the very least, a perception that the human body has become obsolete. The rise of technology has become perceived almost as a sort of rescue from toilsome work. More and more, people have to engage in physical activity for its own sake. They can no longer proverbially kill two birds with one stone—getting their exercise in while fulfilling their daily responsibilities. Bodily exercise must be scheduled. Even then, the health problems that develop from sedentary living take time to develop leaving one with even less incentive, particularly in a culture that prizes instant gratification, to force exercise into their daily routine. On top of that, unless one is accustomed to exercise, the less healthy one has become the more tiring their exercise will be leaving one without the energy to fulfill their daily vocations.

All that said, one would be amiss to simply blame technology, industry and commerce and take up farming instead. At a time of significantly less

---

[403] Berry, *The Art of the Commonplace*, 140-141.

luxury, that is what Karlstadt did and Luther chastised him for abandoning his vocation. These modern developments are neither essentially evil nor good. One can embrace his identity as God's creature even while embracing technology for all its benefits. While some may sinfully perceive the inventiveness of man as man's ascension to godhood, the Christian may rightfully embrace technology and marvel at the latent potential that God wrote into the created order from the beginning. With any significant human development, though, there is a cause-and-effect relationship that impacts how one understands his identity as God's creature. The technological era has allowed man to perceive his daily existence, albeit fictitiously, apart from his dependence upon the ground. It has established new sorts of vocations that involve far less bodily toil than those callings of days gone by. That said, the body has not constitutionally changed. To be God's creature means both embracing one's calling, even if it is not physically rigorous, while at the same time caring for the body with intentional exercise.

Even while embracing a changing world that is dominated by industry and commerce, one can also embrace the emergence the physical fitness industry—albeit with certain qualifications. Technology has, in fact, risen to the occasion to provide opportunities for physical activity through the development of exercise equipment and in-home workout programs that can be followed along with on the television or even streaming on-demand. Technology has been employed to solve a problem that technology itself caused. That said, the commercialization of physical fitness is not without its correlative downside. Where money is to be made, marketing and advertising will emerge alongside it to exploit felt-needs and create demand. If one's godly health, or disciplining the sinful flesh, is not enough to encourage one to exercise his body, an appeal to "body image," vanity, and the sinful nature is at least as marketable. While physical fitness can and should be used to care for the body due to one's affirmation of the body's goodness and creaturely identity before God and the world, the marketing of "body image" has frequently done the opposite by creating dissatisfaction with one's body. Berry reflects on this problem, particularly as it involves young people.

...our young people are offered the ideal of health only by what they know to be lip service. What they are made to feel forcibly, and to measure themselves by, is the exclusive desirability of a certain physical model. Girls are taught to want to be leggy, slender, large-breasted, curly-haired, unimposingly beautiful. Boys are instructed to be "athletic" in build, tall but not too tall, broad-shouldered, deep-chested, narrow-hipped, square-jawed, straight-nosed, not bald, unimposingly handsome. Both sexes should look what passes for "sexy" in a bathing suit. Neither, above all, should look old. Though many people, in health, are beautiful, very few resemble these models. The result is widespread suffering that does immeasurable damage both to individual persons and to the society as a whole. The result is another absurd pseudo-ritual, "accepting one's body," which may take years or may be the distraction of a lifetime.[404]

Particularly for young people, countering the powerful cultural message of "body image" with an affirmation of God's unconditional love is not necessarily sufficient. The commercial exploitation of "body image" is targeted at one's self perception amongst one's peers; it is directed at one's interpersonal relationships rather than one's perception from God's point of view. One can fully recognize his or her acceptance by God, being righteous *coram Deo*, while still feeling insufficient or unaccepted *coram hominibus*. Recognizing that as God's creatures all human beings have a creaturely identity both before God and before men allows Christians to address the above problem in a more nuanced and comprehensive manner.

First, lurking behind the ploy of "body image" is the sexualization of the body. Granted, as affirmed previously, the body is sexual by design. That said, the modern sexualization of the body follows the logic of original shame rather than that of original nakedness. An appeal to "body image" is to deploy the body for the sake of sexual exploitation. By pursuing an image of the body that others may find more attractive is to dangle out one's identity for the sake of objectification. This applies not only to relationships

---

[404] Ibid., 107.

with potential sexual partners but even amongst one's peers. One can feel valued or devalued as a part of a certain clique or class of bodies by which each measures one's worth in comparison to others. Social interaction, pursued on the basis of "body image," still sexualizes the body and objectifies oneself and others. The Christian response to this is not to prudishly desexualize the body. On the contrary, the Christian response to the "body image" conundrum is to properly reorient the sexualization of the body according to God's design. Christian conversation regarding the body and sex cannot be reduced to a set of bedroom behaviors, some of which are sinful others of which are not. A constructive theology of "body image" in the light of God's image in which the body was made must be emphasized.

Second, in order to have a salutary perspective on physical fitness one must begin to comprehend his or her body as a gift from God. This is, of course, closely related to the nuptial nature of the body as expressed earlier in John Paul II's theology. That said, the point here is ultimately far less complex. When one receives a gift from someone else how one cares for and treats the gift reflects on his love for the giver. Many people hold on to gifts out of sentiment that have no practical use simply because they value the relationship they have with the person who gave them the gift. How much more, then, should one care for and value the body which is a gift given by God, the Creator, and is immeasurably useful as well? In spite of the perplexity that sin has cast upon the body, caring for the body is an ongoing act of faith in the Creator's declaration that the body is, in fact, "good."

Third, the body must be comprehended within the framework of a healthy eschatology. More will be said about this in Chapter 5. At this point, it is sufficient to point out that from an eschatalogical perspective the telos of the body should be comprehended through a properly nuanced preaching of the resurrection of the body. Some are tempted, in the light of the resurrection, to neglect the body entirely in view of the "new body" that they will eventually receive. On the other hand, there are those who pursue physical fitness because they are pursuing longevity at all costs by trying to perpetually extend their present lives. As such, the resurrection should be proclaimed as both a present and a future reality. The Christian is called to live according to the resurrection here and now while proleptically participating in the life that has already been promised by Christ. At the same

187

time, though, the fullness of Christian hope is not yet realized and one can hold out hope that one's present bodily sufferings will pass away and a new body, patterned after the bodily image of the resurrected Lord, will be ours eternally. Either extreme, neglecting bodily exercise on account of the resurrection or pursuing longevity at all costs, must be countered by a proper proclamation of the eschatological resurrection of the flesh.

Finally, the issue of physical fitness must be emphasized in the light of bodily discipline and Christian vocation. Much of what should be said here has already been said above in the light of Luther's reflections on monastic discipline. Clearly, in order to fulfill one's daily calling the body must be capable of performing the tasks his vocation demands. For many, then, physical fitness becomes a necessity. There is a more fundamental issue, here, though. Consider Jesus' summary of the second table of the law: "love your neighbor as yourself." The implication of this command is that in order to actually love one's neighbor one should have a certain love of self as well. This is not the sort of self-love that persists according to sinful egoism or narcissism, but a love of self that is comprehended by God's love in Christ Jesus. How can one despise his own body while affirming that Jesus died in the flesh to redeem the body? Fulfilling the first part of Jesus' command, then, to love one's neighbor demands a certain self-value comprehended by the value that God has already placed upon the body by redeeming it. Wendell Berry says it well: "Contempt for the body is invariably manifested in contempt for other bodies - the bodies of slaves, laborers, women, animals, plants, the earth itself. Relationships with all other creatures become competitive and exploitive rather than collaborative and convivial."[405]

The problems posed today as the body becomes more and more commercialized and "body image" becomes marketed is not that people love their bodies too much. What seems on the surface to be too much self-love is actually a hidden contempt for the body that drives many to try and use physical fitness, dieting and even cosmetic surgery in an effort to remake their bodies in a way that they hope to find more pleasing. Egoism is deceptively self-deprecating. In short, the Christian should be encouraged to

---

[405] Ibid., 101.

exercise regularly but not necessarily for all the reasons that physical fitness is marketed by today's world. While the tendency of many is to either neglect the body entirely, or to idolize it, a proper theology of the body alongside a reorientation of physical fitness toward that theology is crucial.

Man's Fallen Relationship with the Earth

The difference between dependence and exploitation is great. Just as man and woman were dependent upon one another in their fulfillment of God's word to "be fruitful and multiply" from the beginning, man and woman were also dependent upon the earth for their sustenance and the earth was likewise dependent upon man that it would be properly governed and worked. Conversely, just as man's mutual dependence and reciprocal gift of one to the other became exploitation of one another through sin, the relationship of man to the ground turned from faithful lordship over the earth into an exploitation of God's creation. What was a relationship of mutual dependence, man and earth as gift to the other, became an adversarial relationship characterized by toil and pain. Not only does the earth seemingly provide for man now only reluctantly, but the earth sometimes strikes back at man randomly through natural disaster. Natural disasters now strike at man's hearth and home causing human beings significant toil and pain. Without pushing the personification of the earth's ecosystems and natural orders too far, it is nonetheless clear that man is both dependent upon creation for the sustenance of his body and is threatened by it. While the ecological responsibility of man is not the primary concern of this book, one could argue that the same might be said of the creation itself. The earth is both dependent upon man for its continued care and is at the same time threatened by him. In short, what was depicted as a great communion of mutual dependence between the human creature and the earth in Genesis 2 becomes a relationship strained, and broken, by the end of Genesis 3. While the natural law of God's original design remains, man's rebellion has consequences evidenced across the entire creation.

Recalling that it was from the very dust of the ground that God fashioned the human body in the beginning, the strained relationship that persists after sin between man and the earth certainly impacts the body in sin as well. While man remains dependent upon the ground to yield food for the body, man nonetheless struggles to find proper sustenance and good health. Even as man was once formed from the dust of the ground, the earth will eventually claim man again as his body returns to the ground. While man was given dominion over the earth, through death, the earth now rules over man by claiming his body and returning it to dust. While the earth sustains the body for a time, man no longer has access to the tree of life by which he would live eternally.

Excursus: Nutrition and the Foods of the Earth

Some further reflections on the manner of the serpent's temptation in Genesis 3 are apropos here. It is fascinating that the chief transgression by which man would fall is through the eating of food. Food, both throughout Scripture and even in today's culture, occasions relationship. It is a decisively bodily act, both as it is necessary to sustain the health of the body and as it has an effect of uniting the bodies of different individuals in the sharing of a common meal. For this reason, this excursus will elaborate upon the theological dimension of food with regard to both of these roles. Both of these roles have to do with the body, either the personal body of an individual or the corporate body of believers in Christ. Contemporary concerns regarding the same will also be addressed. Much of what could be said here was already addressed in the previous excursus on "physical fitness." While those points apply to healthy eating, as well as physical fitness, this excursus will focus exclusively on the relationship between man and the food he eats.

Food bridges man's connection to the earth itself. Whatever benefit man derives from the food he eats he gets from the earth from which the food first sprouted. Those nutrients and minerals, taken from the earth, become building blocks of the human body. Thus, even today we who are born from our mother's wombs continue to be "created" anew from the earth as we grow and our cells are replenished. God first formed Adam from the soil. Like Adam, human creatures today owe their origins and continued sustenance to the nutrients in the ground. Man's dependence upon the creator and his design persists in spite of our attempts to master our own bodily welfare. There is a dependence in relationship, expressed through man's righteousness *coram mundo*, between the human creature and the ground. Eating, by definition, expresses man's dependence upon the earth which, in turn, reflects man's dependence upon his creator's provision.

190

Wendell Berry has picked up on this point by affirming genuine eating as an "agricultural" act. Berry's "agricultural" understanding of eating is set in contrast to how eating is commonly perceived in more "industrial" and "commercial" terms.

> I begin with the proposition that eating is an agricultural act. Eating ends the annual drama of the food economy that begins with planting and birth. Most eaters, however, are no longer aware that this is true. They think of food as an agricultural product, perhaps, but they do not think of themselves as participants in agriculture. They think of themselves as "consumers." If they think beyond that, they recognize that they are passive consumers. They buy what they want – or what they have been persuaded to want – within the limits of what they can get...The industrial eater is, in fact, one who does not know that eating is an agricultural act, who no longer knows or imagines the connections between eating and the land, and who is therefore necessarily passive and uncritical, in short, a victim. *interesting*
> When food, in the minds of eaters, is no longer associated with farming and with the land, then the eaters are suffering a kind of cultural amnesia that is misleading and dangerous.[406]

disordered eating

While food is necessary for the growth and health of the body, overeating or irresponsible eating can also harm the body. One might say, in a concrete way, it is through inappropriate eating that man first departs from the will of God in creation. The disruption of man's dual-relationship before God and before the world is embraced in this single act of disobedience. First, by eating forbidden food man dishonors the body that God had given him and God's abundant provision for it. It is not as though Eve was wrong when she saw that the fruit of the forbidden tree was "good for eating." Her sin, and the one the man would also partake in, has nothing to do with the fruit *per se*. There is no reason given in the Genesis text to suspect that there was anything wrong with the fruit itself. The original sin, though, has a great

---

[406] Berry, *The Art of the Commonplace*, 321-322.

deal to do with trying to seize for themselves what God had not given them. Through this act, man abandons his relationship *coram Deo* previously defined by passivity. Rather than simply receiving every good gift the Lord had provided for man, for the first time, man and woman actively seize for themselves what had not been given them. They thanklessly begrudge their Creator's generosity and determine to be gods unto themselves who take whatever they please. The passivity that defines their bodily dependence in relationship with God is exchanged for man's own active provision which will become a cursed and toilsome labor as man works the ground. As man begrudges his own creaturely origins dependent upon the ground, the ground in turn responds to man's attempts to reap food from it and yields its fruits only by the sweat of man's brow. That said, it was only to Cain toward whom the Lord declared that the earth would not bring for its strength. The ground continues to produce for men, no longer bearing Cain's curse, abundantly though still with the toil that corresponds to the curse spoken upon Adam.

Second, by taking the forbidden fruit at the serpent's temptation man essentially establishes "table fellowship," or "communion" with the serpent as opposed to the communion he had shared with God as he previously took and ate all God had provided through the garden. Eating had previously been an expression of man's creaturely identity before his creator. When man would eat the food that God had abundantly given him in Eden he was able to eat in communion with his creator as he embraced his dependence upon God and his provision for all things required in this body and life. It also was an expression of man's communion with the earth itself. Due to God's previously spoken prohibition regarding the fruit of the tree of the knowledge of good and evil, the communion man enters into with the serpent cannot coexist alongside man's communion with his creator. Man essentially exchanges his fellowship with God and his word for fellowship with the deceiver and a word of sin.[407]

---

[407] It is worth noting, here, that a significant component of Adam's and Eve's original sin is a question of eucharistic fellowship. Through partaking in a meal at the behest of the tempter's word man and woman essentially unite themselves in communion with sin and the devil. Negatively speaking, they abandon God's word of truth. It is a matter of eucharistic fellowship precisely because their disobedience is a sin of thanklessness. In thanks, man receives every good gift from God. Thanklessly the first couple

In short, just as the body is rightfully defined in terms of "relationship" (nuanced by the Two Kinds of Righteousness) eating food is a means by which those relationships are fostered and expressed. In the beginning as man would eat what was provided it expressed communion between man and his creator, and between man and the creation itself. In sin, through inappropriate eating, man's relationship with his creator is fractured and man's dependence upon the ground is frustrated by labor that now requires toil and pain. That said, even confounded by sin, eating continues to express man's dependence upon God's provision and maintains a connection with the ground. Sin had corrupted every relationship man has, according to both kinds of righteousness, but the essential design has not changed. The essence of God's good creation persists with respect to man's body and the earth itself. The relational terms expressed through eating remain intact, even as man seeks to sinfully exploit those relationships.

Martin Luther's Body

Even the casual reader of Luther is likely to encounter some rather crude, sometimes shocking, descriptions of his own body. What people today consider to be rather private matters, such as bowel movements or bodily functions, were neither so personal nor shameful for the sixteenth century person. Without the luxury of private bathrooms plumbed directly into an underground sewer system, dealing with human excrement was by necessity a community affair. Without the luxury of modern medicine, sickness and disease could not be treated in the privacy of a doctor's office or a hospital after which one would simply resume the normal course of life. Sickness and disease was simply a reality of daily life. As such, one ought to refrain from imposing modern taboos on Luther or his contemporaries. The discomfort or embarrassment with which one discusses his own bodily ailments or functions today would not have affected the sixteenth century person in the same way. Few in Luther's day could describe their bodily existence as a comfortable one as their situation at the time forced them to deal with the less pleasant realities of the embodied life on a daily basis.

---

seizes for themselves what had not been given them. Questions of eucharistic fellowship in the church ⟩ *nah* today, harken back to this moment. By partaking in the eucharistic meal as "one body" the church affirms the word of God under which she shares a common unified communion. Indeed, Adam and Eve's communion is cursed as well, because "you obeyed the voice of your wife" (Gen. 3:17).

To examine Luther's body, then, there really are two different "bodies" to examine. First, there is the iconic Luther who survived by legend through art and biographies that became "omnipresent in Lutheran visual culture long after his death," and was "central to the character of Lutheran devotional culture."[408] Second, there is the actual body of Luther that was as human as any other. Luther got sick, rather frequently, and knew pains that were not uncommon for a sixteenth century man.

While Luther was rather frank regarding his own bodily ailments the depictions of Luther in art and biography present Luther in a different manner. Lyndal Roper has provided a thorough analysis of the "iconic" image of Luther, portrayed by the Cranachs.[409] Roper concludes that the depiction of Luther's body according to art presented the image of the reformer as a "stout doctor" who possessed significant bodily strength, power and authority. This "classic" image of Luther's body became, in many respects, a symbol for dignity and strength of the Reformation itself and was revered by subsequent generations of Lutherans.[410]

---

[408] Lyndal Roper, "Martin Luther's Body: The 'Stout Doctor' and His Biographers," *American Historical Review*, 115, no. 2 (April 2010): 354.

[409] Lucas Cranach the Elder [1472-1553] and Lucas Cranach the Younger [1515-1586], father and son, were the court painters for Frederick the Wise, John the Steadfast, and John Frederic. By all accounts, Luther and Cranach the Elder were friends. As Cortright points out, "Because Luther's legal situation kept him relatively constrained from travel, the Cranachs were the only artists who had access to him for portraiture." Cortright, *Poor Maggot Sack that I Am,* 181-182.

[410] "The Cranachs'...standard representation of Luther fused two different iconographic modes into a powerful and novel synthesis. Cranach the Elder's images of the rulers of the Saxon house show them as massive, bull-headed figures, whose impressive solidity underlines their secular power. They stand erect with their feet apart, bestriding their realms; in but portraits, their head and shoulders cram the visual space. The images of Luther used the same means to present an individual who possessed unassailable religious authority. ...This style of depicting Luther found its epitome in Cranach the Younger's full-length woodcuts from 1546 (the year of Luther's death) and 1548, images that the modern viewer may find it hard to comprehend: the large body sits almost comically on the delicate feet. But for contemporary viewers, this monumentalism probably evoked Luther's powerful presence, all the more poignantly because he was no longer with them. His garb marks him out as a doctor and cleric, while the small, expressive hands meet across the massive chest to hold the tiny, precious Bible: when he died, casts were taken of his hands and face. The folds of the talar that he wears create strong downward lines that reinforce the sense of authority, rooting him firmly to the ground. His stance is erect, the shoulders set powerfully back, the neck bull-like, yet the bearing is not that of a man of the sword. The head, with its trademark wayward curl, tilts slightly forward as the eyes gaze into the middle distance." Roper, "Martin Luther's Body," 352.

It is no secret, as mentioned previously, that Luther suffered from various bodily ailments and discussed them freely. In the previous discussion regarding monastic discipline the issue of keeping "sin at bay" through bodily discipline frequently emerged. For Luther the body is often depicted as a sort of wily creature that would be grossly immoral if it were not tamed through Christian discipline. While this sort of thinking may have its origins in his medieval and monastic roots, Luther's experience with his own body certainly confirmed it.

Luther's remarks on his health in his late-in-life Genesis Lectures suggest that he was a relatively healthy man for most of his life as he told his students, "God gave me a healthy body until I was fifty years old."[411] Certainly, in his youth, Luther had a healthy constitution as his journeys by foot to Rome, Heidelberg, and Augsburg were completed without serious strain or injury.[412] In spite of Luther's own reflections on his previous health, however, it appears according to record that his relatively good health only persisted until 1524 when he was forty-one.[413] Even earlier than that, Luther himself remarked in a letter to Staupitz that in his poverty all he truly possessed was a "poor worn body, which is exhausted by constant hardships."[414] While he had told his students he had a "healthy body" until he was fifty, later in his Genesis Lectures he reminisced to his students that during his days in the cloister by "fasting, abstinence, and austerity in the matter of work and clothing I nearly killed myself. My body was horribly tormented and exhausted."[415] While impossible to do a full medical analysis on the causes of his various ailments it is certainly plausible, as Luther indicates, that his early zeal and monastic deprivations combined with the ongoing stress of his work contributed to his chronic health problems. In 1519 an observer at the Leipzig Debate described Luther as "emaciated from

---

[411] *Lectures on Genesis (1535/38), LW* 3:342.

[412] Walter von Loeenich, *Martin Luther: The Man and His Work,* trans. Lawrence W. Denef (Minneapolis: Augsburg, 1986), 375.

[413] Martin Brecht, *Martin Luther: Shaping and Defining the Reformation, 1521-1532,* trans. James L. Schaaf (Philadelphia: Fortress Press, 1990), 204.

[414] *LW* 48:69; *WA* 1:527.

[415] *Lectures on Genesis (1535/38), LW* 8:173.

care and study" to the point that "you can almost count his bones through his skin."[416]

Cortright has chronicled, from the available source material, a lengthy survey of Luther's ailments. While this survey is not exhaustive, it certainly allows one to get a picture of Luther's familiarity with illness. The list of such ailments includes what may have been rheumatic fever (1523), "infections of his upper respiratory tract" that "at various times led to bouts of coughing so violent that they made him too hoarse to lecture," an abscess in his distal left leg that festered throughout his life (1525-1546), dysentery (1525), recurring tinnitus (first occurring in July 1527), frequent headaches, recurring attacks of kidney stones (*i.e.* June 1526 and February-March 1537), declined eyesight requiring reading glasses (1530-1546), gout (1533 and 1538), a ruptured eardrum (1541), and persistent symptoms of heart disease which ultimately led to his death on 18 February 1546.[417]

The above survey of Luther's ailments seems lengthy and extreme. As Cortright points out, however, "in the context of the sixteenth century it was well-within in the curve of normal experience: sickness and disease simply played a large part in the lives of the people of Luther's day."[418] This may explain, in part, why Luther could affirm that he had been blessed with a healthy body until age-50 while modern biographers would challenge his assertion. From Luther's own perspective, his various ailments were within the curve of relative "good health." Regardless, Luther was certainly well acquainted with sickness and disease.

Luther on Disease and Remedy

While Luther lived in a time when the former understandings of the human body rooted in Aristotle, Hippocrates, and Galen were beginning to be revised, as a layman in terms of medicinal arts Luther's views remained

---

[416] Peter Mosellanus to Julius Pflug, 7 December 1519. See *Luther's Correspondence and Other Contemporary Letters,* Preserved Smith, ed. and trans. (Philadelphia: The Lutheran Publication Society, 1913), vol. 1, 261 (letter on pp. 257-262). Cited in Roland Bainton, *Here I Stand: A Life of Martin Luther* (New York: Abingdon-Cokesbury, 1950), 113. Also cited in Cortright, *Poor Maggot Sack That I Am,* 185.

[417] Cortright, 186-203. Luther also suffered from a severe attack of cerebral anemia on July 6, 1527, which he had suffered repeatedly and was typically followed by a period of deep depression. See *LW* 43:119, fn. 1.

[418] Ibid., 203.

mostly traditional. As a product of late medievalism Luther's understanding of human physiology and medical treatments corresponded with the antique theory of humorism. While this analysis will be brief, understanding the paradigm through which Luther viewed the body is helpful toward the goal of understanding Luther's relationship with his body, and how he viewed bodily struggle and sickness from a theological perspective.

Andrew Forbes, Daniel Henley and David Henley have recently published an edited version of the medieval *Tacuinum Sanitatis* originally produced in Rome, 1420. *Tacuinum Sanitatis* could be described as both as a handbook of medieval health and a "uniquely informative and visually appealing iconographic source for everyday life and times in Medieval Europe." The editors of the new edition explain humorism, along with the six things necessary for the daily preservation of health according to the humoral paradigm as follows:

> This concept, rooted in Ancient Greek and Roman medicine, maintains that a necessary equilibrium must be maintained in the four distinct bodily fluids contained in every persona and which influence both health and temperament. These four 'humours' are Black Bile, Yellow Bile, Phlegm and Blood. When a person is suffering from a surplus or imbalance of one fluid, then that person's personality and physical health will be affected. The theory is closely related to the theory of the four elements, Earth, Fire, Water and Air, with Earth predominantly present in Black Bile, Fire in Yellow Bile, Water in Phlegm, all four elements in Blood...The *Tacuinum Sanitatis* is about the six things that are necessary for every man in the daily preservation of his health, about their correct uses and their effects. The first is the treatment of air, which concerns the heart. The second is the right use of food and drinks. The third is the correct use of movement and rest. The fourth is the prohibition of the body from sleep, or excessive wakefulness. The fifth is the correct use of elimination and retention of humors. The sixth is the

corresponds to mental health modern taxonomy

regulating of the person by moderating joy, anger, fear, and distress.[419]

Luther's amateur approach to the medicinal arts seems to reflect, at least, a basic understanding of the above. Reflecting on God's provision for man in the Garden of Eden through fruit and herb bearing trees, Luther affirmed that "from the use of these fruits there would not have resulted that leprous obesity, but physical beauty and health and a sound state of the humors."[420] In his exposition of Ecclesiastes 12, concerning its description of debilities that accompany advanced age, Luther suggests that the aged sleep poorly "for when the humors have dried up, as happens in old people, the source and cause of sleep is lacking. Sleep derives its nourishment from these humors."[421] The function of this perspective was highly significant for how Luther would have understood disease, in general, and consequently the particular way that sin has disrupted the welfare of the body. According to Cortright,

> Disease was not conceived of as an ontologically-specific entity born of pathogens as in most modern western paradigms. Luther would not have understood, in other words, the plague as a *specific* disease cause by the *Yersinit pestis* microbe or any such "bug," but as a diseased state of the whole body cause by out-of-whack humoural balances under attack by environmental conditions conducive for the plague. Such a point of view placed each human person on a continuum of healthy-to-sick in which an overabundance or insufficient amount of one or another of the humours tilted the matter quickly to the side of illness...Practically speaking, most people hung forever between health and illness because of the difficulty of

---

[419] Andrew Forbes, Daniel Henley and David Henley, *Health and Well Being: A Medieval Guide* (Thailand: Cognoscenti Books, 2013), 2.

[420] *Lectures on Genesis (1535/38), LW* 1:72.

[421] *Notes on Ecclesiastes (1526), LW* 15:180.

maintaining equilibrium versus the sheer number of possible dysfunctional combinations between the humours.[422]

Another way to put it is that Luther did not see sickness *as* the result of a microbial invader, such as a virus or bacteria that assaulted the body from without. Sickness was the result of an imbalance within the body itself and an incongruence between man's body and the elements of the earth. While environmental factors may have contributed to such imbalances, and altering one's environment and behavior may have been a prescribed treatment for illness, the ultimate problem was the body's internal inability to properly regulate the humors according to a changing environment. This problem, of course, is due not to the constitution of the body *per se* but due to the sinful nature. Recognizing a close relationship between the humors of the body and the four elements of creation would have made sense from the perspective of Luther's theology of creation. As God had created man from the "dust of the ground," man's dependence upon the earth, along with the earth's dependence upon man, would have cohered well with the elemental treatments associated with humorism. A significant consequence of man's fall into sin is a disrupted relationship between man, his body, and the earth.

That said, while humorism certainly corresponds well with Luther's theology of creation, and his emphasis on the relationship between the body and the earth, in no way is Luther's theological motif dependent upon humorism. Luther's theological propositions regarding man as God's creature, both prior to and after the fall, are able to stand regardless of an already-shifting paradigm in physiology and medicine. Even if humorism, and its correlative remedies, rested on a faulty premise it does not discount the fact that many of the remedies often prescribed seemed to work. For centuries humorism was embraced under the fallacy of a faulty cause, post hoc ergo propter hoc, precisely because the treatments were beneficial. Accordingly, even while embracing the faulty theory of humorism, the reliance upon the elements of the earth in connection with the body was not entirely misplaced. Even today certain conditions require either increased rest or activity. Obesity, diabetes or heart disease often are treated

---

[422] Cortright, *Poor Maggot Sack That I Am,* 206.

medicinally alongside a strict requirement for exercise and a well-balanced diet. Many viral or bacterial infections, when treated today, require the patient to get plenty of rest. Changes in diet, cleaner air and even altering one's mood can benefit one suffering from many different ailments. As such, when Luther cites the "humors" of the body while addressing a theological point, his conclusion is not necessarily invalidated by his faulty premise. His conclusions typically stand independently of humorism even while humorism helps to understand Luther's reasoning and the logic by which he applies bodily metaphors to theology.

The Body in Luther's Rhetoric

As immodest as Luther often was regarding his own body, neither did he hesitate to draw upon the body and its functions in his rhetoric. The body frequently emerges in Luther as a metaphor for theology. As Robert Kolb points out, "The Wittenberg team sometimes called the whole of Biblical teaching a *corpus doctrinae*, a 'body of doctrine,' and the individual topics were members, or *articuli*, of that body."[423] Along with his use of the body for understanding theology, though, Luther often employed bodily imagery that may offend the sensibilities of those who read him today. Luther's "excremental rhetoric," most frequently directed at his opponents, often strikes the modern reader as immature and inappropriate.[424] One would be wrong, however, to either gloss over this feature in Luther's rhetoric or to excuse it. Lyndal Roper emphasizes the importance of this manner of speech for understanding Luther's thought:

> Our Cartesian inheritance, with its separation of mind and body, makes it difficult for us to comprehend the ease with which Luther could see the spiritual in the somatic, or how his body should have conveyed Lutheran identity so powerfully for a whole church. It makes it hard for us even to get the joke. Luther drew on digestive metaphors to convey some of his deepest

---

[423] Kolb, "God and His Human Creatures," 173.

[424] Luther's crudest language emerges in his later polemical writings, particularly *On the Jews and their Lies (1543)* and *Against the Roman Papacy an Institution of the Devil (1545). LW* 47:121-306 and *LW* 41:257-376.

insights, including his conceptions of good and evil, and he had an intuitive understanding of the link between creativity and bodily processes, partly because of the illnesses he suffered throughout his life. Any account of the reformer that wants to do justice to the importance of his body—or to the role of the devil in his thought—must come to terms with his excremental rhetoric, which he regularly deployed against those he considered emissaries of Satan. This is a feature that historians often try to excuse rather than explore.[425]

While it might seem at first glance that Luther's excremental rhetoric reveals an underlying distaste for the body in general, this could not be further from the truth. On the contrary, Luther sees bodily excretion as necessary due to the body's essential goodness. Because the body is essentially good, it must expel whatever is vile.[426] Luther makes this point rather explicitly and, as he was apt to do, employed this aspect of the body as a metaphor for further theological reflection:

> The body is a beautiful and noble creation of God. Yet what comes out of it but a secretion from the eyes, sweat, excrement, urine, snot, pus, and sores? I must say that although sores and pus are in the body, the body is not evil because these things come out of it. For if these things were good, they would remain in the body as other things do. But since the body, together with its members, is sound and healthy, the filth must come out and be thrown away. If you want to reject your body because snot, pus, and filth come out of it, you should cut your head off. Thus Christendom, too, is a living, healthy body of the pious little

---

[425] Roper, "Martin Luther's Body: The 'Stout Doctor' and His Biographers," 354.

[426] "For the human body is not blamed if it defecates, spits, and vomits, since these are its acts of purification. The body is not therefore unsound though it has festering eyes and a scabby skin, because these are purged out with the excrement. Even so the ungodly heretics are not members of the church, but refuse." *Lectures on Isaiah, Chapters 1-39, LW* 16:205.

flock, God's children, Yet filth and stench are mixed in. They must be cast out.[427]

This metaphor, in part, helps to understand Luther's use of bodily functions in his polemic against the papacy. When excrement or farts appear in Luther's writing the devil is typically involved. The pope, frequently addressed as an "ass-fart," or "fart-ass," in Luther's 1545 *Against the Roman Papacy an Institution to the Devil*, is usually addressed as such due to his affiliation with Satan. Viewing the papacy as the Anti-Christ, the theology of the pope is pitted against the theology of Scripture. In this late treatise Luther rehearses a laundry list of biblical doctrines after which the "hellish father" and "farter in Rome" is cited teaching contrary to God's word.[428] Luther is not being crude for crudity's sake. The overall point, solidified through this sort of polemic, is that the devil is the one who speaks lies through the pope and just as the body must expel excrement due to the essential goodness of the body, the lies of the devil that corrupt the body of Christ must be expelled as "farts" and excrement. What the "Lord wills" is set against what the pope "farts" revealing the papacy as an instrument of the devil. The implication, of course, is that the identification of the papacy

---

[427] *Sermons on the Gospel of St. John, LW* 24:206.

[428] For example, "First, as heard above, the Lord wishes to have his church built on himself, the rock, that is, he who wishes to be a Christian should believe in him. 'No,' says the ass-pope, 'it means that one should obey me and regard me as a lord; works like this save—and disobedience or refusal to consider me a lord damns.'...Again, the Lord wills that according to faith and brotherly love, the customs of all creatures should be free, and no sin or justification be looked for therein. 'Oh, no,' speaks the most hellish father, 'Christ is drunken, raving, and mad; he has forgotten what great power he, with the keys, gave me to bind—namely, I have the authority to bind and to forbid that 'Whoever drinks milk on Friday, Saturday, on the eve of Apostles' Day or of my saints' days, which I have made, is guilty of a deadly sin and eternal damnation; except that I am not bound to observe this. Whoever eats butter, cheese, or eggs on those same days is guilty of a deadly sin and hell. Whoever eats meat on these days, however, is damned far more deeply than hell—except me and my cardinals, who are not subject to such binding, because he who has the authority to bind will undoubtedly not bind himself but others. Whoever does not fast and celebrate the saints I have created is guilty of a deadly sin and damnable disobedience. The reason for this is that I have authority to bind and loose.' Perhaps even: 'Whoever does not worship my fart is guilty of a deadly sin and hell, for he does not acknowledge that I have the authority to bind and command everything. Whoever does not kiss my feet and, if I were to bind it so, lick my behind, is guilty of a deadly sin and deep hell, for Christ has given me the keys and authority to bind all and everything." *Against the Roman Papacy an Institution to the Devil (1545), LW* 41:335.

as an "institution of the devil" is not tied to the pope's person *per se*, but to the lies that emerge from the papal chair.

According to Roper, Luther's struggle with the devil is both cosmic and comic. At times his excremental rhetoric is meant to seriously convey the despicability of Satan's lies, and at other times it is employed to comically address the absurdity of the devil and his opponents.[429] That said, the "comical" use of this rhetoric is not necessarily a mere joke, but is intended to emphasize the absurdity of the devil's attacks and his opponents' positions. Directed at the devil directly, Luther is recorded to have said that when a reading of Scripture or prayer fail to chase away the devil the best way to get rid of him is to fart at him.[430]

All of the above, including Luther's own experience with illness and his view of sickness in general, is not without theological importance. As Roper affirms, "Luther thinks through his body. For him the spiritual and the somatic are always intertwined."[431] A previous quote above demonstrated, in one instance, how Luther deployed the body as a metaphor to make a point about the necessity of casting out error from the church, the body of Christ. Reflecting on Jesus' words as recorded in the Gospel according to St. John, "If anyone thirst, let him come to Me and drink," Luther reflects on "spiritual thirst" as analogous to bodily thirst: "Christ says that his doctrine is meant for the thirsty...For at such a time the tongue becomes parched, we grow feverish, our distress consumes the humors of our body, and this creates thirst. How much more will our soul grow thirsty from spiritual temptation, when sin and God's wrath stare us in the face!"[432] Many similar examples of Luther's metaphorical use of the body could be cited here. What is consistent throughout them, though, is both the essential goodness of the body as well as the depth of the body's corruption by sin.

---

[429] Roper, "Martin Luther's Body: The 'Stout Doctor' and His Biographers," 374.

[430] See, for example, *LW* 54:16, 78.

[431] Ibid., 376.

[432] *Sermons on the Gospel of St. John, LW* 23:267.

Luther on the Death of the Body

The mortality of the body was a reality that the sixteenth-century person would be unable to ignore. Without the knowledge of medicine that there is today, nor the sanitation and hygienic standards of today's world, sickness was far more common and death was far more likely the final outcome. The sixteenth-century person lived in constant fear of the plague that seemingly struck randomly without a known cause. Also known as the "Black Death" the plague had raged throughout Europe since the fourteenth-century. Luther was personally affected by the plague as well. Two of Luther's brothers were taken by the plague that hit the Eisleben region in 1505, the same year Luther entered the Augustinian cloister in Erfurt. According to Brecht this tragedy partially appeased the anger of Luther's father over his son's "defection" to the cloister instead perceiving the events "as a sort of thank offering."[433] When the plague struck Wittenberg in 1527[434] the University relocated to Jena at the orders of the Elector. At the Elector John's chagrin, however, Luther remained in Wittenberg in order to assist Bugenhagen in serving the sick and consoling the mourning. Having turned his own home into a hospital, Luther wrote to Amsdorf reflecting on the ordeal, "It is a comfort that we can confront Satan's fury with the word of God, which we have and which saves souls even if that one should devour our bodies."[435]

In the process of his *Lectures on Genesis*, according to Veit Dietrich's notebooks, Luther's commentary on Genesis 3:14 was interrupted by an outbreak of the plague in Wittenberg in July of 1535. He resumed lecturing on January 26, 1536, appropriately reflecting on the stark reality of death in the light of the hope the "seed" of Genesis 3:15.[436]

> This, therefore, is the text that made Adam and Eve alive and brought them back from death into the life which they had lost

---

[433] Brecht, *His Road to Reformation*, 58.

[434] The first of four occasions when the plague struck Wittenberg during Luther's tenure there. The plague also struck Wittenberg in 1535, 1538, and 1539. See Cortright, *Poor Maggot Sack That I Am,* 191.

[435] Brecht, *Shaping and Defining the Reformation*, 207. See also the editor's introduction to *Whether One May Flee From a Deadly Plague (1527) LW* 43:115

[436] See the editor's introduction to Luther's *Lectures on Genesis (1535/38), LW* 1:ix

through sin. Nevertheless, the life is one hoped for rather than one already possessed. Similarly, Paul also often says (1 Cor. 15:31): "Daily we die." Although we do not wish to call the life we live here a death, nevertheless it surely is nothing else than a continuous journey toward death. Just as a person infected with a plague has already started to die when the infection has begun, so—because of sin, and death, the punishment for sin—this life can no longer properly be called life after it has been infected by sin. Right from our mother's womb we begin to die.

Through Baptism we are restored to a life of hope, or rather to a hope of life. This is the true life, which is lived before God. Before we come to it, we are in the midst of death. We die and decay in the earth, just as other dead bodies do, as though there were no other life anywhere. Yet we who believe in Christ have the hope that on the Last Day we shall be revived for eternal life. Thus Adam was also revived by this address of the Lord—not perfectly indeed, for the life which he lost he did not yet recover; but he got the hope of that life when he heard that Satan's tyranny was to be crushed.[437]

The utter depravity of the body in sin is evident by the fact that the body not only dies, but is in the process of dying even from the womb. Cortright reflects on Luther's use of the term "maggot-sack" (*Madensack*) regarding the body in death.[438] As demonstrated previously, seeing human

---

[437] *Lectures on Genesis (1535/38), LW* 1:196.

[438] Cortright's focus on Luther's reflection upon his body, "Poor maggot sack that I am," is probably overemphasized. Using this as a title for his dissertation, Cortright neglects the essential ╱ goodness of the body that Luther affirms even on this side of the resurrection. Granted, while Luther employs the language of *Madensach* to console Christians in death to "let go" of their bodies and look forward to the resurrection, this does not mean that his description of the body as a "maggot sack" was particularly significant for his overall perspective on the body. As already demonstrated, Luther showed great concern for the wellbeing of the body here and now and chastised those who neglected their bodies. Cortright overemphasizes the importance of this phrase for Luther's fundamental theology of the body to the neglect of the body's creaturely goodness. Cortright, in fact, says that Luther's use of *Madensach*, "far from bring simply a disparagement of the body's future in the grave, was used by him to convey the hopelessness of the body in death because of sin. Yet it was through death that his 'maggot sack' would rise to new life in the resurrection." Cortright, 220. In other words, and Cortright is correct on this point,

excrement as the body's dispelling of what is "vile," the sinful nature inheres in man to the point that even in the grave the body brings forth maggots and worms. According to Cortright, consistent with the prevailing opinion of his day, "Luther evidently believed that maggots and worms (and adders and toads) were spawned by the body from its sinfulness in decomposition, just as he held to the medieval notion that rot spawned mice."[439] Though, as also affirmed earlier, what the body expels or produces gives no warrant for despising nor denigrating the body. The body is "a beautiful and noble creation of God" even as it expels filth and produces maggots in death.[440]

The human creature of God continues to live in hope of a resurrected body through Baptism into Christ even as his body at present is on course for the grave. Adam and Eve are able to "both live and die" in hope and are deemed "truly holy and righteous" according to the promised seed. Even while it is impossible to "become wholly righteous, that we love God perfectly, and that we love our neighbor as we love ourselves" in this life, Luther affirms that this life is to be lived according to hope, rather than according to the rule of sin and the body of death.[441] Even as this very body is baptized into death, it is this very body that clings to the hope of the seed, to Christ who will raise the body again. The evocation of the "seed" as man's hope inextricably links man's redemption to an embodied reality—hope is consummated through the body's sexual and reproductive functions. Accordingly, the Christian is to regard his body according to hope rather than write it off because it is presently ruled by death. Regarding one's body in hope, then, means that one need not despair of the body in death but can see beyond the grave to the redemption of the body.

Luther seems to speak in a disparaging way about the body in sin to console those who mourn the death of loved ones and direct their focus, instead, to the resurrected body. This point is well made. That said, this is an instance of pastoral care and reflects a nuance of Luther's proclamation of Law and Gospel more than it summarizes his theology regarding the body *per se*. Even while Luther consoles the mourning by exhorting them not to place their hopes in their earthly bodies, Luther nonetheless exhorts Christians to embrace their bodily existence as God's creatures.

[439] Cortright, *Poor Maggot Sack That I Am*, 219.

[440] *Sermons on the Gospel of St. John, LW* 24:206

[441] *Lectures on Genesis (1535/38), LW* 1:197.

206

Conclusion

While John Paul II's description of the body as revelatory, even a primordial sacrament, can be embraced to a certain degree it must only be embraced with certain qualifications. After the fall into sin, man's relationships *coram mundo* consistently fall short as revelatory of God's relationship with man. While the body may be revelatory, particularly in spousal union, sin has so confounded the revelation man perceives from the body that if one were to project what one learns from the natural revelation of the body alone upon God he would miss the mark completely. This does not stop Luther, though, from deriving significant insight from the body even it its crudest form. The body, albeit corrupt in sin, is fodder for theological insight even as deployed metaphorically for Luther's understanding of other theological matters. As the body is corrupted by sin, so is the church and the entirety of the Christian life according to both kinds of righteousness. As essentially good, the body still testifies to the goodness of God and the ongoing dynamic between the creature and his Creator. No matter how much man may attempt to deny his creaturehood by commercializing and industrializing food distribution systems, man's ultimate sustenance still has its origins in the ground. In spite of increased technologies that perpetuate sedentary lifestyles, the body nonetheless testifies to God's original plan that man be active and working rather than idle. That God continues to provide for man, through the earth, in spite of the toil and pain with which man now works the ground, testifies to the fact that God has not abandoned his responsibility as Creator. God continues to provide for and preserve his good creation. God graciously does this even in and through man's disobedience. Corrupted by sin, the suffering one endures in the body through pain, toil and sickness testifies to man's need for bodily redemption. The present body will die, but even death need not overcome the Christian in despair. From the body emerges the promised "seed." The human body will play a role in God's redemptive plan. The Christian, even though fully depraved by sin, can continue to live this life in the hope of the body in redemption. This is the focus of the next chapter.

CHAPTER 5:
THE BODY IN
REDEMPTION

N O MATTER HOW ASSUREDLY ONE MIGHT affirm the essential goodness of the body according to creation, due to sin, if the body is not redeemed its "goodness" is purely historical and academic. It does no good to affirm man's somatological goodness if, for all practical purposes, the body is irrevocably corrupted by sin at every level. There would be plenty of reason to despair of the flesh if there were not a redemption of the body. Apart from the theology of the body's redemption, any notion of the body's original goodness in creation would be nothing but long-lost nostalgia. If bodily redemption were not a reality, and eternal salvation was only a salvation of disembodied souls, the gnostic heresy of Manichaeism would become orthodoxy. Life in creation would become meaningless and death, rather than resurrection, would be one's ultimate hope. In short, the devil through the serpent's temptation would have accomplished an irrevocable victory over God and creation if man's ultimate hope were merely a redemption of the soul. The victory, however, belongs to the Lord. The redemption of the body affirms both man's original righteousness as well as the ability of man to live according to the hope of his redemptive future. In Christ, the body's righteous redemption before God and man is both a present reality and a future hope. The redemption of the body is necessitated by Christ's victory and solidifies the defeat of the serpent, who is Satan, and the deathly consequences of his temptation.

Differently than previous chapters, where Pope John Paul II's work was treated at the onset, this chapter will begin by engaging Luther's perspective of bodily redemption first. Having already established the conversation across the centuries between the oddly coupled reformer and pope, the consummative theology of the redeemed creature in Luther is nuanced across a variety of theological loci. As Luther's theology functions as a cohesive whole *Scripturally — not Systematically* rather than as a sum of various disjointed parts or doctrines, it will be most helpful to draw these connections across Luther's *corpus doctrinae* before engaging John Paul II's work. Continuing the analysis of Luther's *Genesis Lectures* his emphasis on the promised "seed" of Genesis 3:15 will be given first consideration. Luther traces this promise through the patriarchs and beyond until the promise's consummation in Jesus Christ. The particular importance of Jesus Christ's body from incarnation through death and resurrection will be discussed followed by an analysis of the unity of spirit and flesh according to Luther's pneumatology. Luther's emphasis on God's employment of corporeal elements in the means of grace in his economy of salvation will be engaged at length. Luther's understanding of the church as "body" will be briefly touched upon. Finally, the body of the Christian in eschatological hope will conclude the discussion of Luther on the redeemed body. John Paul II's perspective on the resurrected body will then be summarized. Appropriate comparisons and contrasts between John Paul II and Luther will be considered.

The Promised Seed and the Redeemed Body

The promise of the "seed" of woman is Luther's prevailing gospel motif in the Genesis Lectures. Redemption would come through childbearing, meaning that the very curse upon woman to bear children in pain would also be the process through which God would bring about salvation for the elect. Here the futility of the devil's temptation is exposed. What might have seemed to be the serpent's victory will ultimately result in his very defeat. From the onset, redemption is intimately linked to the body. Through the nuptial unity of man and woman children would be born. Childbearing, while cursed in pain, would also be the source of man's hope. "Marriage," Luther says, "should be treated with honor; from it we all originate, because it is a nursery not only of the state but also for the church and the kingdom of Christ (until) the end of the world."[442] As such, the centrality of God's blessed word to be "fruitful and multiply" becomes even more pronounced.[443] In death, man would be subdued by the earth itself as his body returns to the ground. Through childbearing, though, the promised messianic seed would one day fulfill man's original call to subdue the earth by rescuing man from the grave in the ground and returning man to his proper vocational lordship amongst the creatures. Only in faith and hope could man fulfill his creaturely calling. Against all tangible evidence, as the cursed ground rebels against man's effort to work it and childbearing consumes the woman in pain, Adam and Eve are able to live again through hopeful faith according to the promise of the seed. As such, through faith alone, man is able to live out the fullness of his bodily, creaturely, life. Man and woman live by faith, trusting that God will deliver them beyond the curse of sin and the grave. This faith is not mere intellectual ascent, but is expressed through the trust of God's promise as man continues to fulfill his creaturely calling even through toil and pain. Faith is an exercise of the body as much as the mind—it encompasses the total person. Man's vocation becomes normed by worship, as man bears his cross in painful work trusting in the hope of the promised redeemer. By working the ground, in faith, and continuing to bear children Adam and Eve live proleptically as participants in the redeemed life. Eve can joyfully bear children, even through the painful curse, knowing that through her pain a redeemer will come to crush the serpent's head. Man can continue to work the rebellious soil knowing that, through the promise, he remains lord over creation and that the ground will not hold his body in its grave forever.

---

[442] *Lectures on Genesis (1535/38)*, *LW* 1:240.

[443] "Although Adam had fallen because of his sin, he had the promise...that from his flesh, which had become subject to death, there should be born for him a shoot of life. And so he understood that he was to produce offspring, especially since the blessing, 'Increase and multiply' (Gen. 1:28), had not been withdrawn, but had been reaffirmed in the promise of the Seed who would crust the serpent's head (Gen. 3:15). Accordingly, in our judgment, Adam did not know his Eve simply as a result of the passion of his flesh; but the need of achieving salvation through the blessed Seed impelled him too." Ibid., 237.

Cain and Abel

In the *Lectures on Genesis* Luther traces the promise of the "seed" from Adam and Eve's children to the patriarchs and beyond. Adam and Eve, albeit from pious intention, rejoice at Cain's birth supposing he would be the seed that would crush the serpent. Eve was "a saintly woman and...she believed the promise concerning the future salvation through the blessed seed...Her extreme trust in the promise causes Eve to reach a hasty conclusion, and she believes that her first son is the one about whom the Lord had given His promise."[444] That his parents thought him the promised seed is evidenced by the name their firstborn receives, "Cain" meaning "possession." While the etymology Luther discerns from the Hebrew names is debatable, he nonetheless affirms that "Cain is called Cain as if he were the one who would restore everything; by contrast, Abel means vanity and something that is worthless or cast aside."[445] Luther also identifies Adam and Eve's mistaken assignment of primogeniture to Cain through the vocation each receives. Cain is trained to tend the ground, following in his father's footsteps while Abel is given another vocation, albeit a noble one as well, to tend the flock as a servant.[446] Moses' narrative account of Cain's birth indicates, though, that the promise would not come through Cain.

> Here the question arises why Moses says: "She bore Cain" and not rather, as below, "She bore her son Seth." Yet Cain and Abel were also sons. Why, then, are they not called sons? The answer is that this happens on account of their descendants. Abel, who was slain by his brother, perished physically; but Cain perished spiritually through his sin, and he did not propagate that nursery of the church and the kingdom of Christ. All his

---

[444] Ibid., 242.

[445] Ibid., 234, 314.

[446] "Just as the names do, so the occupation to which each is directed by his parents reveals the parents' glorious hope concerning Cain. Although each pursuit is honorable, nevertheless Abel's is concerned with the home only; but Cain's has to do with the government. Because Adam was a husbandman, he trains Cain, for whom he has the greater love, for his father's occupation. To Abel meanwhile is assigned the chore of tending the flock, so that it might appear that the latter is regarded by his parents as a servant, the former as lord." Ibid., 246.

posterity perished in the Flood. Therefore neither blessed Able nor cursed Cain has the name of son; but it was Seth from whose descendants Christ, the promised Seed, would be born. And so Seth was the first who received the name of son.[447]

Luther speculates that Adam would gather his family together every Sabbath, preaching to them a sermon concerning the promised seed.[448] The importance of the "seed" and what was supposed to be Cain's inheritance of that promise would have been impressed upon the brothers from childhood on. The strife between brothers reveals what is already a misappropriation of the second article over and against the first. The elder brother takes pride in his supposed status as the "seed" that will redeem mankind while losing sight of his identity as God's creature. Cain is more concerned to assert his right of primogeniture over and against his brother than he is concerned to fulfill his daily calling in faith and hope as God's creature.[449]

---

[447] Ibid., 241.

[448] Ibid., 246-247.

[449] Luther makes similar comments returning to the Cain and Abel account regarding the controversy over Jewish purification rites in John 3:25. These comments were from a sermon preached by Luther between 1537-1540, within the timeframe in which he was also lecturing on Genesis to his students. "The pious son Abel sacrificed a fatted lamb; yet he was not saved because of the sacrifice but because of his faith in the promised Christ. It was the promise that did it, the promise that the woman's Seed would crush the serpents head (Gen. 3:15). Abel believed in this promise, and on the basis of his faith in the future Seed he was graciously accepted by God. Cain, however, came swaggering along with his sacrifice, a sacrifice of good quality, which his field had yielded and which had been God's gift and present to him. But what was missing? He did not look to the future Seed of the woman; he was an unbeliever and assumed that since he was the first-born and the only prince in the human race, he would prove acceptable to God for the sake of his own person. Therefore he did not look to, and hope for, the woman's Seed which was to crush the serpents head. Abel, on the other hand, gave ear to the message of the woman's Seed; he believed it, and as proof of his faith he offered his sacrifice. Cain, however, thought: 'Oh, even if I sacrifice but three kernels of wheat and my brother places a hundred lambs on the altar, I am still everything, while Abel is nothing.' But our God has a different system of accounting, and according to it, the one who is nothing must be everything; for he believes in the future Seed, Christ. And Cain, who presumed to be everything, is nothing; for his faith does not rely on the future Seed of the woman. It is Abel who is purified, not Cain. About this a horrible quarrel ensued, so that in the end he who wanted to be everything slew Abel. This has always been the course of history. Just read the records, and see how all the patriarchs and fathers sacrificed and how the fire consumed their offerings. Then the ungodly Jews remarked: 'God regards the gift and the sacrifice!' Now Cain had offered nothing but chaff. However, God is not interested in oxen, sheep, and sacrifices; as is evident from Ps. 50:8–9 and from Is. 1:11." *LW* 22:427.

Luther forcibly rejects any interpretation of the brothers' offerings that would suggest God's pleasure in Abel's over Cain's has anything to do with the offering itself.[450] In spite of being considered "vanity" by his parents, Abel offers God his true worship in faith. In spite of being surely taught that it was his elder brother who would be the deliverer of mankind, Abel trusts in God's promise and grace giving no regard to his own stature. Abel simply goes about his daily vocation in joy, freely offering his sacrifice to God, recognizing in faith that his toil is not in vain. Abel embraces his identity as God's creature. It is Cain, who considers himself righteous according to birthright rather than by faith, whose worship is rejected.

> God is not interested in works, not even those which He Himself has commanded, when they are not done in faith...Cain's offering did not please because the unbelieving Cain did not please. On the other hand, Abel's offering pleased because Abel pleased; and this was so because of his faith, since it did not rely on his own worthiness...Accordingly, this text has to do with our conviction concerning justification, namely, that a human being, rather than his works, must be just...solely through grace, which faith believes and apprehends...the works which follow are evidences, as it were, of this faith; they please God, not simply on their own account but because of faith or because of the believing person.[451]

Imagining that one can only be blessed if it is through his own lineage that the promised redeemer in born, Cain fears that he will be consigned to

---

[450] "If you look at the work itself, you cannot prefer Abel to Cain. The Jews, in their folly, have a silly idea when they dream that Cain did not offer selected grain but chaff, and that for this reason he was rejected by God. From them this is to be expected, for they act as judges and pay attention only to works. But the verdict of the Epistle to the Hebrews is different; it declares that because of his faith Abel brought the more excellent offering (Heb. 11:4). And so the fault lay not in the materials which were offered but in the person of him who brought the offering. The faith of the individual was the weight which added value to Abel's offering, but Cain spoiled his offering. Abel believes that God is good and merciful. For this reason his sacrifice is pleasing to God. Cain, on the contrary, puts his trust in the prestige of his primogeniture; but he despises his brother as an insignificant and worthless being." *Lectures on Genesis (1535/38), LW* 1:251.

[451] Ibid., 259.

his brother's place of "vanity" if he not inherit the promise of the "seed" for himself and his children. That Abel's sacrifice is accepted, while Cain's is not, causes Cain to fear that the promise will fall in line with Abel or his heirs rather than himself and his. He fears he is losing the priority his parents had surely taught him was his by birthright. Cain kills Abel imagining that it would secure his place as the only "seed" of Eve who remains. He forcibly eliminates what he perceives to be his competition.[452] Imaging that he could force God's hand in this way to secure for himself the position of blessing further demonstrates that Cain failed to embrace his identity as God's creature. He repeats the sin of his parents by trying to attain godhood for himself, as if he were the creator rather than a creature.[453] Cain attempts to claim righteousness for himself rather than receiving righteousness passively in faith as God's gift.

Abraham and the Patriarchs

While the details vary by account, throughout Genesis and beyond, what occurs between Cain and Abel is repeated time and time again demonstrating an ongoing struggle between works righteousness and righteousness by faith. It is a struggle between man's embracing his identity as God's creature and trying to act as a creator unto himself. This is a struggle that will persist until the redemption of our bodies. On many occasions, throughout Genesis, the lineage of the seed seems to be in jeopardy. Wherever God's promise coheres there the serpent, understood as Satan, is nearby striking at the very heel that would eventually crush his head.

Luther evokes the promise of Genesis 3:15 and the blessed seed so frequently in his Lectures on Genesis that it is impossible to treat every instance sufficiently for these purposes. Neither is it necessary to fully explore every instance when Luther discusses it to decipher the significance

---

[452] "In Cain's instance there is no doubt that he hoped to keep his glory of primogeniture after Abel had been destroyed. Thus the ungodly believe that their cruelty will benefit them; but later on, when they realize that their hope was vain, they sink into despair." Ibid., 281.

[453] "[Adam's and Eve's] thoughts ran as follows: 'Behold, this is our sin. In Paradise we wanted to become like God, and through our sin we became like the devil. The same thing has happened to our son. Him alone we loved, and him we regarded most highly. To us the other was righteous compared with this 'Abel,'" that is, this worthless person. We hoped that he would crus the serpent's head. And behold, he himself has been crushed by the serpent..." Ibid.

of the promise for Luther's thought. Regardless of who Luther is attributing the promised seed to, be it Abraham, Isaac, Jacob, or others, similar themes emerge throughout. For the sake of both brevity and clarity, instead of discussing the relevance of the promise to each patriarch this discussion will address it thematically.

The struggle between the serpent and the seed is a story that often repeats itself, albeit through different conditions and contexts. Luther's *theologia crucis* coheres throughout his treatment of the pre-messianic seed. The struggle between Cain and Abel already addressed exhibits the struggle initially. Seth, who otherwise has very little attention drawn to him, becomes the unlikely heir of the promise. Genesis similarly tricks the reader into assuming the promise would cohere through Esau, or Joseph, when at either instance it is an unlikely brother who ends up as God's chosen seed-bearer. If Cain was cursed for trying to secure the promise for himself and his heirs, why would not Jacob be condemned for his deception of his father and brother by similarly securing the "blessing" through his own means? When one "underdog" seems to gain the favor of God, another "underdog" may not be granted the same preference. There seems to be no logical pattern, at all, regarding man's role or activity when God chooses to propagate his seed through the heirs of Abraham's descendants. The blessing and curse of the nations revealed through Abraham's call expresses the ongoing struggle between the seed of the serpent and the seed of woman. This struggle, revealed to Abraham, would continue to persist where ever God's true church would be found.[454]

Thematically, faith in the promise of the seed is what justifies and makes one righteous *coram Deo*. This is a justification not only of the soul or spirit, but of the entire person, including the body.[455] As already established,

---

[454] If you desire to reduce to a few words the history of the church from the time of Abraham until today, carefully consider these four verses. You will see the blessing, and you will also see some who curse; but these, in turn, God has cursed so that they utterly perished, while the eternal blessing of the church has remained unshaken. Hence this passage is in agreement with the first sermon about the Seed who crushes the head of the serpent (Gen. 3:15). The church does not lack enemies; it is troubled, and it sighs; and yet it overcomes through the Seed and finally triumphs forever over all its enemies. But just as the Lord gave a warning above about the bite of the serpent, so here He warns that the seed of Abraham will encounter some who will curse it." *Lectures on Genesis (1535/38), LW* 2:265.

[455] For example Luther says, "For the promise does not depend on my merits or works; it depends

one's birthright is seemingly irrelevant in terms of one's justification.[456] Luther praises Abel, Joseph, and others who demonstrate great faith even though their names never appear in the genealogies of the coming Christ. Noah is deemed righteous because he considered the promise of the seed "of greater weight than the destruction of all the rest of the world."[457] Luther praises the faith of unlikely characters, such as King Abimelech, even though they have no genealogical role in the propagation of the promised seed.[458]

Perhaps most significant, for these purposes, is the recurring theme that the propagation of the seed testifies to the bodily human nature of Christ. Recognizing that redemption occurs by agency of the corporeal nuptial act of man, the human body becomes particularly significant in terms of both the subject and object of man's redemption. Jesus Christ becomes fully human through the lineage of man, and as the bodily subject of man's justification saves the human creature in the body as well.

*which is Gospel
why the reales*

---

on the Seed of Abraham. By Him I am blessed when I apprehend Him in faith; and the blessing clings to me in turn and permeates my entire body and soul, so that even the body itself is made alive and saved through the same Seed." *Lectures on Genesis (1535/38), LW* 4:158.

[456] "From the womb of Sarah there came not only kings—David, Solomon, etc.—but also peoples, the Edomites and others, who are reckoned among the descendants of Esau. This is the physical promise. When Christ was born of the Virgin Mary, the spiritual promise was also fulfilled. That was the real time of blessing. Then there were valiant kings: the apostles and their successors. Next came Gentiles who, because of faith in the Blessed Seed, are also descendants of Abraham, not according to the flesh or by nature but 'grafted,' as Paul calls them in Rom. 11:17. Of course, the promise concerns the spiritual seed, that is, the believers, more than it does the physical descendants. And although Isaac himself was born from the flesh of Abraham, he was nevertheless a son of the promise; for he was not born according to the flesh, inasmuch as the bodies of Sarah and Abraham were dead, as it were, so far as procreation was concerned." *Lectures on Genesis (1535/38), LW* 3:152.

[457] *Lectures on Genesis (1535/38), LW* 2:97. Luther later praises Noah's discernment about the fulfillment of the promise regarding his treatment of his sons: "Great must have been the enlightenment in the heart of Noah, who thus distinguishes between his sons: Ham with his descendants he repudiates; but Shem he places among the line of the saints and the church, because on him would rest the spiritual blessing that was given in Paradise concerning the Seed (Gen. 3:15). It is for this reason that the holy man blesses God and thanks Him." Ibid., 178.

[458] "Abimelech knew God even before Abraham's arrival and had ruled his people in a godly fashion, but that knowledge of God was of a more general nature. Now, when he happens to hear Abraham, he learns to look at God more closely, as it were, since he knows that Abraham will be the father of the Blessed Seed. This knowledge of God Abimelech spreads among his subjects." *Lectures on Genesis (1535/38), LW* 3:340.

Therefore we have His ancestors, who were true men. Nor can He be named without these fathers, without Abraham, Isaac, Jacob, and Adam, in order that He may have a definite lineage, a true father, a true mother, and that it may be certain that He is from a human seed and that He took upon Himself human nature, not the angels, not any other creature. Accordingly, a definite place was assigned to the nativity of Christ for the fathers and the prophets, and definite persons from whom He had to descend were named. Consequently, we cannot doubt that He is in very truth our flesh and blood, bone of our bones.[459]

Accordingly, that the promised seed would have a particular lineage by no means implies any special favor before God for those who are genetic children of Abraham, Isaac and Jacob. The specificity of Jesus' lineage, rather, is indicative of his true flesh-and-blood humanity. Just as no human creature is born apart from a true human lineage, Jesus would be born with a true lineage as he assumed a true human body. Accordingly, the specificity of Jesus' lineage gives no priority to anyone nor does it limit the scope of the atonement. On the contrary, that Jesus possessed a true human lineage testifies to the fact that the true body he assumed by being born of woman would stand in the place of every human body. The promised seed's victory, as he would crush the serpent who strikes at his heel, would be for all whom the Lord would call to Himself. Just as it was faith in the promise that justified Abraham, only those who receive the victory in faith would be saved.

Jesus Christ: The Seed of the Woman

Luther can hardly help, at times, to jump from Abraham, Isaac or Jacob, directly to David and then Jesus.[460] Luther has difficulty pretending he

---

[459] *Lectures on Genesis (1535/38), LW* 5:228.

[460] Commenting on Genesis 22:18, "And by your Seed shall all the nations of the earth be blessed, because you have obeyed My voice," Luther remarks, "These words are the subject matter and the gushing fountain, as it were, of many of the prophecies and addresses of Isaiah, David, and Paul. Moreover, they agree with the preceding promises, which are found in Gen. 12:3: 'In you all the families of the earth will be blessed' and in Gen. 15:5: 'Look toward heaven, and number the stars, if you are able; so shall your descendants be.' But this promise is clearer and more explicit. Above God said: 'In you, Abraham, all the families of the earth will be blessed.' There his Seed is included, but it is not expressed. But in this passage it is expressly stated: 'In your Seed.' In opposition to the nonsense of the Jews,

is as unaware of God's actual fulfillment of the promise as the actual initial hearers or readers of Moses' writing. Lecturing to his students across the greater part of a decade, it should not be expected that Luther would feign ignorance about the fulfillment of God's Old Testament promise. Obviously Luther is lecturing from the perspective of one who knows the "end" of the story. Luther and his students know, from the onset, that the promise of the seed is fulfilled in Jesus Christ. As such, references to Jesus abound in the Lectures on Genesis as frequently as the theme of promise is discerned from the text.

That the redemption of man would happen through the "seed" is particularly significant for a theology of the body. It is precisely through the definitive act of creaturely identity, the nuptial union, that God promises to deliver bodily redemption. There is, of course, a glaring caveat to this notion that cannot be ignored. The promised "seed," Jesus Christ, ultimately becomes incarnate through a virgin birth, apart from the sexual union of man and woman. Luther explicitly asserts that the reality of the virgin birth was not yet known to Adam and Eve, though, and only was gradually revealed through the prophets. For Luther, the promise that redemption would come by the "seed of the woman," rather than the "seed of man," is necessarily fulfilled by the virgin birth.[461] Nonetheless, the presence of Jesus' genealogies in the Gospels still affirms the importance of the sexual union for bringing about the fulfillment of the promised seed. Being produced apart from the sexual union diminishes Jesus' humanity no more than it would

---

however, Paul declares and explains that this Seed is Christ (Gal. 3:16)." *LW* 4:151.

[461] "Women gave birth up to the Flood and later until the time of Mary; but their seed could not in truth be called the Seed of the woman, but rather the seed of a man. But what is born from Mary was conceived by the Holy Spirit and is the true Seed of Mary, just as the other promises given to Abraham and David testify, according to which Christ is called the Son of Abraham and the Son of David. This meaning Isaiah is the first to point out when he says that a virgin will give birth (7:14). Then, in the New Testament, it is more clearly explained by the angel (Luke 1:35). Therefore I have no doubt that this mystery was not understood even by many saints; although they expected that Christ would have to be born into this world by a woman and that He would deliver the human race, they did not know the manner of His birth. With this general knowledge they were satisfied, and they were saved even though they did not know how He would have to be conceived and born. This had to be reserved for the New Testament as a clearer light and had to be announced to the first world rather obscurely because of Satan, whom God wanted to mock and irritate in this fashion so that he would be ill at ease and would fear everything." *Lectures on Genesis (1535/38), LW* 1:194.

218

have diminished Adam's humanity by having been formed by God's hand in the "womb" of the earth.

Conversely, however, the testimony of the virgin birth also excludes the notion that the body can be defined as *essentially* nuptial, as John Paul II does. For Luther, John Paul II's move would have been judged a reversal of cart and horse. While the union of man and woman *fulfills* God's vision for man in Genesis 1-2, before the creation of woman man is still *essentially* man. To render the nuptial significance of the body as an essential component of the human creature would inevitably encounter a Christological problem— one which John Paul II never anticipates. In other words, how can Christ be deemed fully human if the nuptial union is what effectively furthers and defines humanity essentially? Rather than the sexual union, *per se*, it is the birthing of children that ultimately promulgates both the human race—as mankind exercised dominion over creation accordingly—and brings about our Lord's incarnation.

The Body and the Spirit of God

> The Holy Spirit gives people faith in Christ...that is, he renews heart, soul, body, works, and conduct, inscribing the commandments of God not on tables of stone, but in hearts of flesh...That is the work of the Holy Spirit, who sanctifies and also *awakens the body to such a new life* until it is perfected in the life beyond. That is what is called "Christian holiness."[462] *theosis roots*

It has already been established that Martin Luther saw the Holy Spirit from "the beginning" in creation. It was the Holy Spirit whom Luther identified as the "spirit of God" hovering over the waters, and it was the Holy Spirit whom Luther also termed the "breath" of God that gave man life itself. Having further established that Luther viewed creation as a present reality— not merely an event in history—and linked his theology of creation to his theology of redemption it follows that the very same Holy Spirit breathed into man "in the beginning" would likewise give man new life in Christ. As the locus of the Spirit's life given to man "in the beginning" was the body,

---

[462] *On the Councils and the Church (1539), LW* 41:145-146.

through man's nostrils, it is the Spirit who enters man's ear canals through proclamation as He redeems and awakens the body to a new life.

As discussed in chapter two, the "breath" of God into man's nostrils in the beginning reveals the immediate concern of the body for genuine spirituality. Later biblical descriptions of the body as a "temple of the Holy Spirit" harken back to this original description of the breath, or Spirit, of God vivifying man in the beginning. In the above quotation Luther defines "Christian holiness" as such an awakening and sanctifying of the body itself. In the economy of God's Trinitarian act of creation, it is the Spirit who most immediately engages man in the flesh.

Luther sees the Holy Spirit actively engaging man throughout the Genesis Lectures. It is the Holy Spirit whom Luther identifies as the person of the Godhead who pronounces the curse upon Cain and excommunicates him after he murdered Abel.[463] Calling him a "minister of the Word," Luther indicates an emotive connection between Noah and the Holy Spirit. As Noah grieves over the state of the fallen world, and wishes man had never been made, the sentiment is applied to the Holy Spirit as Noah is his representative in creation.[464] It is the Holy Spirit who works faith in the heart of Abraham who, against all odds and contrary to all evidence in his advanced years, believes that God would make from his descendants a great people and the seed of promise will come from his lineage.[465] These are but a few examples of the intimate activity of the Holy Spirit in the lives of his chosen people throughout Genesis. Wherever God's people are, particularly (though not exclusively) those whom Luther calls "ministers of the Word," the Holy

---

[463] *Lectures on Genesis (1535/38), LW* 1:290.

[464] "It is in this manner that God saw human wickedness and repented. That is, Noah, who had the Holy Spirit and was a minister of the Word, saw the wickedness of men and through the Holy Spirit was moved to grief when he observed this situation. Paul also similarly declares (Eph. 4:30) that the Holy Spirit is grieved in the godly by the ungodliness and wickedness of the ungodly. Because Noah is a faithful minister of the Word and the mouthpiece of the Holy Spirit, Moses correctly states that the Holy Spirit is grieving when Noah grieves and wishes that man would rather not be in existence than be so evil." *Lectures on Genesis (1535/38), LW* 2:44.

[465] "Therefore the power of the Holy Spirit was great and extraordinary in Abraham, because he was able to apprehend with his heart these impossible, unbelievable, and incomprehensible things, as though they were real and already present. Such must have been the case, especially since he was already approaching old age. For he was seventy-five years old, but Sarah was ten years younger and barren at that." Ibid., 254.

Spirit is active. From a literary perspective, one might suggest that for Luther the protagonist in the book of Genesis is not any particular man, as the characters keep changing, but the Holy Spirit who is the true "actor" bringing about God's plan according to the promise. It is the Holy Spirit who carries along God's story as he works through his chosen agents and means.

For Luther, true spirituality always has the Holy Spirit, the third person of the Trinity, at its heart. Regin Prenter contrasts Luther's "spirituality" from the spirituality of the enthusiasts, and even the scholastics, who oriented spirituality from the point of view of a "metaphysical dualism between the body and the soul, between the visible and the invisible, between matter and thought."[466] For Luther true spirituality is not derived from anthropology, or even metaphysics. There is nothing "spiritual" about man apart from the very Spirit who was first breathed into Adam's nostrils in the beginning. Nothing is truly spiritual apart from the Holy Spirit. In fact, the things man often deems "spiritual" are in fact anti-spiritual in Luther's perspective. The popular trend today to call oneself "spiritual" apart from any particular theological commitments Luther would deem not spirituality, but depraved carnality. True spirituality is not a metaphysical ascent to something "above" temporal experience, but is decisively corporeal. True spirituality is not found by climbing a mystical latter to a higher realm, nor by discerning spiritual whims in the world with the enthusiasts. When man attempts to "ascend" to the Spirit, he does not truly find the Holy Spirit, as the Spirit has already "descended" to man in the world. True spirituality is found where the Spirit descends and reveals Christ. Accordingly, for Luther we can speak of Christ's "spiritual" presence, even in the Lord's Supper, so long as by doing so we do not mean "immaterial." As Cooper summarizes Luther's perspective, "only the super-spiritualists think that "spiritual" consists in non-material, non-physical inward realities."[467] For Luther, a false dichotomy placed upon John 6:63 ("The Spirit gives life; the flesh counts for nothing") results in abundant error. Luther emphasizes the proper definition of "spirit" and "flesh" according to its biblical usage:

---

[466] Prenter, *Spiritus Creator,* 288.

[467] Cooper, *Life in the Flesh,* 118.

221

We do not call "flesh" that which can be seen by the eyes or touched by the fingers, as the fanatics do when they call Christ's body useless flesh; but...all is spirit, spiritual, and an object of the Spirit, in reality and in name, which comes from the Holy Spirit, be it physical or material, outward or visible as it may be; on the other hand, all is flesh and fleshly which comes from the natural power of the [sinful] flesh, without spirit, be it as inward and invisible as it may.[468]

Correct categorizing of the terms

When trying to find a "spiritual" life man often works too hard, as the Spirit has already placed himself in plain view of man's natural senses. Specifically, genuine spirituality is found through the means of grace where the Spirit delivers the benefits of Christ through a physical encounter with man. God did not create man in the flesh and then expect man to find a relationship with the Triune God by escaping his bodily nature. God, rather, encounters man through the Spirit by revealing Himself through the means of grace as man meets God sensibly. To be truly "spiritual" is nothing more than embracing one's bodily creaturehood when and where God has chosen to locate Himself for and among men. More on Luther's theology of the "means of grace" must be addressed.

exactly as

"here I promised" and anywhere but "here" who look else, to you

The Means of Grace

YES.

The means of grace, for Luther, are very physical corporeal acts. Holy Baptism involves a participation of the entire person–*totus homo*–in the water. The Baptism of the Holy Spirit cannot be divorced from the baptism of the entire person in the water any more than man's very body can be separated from his spirit. The Lord's Supper similarly meets man as he takes and eats, with a human mouth, the body and blood of Jesus for the forgiveness of sins. This new life in the Spirit is realized in the present, yet still awaits a consummative hope in the eschaton. The now/not yet character of the sanctification of man in the Spirit is evident in the means of grace, and is experienced in the embodied life of every Christian.

---

[468] *That these Words of Christ, 'This is My Body,' etc., Still Stand Firm Against the Fanatics (1527), LW* 37:135-136.

All of that said, for the purposes of addressing a theology of the body according to Luther's theology it is more appropriate to speak of his theology of the "means of grace" than of the "sacraments" *per se*. Luther identifies many "means of grace" in Scripture, particularly in his Lectures on Genesis, while avoiding using the term "sacrament" to define them. That said, he often links such means of grace to the sacraments in his effort to draw parallels between God's manner of engaging his creatures then and now. For Luther, even before the sacraments are explicitly instituted, God is a "means of grace" God who localizes himself for the sake of his human creatures. According to Cooper, Luther "found it characteristic of God to 'clothe' or 'cover' himself in tangible, accessible forms, to hide his naked divine majesty and limit himself to specific, circumscribed avenues of apprehension, designated and recognized as such exclusively by his sovereign but explicit word."[469] Reflecting on the sacrifices offered by Cain and Abel affords Luther the opportunity to engage a rather lengthy excursus on God's tangible presence among man through the means of grace.

> ...all the sacred accounts give proof that by His superabundant grace our merciful God always placed some outward and visible sign of His grace alongside the Word, so that men, reminded by the outward sign and work or Sacrament, would believe with greater assurance that God is kind and merciful. Thus after the Flood the rainbow appeared in order to serve as a convincing proof that in the future God would not give vent to His wrath against the world by a similar punishment. To Abraham, as we shall hear, circumcision was given, so that he might firmly believe that God would be his God and that He would give him the Seed in who all the nations would be blessed. To us in the New Testament, Baptism and the Eucharist have been given as the visible signs of grace, so that we might firmly believe that our sins have been forgiven through Christ's suffering and that we have been redeemed by His death. Thus the church has never

---

[469] Cooper, *Life in the Flesh*, 112.

been deprived to such an extent of outward signs that it became impossible to know where God could surely be found.[470]

i.e. it is always possible to 'locate' God, thus duty of ... assembly

Luther continues this line of thought, reflecting on Proverbs 8:30, "I was delighted every day, playing before Him, playing in the world, and My delight was with the children of men." Here, Luther suggests that the word "play" is an insufficient rendering of the Hebrew verb qx;f.

> What Wisdom is saying is that Its concern was for men and that it revealed Itself to them. It is as if it were to say: "I have always displayed Myself to the eyes and ears of men in such a way that they could become aware of My presence in the sacrifices, in circumcision, in burning incense, in the cloud, in the Red Sea, in the manna, in the brazen serpent, in the tabernacle of Moses, in the temple of Solomon, and in the cloud. And it was my delight to display and reveal Myself in this manner to the children of men.[471]

The signs of grace are offered precisely to man's senses, "to the eyes and ears of man" in order that man may truly be aware of God's genuine presence. As man is constituted in the body, with all his corporeal senses, God intends to reveal himself to man according to the very form in which he first made man. The body, as it was when God first created it from the dust, is the locus where God initiates and fosters his relationship with man. It is, likewise, through the bodily senses that the total man should take hold of God's promises.[472]

---

[470] Luther continues, "It was a great comfort for Adam that, after he had lost Paradise, the tree of life, and the other privileges which were signs of grace, there was given to him another sign of grace, namely, the sacrifices, by which he could perceive that he had not been cast off by God but was still the object of God's concern and regard." *Lectures on Genesis (1535/38), LW* 1:248-249.

[471] Ibid.

soul is provided for by what?

[472] Luther identifies the "soul" as the life of man in the "external senses" reflecting on the necessity of man to follow certain liturgical patterns or ceremonies. Reflecting on the ceremony around which Isaac's blessing, intended for Esau but received by Jacob, occasions this insight. "The soul is the spirit or the life of man in the external senses. The soul sees, hears, speaks, weeps, and laughs. This is what Isaac wants to say: "Inside, in my heart, it had been decided that I want to bless you. Now my soul will bless you; that is, I will bless you with the external senses. You have been blessed according to the spirit. Now I will bless you with my soul." For this reason ceremonies are added. For even spiritual things that are

God in His divine wisdom arranges to manifest Himself to human beings by some definite and visible form which can be seen with the eyes and touched with the hands, in short, is within the scope of the five senses. So near to us does the Divine Majesty place Itself. It is the height of wisdom to hold fast to these visible forms. But the examples of all the patriarchs, prophets, and godly men teach that Satan strives continually to find ways to obscure those forms and to set others before us.[473]

God prefers to attach this word of promise to external signs within the prevue of the five senses both so that man may comprehend his word in total, as a creature both in body and soul, and also so that man may always know where he can find God's grace. That God chooses to attach his promise to means that man apprehends corporeally through the five senses is certainly consistent with the fact that God's redemption applies to the total man. It is in God's grace and mercy that he has instituted particular means whereby man may cling, with his senses, and know the forgiveness of sins. Even though God engages man mediately, through the senses, it is not merely the body that God blesses through His gifts of word and sacrament. Indeed, recalling Luther's metaphor of the human creature as tabernacle, it is through the outer courts (the body) that the Spirit ultimately comes to reside in man's soul and spirit, or the holy of holies.[474] That man would be forgiven is known, in the case of the Old Testament signs, according to the promise of the seed. According to the New Testament it is according to the suffering and death of Jesus Christ that was already accomplished.[475] In his

---

external cannot be administered without external ceremonies. The five senses and the entire body have their own gestures and rites under which the body must live as if under certain masks. Therefore Isaac blessed not only in his heart but also with the external senses and ceremonies." *Lectures on Genesis (1535/38), LW* 5:135. *i.e. faith necessarily externalizes (faith without works is dead!)*

[473] *Lectures on Genesis (1535/38), LW* 3:109.

[474] *The Magnificat (1521), LW* 21:303.

[475] "We treat the forgiveness of sins in two ways. First, how it is achieved and won. Second, how it is distributed and given to us. Christ has achieved it on the cross, it is true. But he has not distributed or given it on the cross. He has not won it in the supper or sacrament. There he has distributed and given it through the Word, as also in the gospel, where preached. He has won it once for all on the cross." *Against the Heavenly Prophets (1524), LW* 40:213-214.

mercy, God has always given his people such external signs. Apart from such signs of God's grace, Luther insists, it would have been "impossible to know where God could surely be found."

Luther frequently terms these tangible means by which God reveals himself to men as "masks," "faces," or "coverings." Luther employs, within the Lectures on Genesis, nominalist categories and terminology distinguishing between *Deus nudus* and *Deus revelatus*.[476] Furthermore, he distinguishes between God's *potentia absoluta* and *potentia ordinata*. While God is capable of working apart from means, and does from time to time, such instances are the exception rather than the rule. One cannot expect God to act, as he once helped Daniel walk through fire, ordinarily.[477] Such examples, while within the scope of God's *potentia absoluta* are not a part of his *potentia ordinata* to which he attaches the surety of his promise and word. As the creator, infinitely beyond the comprehension of his creatures, man cannot nor should he attempt to discern God in his bare majesty, *Deus nudus*. To make such an attempt, as the enthusiasts do, is inconsistent with our identity as God's creatures.

It is not just that God "masks" himself behind created matter, but he reveals himself even while hiding himself behind what appears to be his

---

[476] "...when we approach the unrevealed God, then there is no faith, no Word, and no knowledge; for He is an invisible God, and you will not make Him visible...God has most sternly forbidden this investigation of the divinity...And it is true that God wanted to counteract this curiosity at the very beginning; for this is how He set forth His will and counsel: "...From and unrevealed God I will become a revealed God. Nevertheless, I will remain the same God. I will be made flesh, or send my Son. He shall die for your sins and shall raise again from the dead. And in this way I will fulfill your desire, in order that you may be able to know whether you are predestined or not." *Lectures on Genesis (1535/38), LW* 5:44-45.

[477] Commenting on Genesis 19:14, "...if at times some things happen without the service either of angels or of human begins, you would be right in saying: 'What is beyond us does not concern us.' We must keep the ordered power in mind and form our opinion on the basis of it. God is able to save without Baptism, just as we believe that infants who, as sometimes happens through the neglect of their parents or through some other mishap, do not receive Baptism are not damned on this account. But in the church we must judge and teach, in accordance with God's ordered power, that without that outward Baptism no one is saved. Thus it is due to God's ordered power that water makes wet, that fire burns, etc. But in Babylon Daniel's companions continued to live unharmed in the midst of the fire (Dan. 3:25). This took place through God's absolute power, in accordance with which He acted at that time; but He does not command us to act in accordance with this absolute power, for He wants us to act in accordance with the ordered power." *Lectures on Genesis (1535/38), LW* 3:274. "*Sed in Babylone in medi igni Danielis socii incolumes vivebant. Haec fuit potentia Dei absoluta, secundum quam tum agebat, sed secundum hanc nihil nos iubet. Vult enim nos facere secundum ordinatam potentiam.*" *WA* 43:71, emphasis added.

226

alien / proper distinction

opposite, sub contraria specie. God employing what seems to be his "opposite" for his means of redemption begins at the onset when what is cursed, bearing children in pain, is also the means through which God promises the eventual "seed" who will "crush" the serpent's head. The ultimate evidence of God's desire to save man through what seems to be his opposite, though, is that through Jesus Christ it will be through the ultimate curse man experienced, death, that man's ultimate salvation is achieved. Discerning this truth in the means of grace is consistent with Luther's *theologia crucis.*

Luther expressly defines the external elements in the means of grace as "creatures apprehended by the Word."[478] The relationship between the word and the element needs some clarification. Most frequently, throughout the Genesis Lectures, the word appears not only as that which is joined to external signs, but also appears alongside (*iuxta*) baptism, the eucharist, and the Old Testament signs of grace. Verbum occurs in a variety of ways.[479] Recalling the creative prowess of God's spoken word in creation, as discussed in chapter one, the significance of God's verbum as a means of grace itself, alongside the explicitly instituted sacraments, is not difficult to imagine. Luther's theology of the means of grace is explicitly tied to his theology of creation, indicating a further connection between creation and redemption. God's act of redemption is not altogether different than his act of creation,

---

[478] On Gen. 3:23f. "...the Word must always be taken into consideration and honored as that by which God takes hold of and, as it were, clothes the creatures; and a difference must be made between the creature and the Word. In the Sacrament of the Altar there are bread and wine; in Baptism there is water. These are creatures, but creatures apprehended by the Word. As long as the creature is apprehended by the Word, so long it is and does what the Word promises." Ibid., 228. In the Latin, "*Hae sunt creaturae sed apprehensae per verbum.*" WA 42:170. Here Luther is engaging Lyra's view, which he sees exemplified in Aquinas and Bonaventura, about the inherent properties of such external things as the brazen serpent, etc., apart from any threat or promise of God.

[479] Jonathan Trigg discusses Luther's various uses of *verbum* in the *Genesis Lectures*. "At the root of the complexity in the relationship of word and sacrament is the polyvalence of *verbum*. There is clear evidence within the Lectures of this polyvalence. Sometimes, when he places *verbum* alongside the sacraments as one of the 'masks' Luther appears to be thinking of the ministry of the word, which in turn seems on occasion to be equivalent to the keys, added to baptism in accommodation to human weakness. At other times *verbum* is the divine word to which the sign is joined. The tension between *verbum* as the divine self-disclosure and *verbum* as the human speech which conveys it (or Him) is fully reflected int he Lectures...it is important to note the danger of attempting to move too quickly to a clear-cut view of the priority of word over sacrament which does not account for the fluidity to be observed in Luther's actual usage." Jonathan Trigg, *Baptism in the Theology of Martin Luther* (Boston: Brill, 2001), 35.

though through redemption God chooses to unite his verbum to tangible means so that his favored creature, man, can comprehend his redemptive word as a gift. The pro me of the Small Catechism ingrains this truth in the heart of every Christian who learns it.   *pro me God unites verbum*

Just as God did not constantly speak from the heavens to the people of Israel, but spoke through Moses and instituted corresponding tangible signs of his presence, God chooses to speak through those whom he calls and attaches his word of forgiveness to tangible elements. Clearly, God can work immediately and speak to his people directly. This, however, is not the normative way God chooses to make himself known. Even when the Genesis text says that God is speaking, Luther frequently imagines that it is God's voice heard through another vessel. When God confronts Cain for murdering Abel Luther prefers to think that it was Adam who was, in fact, speaking authoritatively on God's behalf.[480] Luther is convinced that the call of Abram recounted in Genesis 12:1 was not likely direct, but was mediated through someone who held "the ministry," likely Shem.[481] While Luther's point here is certainly disputable, it testifies to the pervasiveness by which Luther discerns God's preference to address man through appointed means. God prefers to work through means so consistently that Luther seems to assume a mediated voice whenever possible unless the text explicitly warrants another interpretation to suggest God spoke directly. In other words, Luther assumes that God is working normatively by employing means and agents unless the text provides particular details to indicate otherwise.[482]

---

[480] "I take Moses' statement to mean that God spoke in the same sense as above, namely, that Adam spoke these words through the Holy Spirit and as God's representative, a position which he, as the father, held toward his son. And so this expression of the Holy Spirit is concerned with extolling the authority of parents. When children listen to and obey them, they are listening to and obeying God." *Lectures on Genesis (1535/38), LW* 1:283.   *interesting, a mediator of sort ...*

[481] "But here the question arises: How was Abraham called, and did he hear this voice from God Himself? I am convinced that he was not called directly by God without the ministry, as it is related below (Gen. 18:2) that God visited him, conversed with him, and was even the guest of Abraham; but I believe that this command was brought to him either by the patriarch Shem personally or by some others who had been sent by Shem." *LW* 2:249.   *careful, Marty ... can't have your plain reading both ways ...*

[482] Further examples of the above abound in the *Genesis Lectures*. For example, when God "repents" of having made man upon the earth, prior to destroying the world by the flood, Luther explains God's repentance here as occurring "in the hearts of men who carry on the ministry of the Word." Ibid., 44.

The means of grace become (loci) where God can truly be found. Christianity is not a religion based on man's quest to "find God," but it confesses the reality that God comes to save man. As such, notions that one would "find" God in ethereal existence runs counter to this foundational truth. God comes to man, continually, through external signs where man can find him assured of his gracious presence. As Jonathan Trigg writes, "the signs or means of grace are also spoken of as 'places,' chosen by God for his tryst with mankind."[483] Because God has so clearly and assuredly located his good presence for man through external means, there is no reason to envy either those such as Abraham to whom God appeared visibly, or to the Apostles and others who witnessed Jesus' earthly life.

> If Abraham should be compared with us who live in the New Testament, he is, for the most part, less important than we are, provided that one considers the matter impartially. To be sure, in his case the personal gifts are greater; but God did not manifest Himself to him in a closer and more friendly manner than He does to us. Let it indeed be a great glory to have those appearances, but what greater or better advantage did Abraham have from them than the fact that God spoke with him? This happens to us too, however, and indeed daily, as often as and wherever we wish. It is true that you hear a human being when you are baptized and when you partake of the Holy Supper. But the Word which you hear is not that of a human being; it is the Word of the living God. It is He who baptizes you; it is He who absolves you from sins; and it is He who commands you to hope in His mercy.[484]

Since God has located himself in specific places for man's sake, he should not be sought elsewhere. Certainly God is present everywhere. He may even present himself according to his *potentia absoluta* somewhere unprecedented for man's benefit. It is only through the means of grace,

---

[483] Trigg, *Baptism in the Theology of Martin Luther*, 23.

[484] *Lectures on Genesis (1535/38), LW* 3:166.

wherewith he has attached his word of promise, that man can be sure God is there in his grace for his children. God should not be sought in self-appointed locations. Throughout Genesis Luther finds evidence of man searching for God in ways of his own choosing. Cain, the citizens of Ur, the idolatrous worshippers at Bethel in the time of Hosea, and the papists of Luther's own day are chastised for despising the places of God's choice and manufacturing signs and places of their own.[485]

> ...the right hand of God, although this is everywhere...you can actually grasp it nowhere, unless for your benefit it binds itself to you and summons you to a definite place. This God's right hand does, however, when it enters into the humanity of Christ and dwells there. There you will surely find it, otherwise you will run back and forth throughout all creation, grasping here and yet never finding, even though it is actually there; for it is not there for you.[486]

Trigg points out how in Luther's comments on Genesis 22:19, Abraham's departure to Beer-sheba after the events on Mount Moriah, he finds it "remarkable that the patriarch erected no altar and established no shrine on the mountain where he has received such a wonderful revelation and promise concerning the future Seed."[487] Abraham declined to erect any altars or offer any worship there because God had not commanded it so. Most of us lack Abraham's profound piety:

> Such is the deplorable perversity of our nature that we do not keep what God commands or value it highly; but whatever the devil commands, this we receive and observe the utmost eagerness and deference; we erect altars, chapels, churches; we

[485] See *LW* 1:249; 2:242, 244; 5:241.

[486] *That these Words of Christ, 'This is My Body,' etc., Still Stand Firm Against the Fanatics (1527), LW* 37:68.

[487] Trigg, *Baptism in the Theology of Martin Luther*, 25.

run to Rome and to St. James. But meanwhile we slight Baptism, the Eucharist, absolution and our calling.[488]

The reality of man's creaturely, bodily, existence indicates the importance of God's means of grace as the primary avenue through which God engages his creatures. The prominence of the means of grace, throughout scripture, should in turn thwart any inclinations to despise the body. One cannot apprehend the means of grace apart from his body. Baptismal waters cover the body. The body and blood of Christ, no matter how literally or symbolically one comprehends the modality of Christ's presence therein, are consumed by the mouth. The word of God is heard by the ears. As such, a positive theology of the body and a theology of the means of grace go hand in hand.

Matthew Lee Anderson's intriguing book, *Earthen Vessels*, attempts at its onset to answer the question, "Why has the body been seemingly neglected in Evangelicalism?" It is this author's contention that it is the explicit absence of a theology of the "means of grace," misguidedly aided by the error of dispensationalism that would suggest that God works differently in different historical eras, that makes it difficult to uphold the reality and significance of bodily existence for the Christian life. While not found in Luther (this will be addressed in the conclusion) a covenantal hermeneutic and framework can overcome both of these deficiencies in evangelical thought. Apart from a recognition of the means of grace, encounters with God become relegated to either the intellect or the emotions. While one may recognize a bodily resurrection apart from the means of grace, the importance of bodily resurrection for the daily life of the Christian becomes incomprehensible. It is difficult to conceive of any positive theology of the body apart from a recognition that God engages human creatures corporeally. If God encounters man, in redemption, apart from the way man was constituted with all his senses, it makes sense that man's physical constitution would necessarily be denigrated, or at least neglected, in corroborating theological discourse. If the "means of grace" of the Old Testament along with the New Testament sacraments are reduced to *mere*

---

[488] *Lectures on Genesis (1535/38), LW* 4:179.

symbols with little spiritual significance beyond cognitive recollection it is difficult to perceive of bodily living apart from mere "temporal" categories. For Luther faith involves the total man, *totus homo*, thus the objects to which man's faith must cling are likewise objects that can be comprehended by the total man, body and soul.

Considering the centrality of the New Testament means of grace for Luther's conception of creaturely identity, it is necessary to discuss the specific somatic proprium of the sacraments. These "signs" of grace that Luther identifies in the Old Testament are directly related to the sacraments of the New Testament.

> These [signs] were true manifestations of the divine mercy which the wretched people needed in order not to be without some light of the grace of God. In the same way the very Word, Baptism, and the Eucharist are our lightbearers today, toward which we look as dependable tokens of the sun of grace. We can state with certainty that where the Eucharist, Baptism, and the Word are, there are Christ, forgiveness of sins, and eternal life. Contrariwise, where these signs of grace are not present, or where they are despised by men, there is not only no grace, but execrable errors follow, and men set up for themselves other forms of worship and other signs.[489]

Luther's enumeration of the sacraments varies according to the definition of "sacrament" with which he is operating in any given discourse. Baptism and the Lord's Supper always make his list. While Luther's enumeration of the sacraments is not always consistent, the following discussion will be limited to Holy Baptism and the Lord's Supper.

Holy Baptism

> Thus, we must regard baptism and put it to use in such a way that we may draw strength and comfort from it when our sins or conscience oppress us, and say: "But I am baptized! And if I

---

[489] Ibid.

have been baptized, I have the promise that I shall be saved and have eternal life, both in soul and body." This is the reason why these two things are done in baptism; the body has water poured over it, because all it can receive is the water, and in addition the Word is spoken so that the soul may receive it. Because the water and the Word together constitute one baptism, both body and soul shall be saved and live forever: the soul through the Word in which it believes, the body because it is united with the soul and apprehends baptism in the only way it can. No greater jewel, therefore, can adorn our body and soul than baptism, for through it we become completely holy and blessed, which no other kind of life and no work on earth can acquire.[490]

These words from *The Large Catechism* explicitly link the externality of Holy Baptism to the redemption of the total man, *totus homo*. The paragraph above was written as a concluding summary to his section concerning the nature, benefits and use of baptism. Luther, here, employs a dichotomous view of man composed of body and soul. Elsewhere, Luther defines the "soul" as that which gives life to the body.[491] Accordingly, even noting that the "water" applies to the body while the "word' applies to the soul, all of it coheres in the total person who is a soul–animated body.

There were those, namely the enthusiasts and anabaptists, who argued that the use of external means was a "work" and contradicted the doctrine of justification by faith alone. Luther forcibly rebukes this position. Faith, as a function of the body as well as the soul, must have "something to which it may cling and upon which it may stand." Faith, then "clings to the water."[492] If one separates faith from the object to which faith is bid to trust by God's word, one only has faith according to an excised component of man. The total man, though, must have an object of faith. "Yes, it must be external so

---

[490] Kolb, Wengert and Arand, eds. *The Book of Concord: The Confessions of the Evangelical Lutheran Church*, 462.

[491] *The Magnificat, LW* 21:303.

[492] Kolb, Wengert and Arand, eds. *The Book of Concord: The Confessions of the Evangelical Lutheran Church*, 460.

deeply pastoral concern

that it can be perceived and grasped by the senses and thus brought into the heart, just as the entire gospel is an external, oral proclamation."[493]

As baptism signifies a true burial of the Christian with Christ and a true resurrection into the fullness new life, baptism links the baptized Christian to Christ's body. Being baptized does not mean that the Christian will not die in this body and life, but it means that the Christian's body goes through death the same way Christ did. It means that a resurrected body, like the resurrected body of Jesus, will be the Christian's full realization of his creaturely baptismal identity. It further means that as surely as the Christian can say in the present tense, "I am baptized," taking hold of what the sign signifies by faith, he lives in the reality of resurrection even now.

because God does not lic

As a specifically appointed means of grace, instituted by Christ, baptism is especially prominent in Luther's thought. As was frequently the case, Luther's defense of baptism was a two-front battle. On the one side there were the radicals who denied the efficacy of baptism, refused to baptize infants, and understood the sacrament as an act of Christian obedience rather than a gift given by God to man. On the other side were the Romanists who had diminished baptism by denigrating its importance beneath such things as monastic vows. Luther's emphasis on the unity of the total man as a means of grace for the entire creature ultimately thwarts attacks from either side. Against one side, mere symbolic interpretations of the sacrament fail to cohere with God's typical manner of engaging the creatures he made with five senses. The importance of baptism reaching the entire person for justification further thwarts any notion that some other "vow" or work of supererogation could supersede baptismal grace.

The Lord's Supper

That the Lord's Supper contains, in Luther's emphatic view, the true body and blood of Jesus Christ implies some understanding about the nature of this true body. That it is given to men through bodily eating and drinking similarly implies a participation in the body of the human creature who receives the sacrament. In *The Large Catechism* most everything that could be said regarding the externality of Holy Baptism applies to the Lord's Supper as well. Just as Baptism testifies to the salvation of the total man, body and

---

[493] Ibid.

soul, the Lord's Supper delivers Christ's gift of forgiveness to the entire human creature.

The very words "This is my body, which is given for you" indicate not only that Christ's body is relevant to Christian redemption, but his words enact the total gift of his own flesh that manifests the Father's love for the world. It is the language of gift, here, that Luther teaches through The Small Catechism is "the essential thing in the sacrament."[494] It is because God has joined his word and promise to the act of bodily eating and drinking in the sacrament that the gift which conveys the forgiveness of sins is received.

Because the Lord's Supper is received "often," while Baptism is only performed once,[495] there is a particular emphasis in *The Large Catechism* on one's worthiness and the frequency with which one received God's Eucharistic gifts. As Baptism is a bodily act, but would account for nothing before God apart from the word of God attached to its institution and faith's adherence to that word, the Lord's Supper is received through "bodily" eating and drinking that, likewise, would avail nothing before God apart from the mandating word of Christ. As a gift that brings salvation to man, both in body and soul, one may not always feel the need to receive the sacrament. If such is the case, Luther suggests that one consider his body in the light of Scripture.

> Suppose you say, "What shall I do if I cannot feel this need or if I do not experience hunger and thirst for the sacrament?" Answer: For those in such a state of mind that they cannot feel it, I know no better advice than that they put their hands to their bosom to determine whether they are made of flesh and blood. If you find that you are, then for your own good turn to St. Paul's

---

[494] Kolb, Wengert and Arand, eds. *The Book of Concord: The Confessions of the Evangelical Lutheran Church*, 363.

[495] Though Luther does insist that through repentance, and going to confession, one continually returns to baptism daily throughout his life.

Epistle to the Galatians and hear what the fruits of your flesh...
496

Because the scriptures "know your flesh better than you yourself do" simply believing what God has said about the flesh ought to drive everyone to the sacrament even if they feel no pressing need to receive it. That one feels nothing, in fact, testifies on its own right to one's need for the sacrament as we have a "leprous flesh, which feels nothing although it rages with disease and gnaws away at itself."497 Nonetheless, if the sinful condition of the body testifies to the need one truly has to go to the Lord's Supper, it so follows that the Lord's Supper offers something to remedy that need. The forgiveness of sins, here, testifies to the redemption of the entire person. Bodily eating and drinking, a corporeal act accompanied by God's mandating word, offers the human creature salvation both in body and soul.498

The Means of Grace and Christian Vocation

As discussed previously, Luther employs the language of God's "masks," *larvae Dei*, to convey the manner by which God uses his means of grace by engaging the corporeal creature through the senses, to affect spiritual realties. In a very similar way Luther uses this language with regard to Christian vocation as well. The disjunction between God's appointed "means of grace" and Christian vocation is not as great as one might suppose. Recalling that man was, in the beginning, called to exhibit dominion over creation though tending the garden, naming the animals, and the like, man's original calling was to act as God's representative, *larvae Dei*, carrying out his lordship over creation.

---

496 Ibid., 474.

497 Ibid., 475.

498 Luther makes this point with regard to both Baptism and the Lord's Supper in his commentary on 1 Corinthians 15, which will be pondered in more depth later. Luther writes, "For we are baptized not only with regard to the soul; but the body is also baptized. So the Gospel is preached to us, and we are blessed thereby, not only so far as the soul is concerned but also in regard to the whole person, also the body. Likewise, not only the soul but also the body receives the Sacrament of Christ's body and blood. Thus the body accompanies the soul through Baptism and the Sacrament, and on the Last Day it will abide where the soul abides." *Commentary on 1 Corinthians 15, LW* 28, 193.

The connection between Luther's theology of the means of grace, and Christian vocation, is particularly significant for a theology of the body. In the beginning, the human creature is a "mask" of God by which God's lordship over creation would be carried out. This is not an oppressive sort of dominion, but a lordship exercised after God's own image inhering in man in self-sacrificing service for the sake of all God's creatures. The connection between man's original calling, and the means of grace, is profound. In the very same way that God employs created matter to become his means of grace for man, the human body becomes a means of God's lordship and gracious provision for his entire creation. *so domination for the human body to exploit creation is abomination*

The reciprocal dependence of man's body upon the elements of creation and the creation's dependence on man is, in this way, restored in redemption. Just as God employs physical elements that seem to be his opposite, *sub contraria specie*, as his means of grace for man, God employs his fallen human creatures as vessels united to his proclamatory redeeming word. Just as the plain elements of the sacraments are nothing but simple *natural signs* water, bread and wine, apart from the word of God, the human creature is but a plain, even corrupt, body apart from the word of God who puts the human creature to his use. One might say that through God's creaturely means of grace he reintegrates the human body into a proper creaturely identity through which God's lordship over creation is restored. As such, the proper posture of the Christian toward his daily life in redemption is not one that looks always into the heavens in neglect of this world, but the Christian is to direct his gaze outward along with his extended hand in service to his neighbor. This is, in fact, a restoration of man's original vocation albeit particular to each Christian's unique calling to exhibit God's lordship in creation.

This is why, for instance, Adam is said to be able to work the ground joyfully according to the promise even though his joy is experienced through toil and pain. It is not merely that Adam is able to look past his toilsome labor knowing that better things are coming, but his very toil and pain becomes his cross through which he can perceive in God's promise his redeemed identity. Luther's *theologia crucis* is certainly at work here. To imagine that Adam would conceive of his redemption only in some sort of future glory apart from the reality of his experience in his toilsome vocation would make him a theologian of glory. As a theologian of the cross, Adam embraces even his toil and pain as the place where God's promise for him is found most clearly. His painful vocation is a true participation in God's redemption. In his faith, Adam perceives God's redemption in light of the promise not merely in spite of working in toil and pain, but even through his suffering he takes hold of the promise in Christ's suffering and cross.

The importance of disciplining the body and caring for its health and fitness for the sake of one's vocation, then, is not merely of temporal benefit but applies to one's actual participation in God's redemption of creation. Further parallels between how one treats the sacramental elements of bread and wine might help to elucidate the proper care one should render his body. The elements of bread and wine, as those God has chosen for his redemptive purpose, should always be cared for and reverenced (for Luther) but never worshipped. It is deplorable to despise the elements that God has taken to his use as a means of grace and it is equally deplorable to worship the elements themselves. Likewise, the human body, as God's "mask" and means of dominion for the rest of creation should be reverenced but never worshipped. The human body, while easily despised by men on account of its corruption, is the means God employs *sub contraria specie*. The body will suffer its various crosses in this life, but these crosses should not be self-inflicted.

As a younger Luther was apt to say in *The Freedom of a Christian* (1520), in one's vocation the Christian becomes "Christ to the other" for the sake of his neighbor.[499] Baptism consecrates or "seals" the Christian for this life as the body is buried with Christ and resurrected refashioning the human creature in Christ's image as a living sacrifice for the sake of God's creatures.

---

[499] "Therefore, if we recognize the great and precious things which are given us, as Paul says [Rom. 5:5], our hearts will be filled by the Holy Spirit with the love which makes us free, joyful, almighty workers and conquerors over all tribulations, servants of our neighbors, and yet lords of all. For those who do not recognize the gifts bestowed upon them through Christ, however, Christ has been born in vain; they go their way with their works and shall never come to taste or feel those things. Just as our neighbor is in need and lacks that in which we abound, so we were in need before God and lacked his mercy. Hence, as our heavenly Father has in Christ freely come to our aid, we also ought freely to help our neighbor through our body and its works, and each one should become as it were a Christ to the other that we may be Christs to one another and Christ may be the same in all, that is, that we may be truly Christians." *The Freedom of a Christian (1520), LW* 31:367.

Accordingly, the body is restored to its original condition but it is restored in the image of Christ.

At the same time, in *The Freedom of a Christian*, Luther encourages caring for the body precisely for the sake of serving one's neighbor. In his 1520 treatise, Luther began with a paradox—that the Christian is "a perfectly free lord of all, subject to none," while also a perfectly dutiful servant of all, subject to all."[500] At first, it appears that Luther embraces a soul/body dualism here, justifying his distinction on the basis of passages like 2 Corinthians 4:16 (ESV), "Though our outer nature is wasting away, our inner nature is being renewed day by day." Luther discerns, then, a two-fold nature within man—a spiritual and a bodily one.[501] Even as it is a mistake to view Paul's spirit/flesh dichotomy as a corollary to whatever in man is immaterial versus what is material,[502] Luther's distinction does not hinge upon materiality *per se*. As Luther explains this distinction, in fact, he proceeds to assign to the "spiritual" nature of man the locus of faith, and the "bodily" nature of man the domain of good works. What is at play here, already in 1520, is an early articulation of what Luther later termed the two kinds of righteousness. What Luther terms "spiritual," is simply an exercise of faith which depends not on the works of human hands, but upon the believer's trust in God's grace through Christ. What Luther terms "bodily," is not exorcised from faith, but is the outward life of man, upon a horizontal plane, where love motivates good works for one's neighbor's sake. Further, Luther is addressing here the orientation of the Christian life—he is speaking about the orientation of the regenerate man. Luther's famous paradox, then, in the *Freedom of a Christian* is expounded upon by assigning freedom to the spiritual orientation of man, while man's dutiful servanthood is relegated to man's "bodily" nature, as he seeks to offer his body and all its members as a living sacrifice unto God, by loving the least of these, or the Christian's neighbor. Luther's concern here is not a theological anthropology, *per se*, but the proper exercise and orientation of faith and

---

[500] Ibid., 344.

[501] "Man has a twofold nature, a spiritual and a bodily one. According to the spiritual nature, which men refer to as the soul, he is called a spiritual, inner, or new man. According to the bodily nature, which men refer to as flesh, he is called a carnal, outward, or old man, of whom the Apostle writes." Ibid.

[502] See Chapter 2, above.

good works, before God and before man respectively. Thus, when turning to man's bodily duty he exhorts the Christian to care for his or her body:

> This is what makes caring for the body a Christian work, that through its health and comfort we may be able to work, to acquire, and lay by funds with which to aid those who are in need, that in this way the strong member may serve the weaker, and we may be sons of God, each caring for and working for the other, bearing one another's burdens and so fulfilling the law of Christ [Gal. 6:2]. This is truly a Christian life. Here faith is truly active through love [Gal. 5:6], that is, it finds expression in works of the freest service, cheerfully and lovingly done, with which man willingly serves another without hope of reward; and for himself he is satisfied with the fulness and wealth of his faith.[503]

Notice, here, how in spite of the fact that Luther describes bodily care and works within the structure of the second premise of his paradox—that the Christian is a dutiful servant of all—he rends this hands-on Christian lifestyle as comprehensible only through the acceptance of the freedom of his first premise. Solely on account of the freedom that comes to the Christian by justification through faith, the Christian is then able to live an outward life that is not duty-bound to do good works to merit salvation, but is free to do so out of love for neighbor. This, however, comes with certain Christian responsibilities—caring for the body, included. Loving one's neighbor is not merely an attitude of the inner man, but requires that one's body be active and performing acts of service for the benefit of others. Such works, then, are finally pleasing to God not because they merit anything, but solely because they proceed from the freedom that faith grants as it is lived out through Christian vocation. In this way, the soul and body become total man—as the soul (which is the locus of faith) reorients the entire person including, especially, the body as the passions of the flesh are disciplined and restrained, while being replaced with faith's actions in service to others. Luther has effectively taken the *fides caritate formata* of the medieval church and flipped it on its head. Faith is not formed by love. Love, rather, is formed by faith. Such love, in turn, is always expressed as the soul's faith is manifest

yes, so it is not a distorted, self-serving version of 'love'

---

[503] *The Freedom of a Christian (1520), LW* 31:365.

in bodily service. Ultimately, in *The Freedom of a Christian,* Luther distinguishes the "spiritual" from the "bodily" part of man so that by properly distinguishing the activities of each—faith and works, respectively—they might be reunited and a new vision of the Christian life that embraces the total man, body and soul, might be understood.

The Church as Body of Christ

From the worship of Cain and Abel Luther sees the church divided into "two churches:" "the one which is the church in name but in reality is nothing but a hypocritical and bloodthirsty church; and the other one which is without influence, forsaken, and exposed to suffering and the cross, and which before the world and in the sight of that hypocritical church is truly Abel, that is, vanity and nothing."[504] An analysis of Cain's lineage reveals that, by worldly standards, he and his children enjoyed great worldly success. Cain founded what seems to be an impressive city and his descendants become great craftsmen, herdsmen, and musicians. In the lineage of Seth, who replaces Abel as the one through whom woman's seed would come, no such worldly successes are cited.

> It causes surprise that Moses gives a description of the generation of the sons of Cain before writing about the sons of God. But this is done according to a definite plan of God. In this life the children of this world surpass the children of God in accordance with the first promise. The Seed of the woman possesses a spiritual blessing; but the seed of the serpent obtains for itself a physical blessing, for it bites the heel of the blessed Seed (Gen. 3:15). Accordingly, what is carnal comes first; but what is spiritual comes later.[505]

---

[504] Luther continues, "For Christ also calls Abel righteous and makes him the beginning of the church of the godly, which will continue until the end (Matt. 23:35). Similarly, Cain is the beginning of the church of the wicked and of the blood-thirsty until the end of the world." *Lectures on Genesis (1535/38), LW* 1:252.

[505] Ibid., 310-311.

In the Lectures on Genesis similar insights occur as the struggle between these "two churches" emerges time and time again. After the flood, although Cain's descendants are no more, the Cainite church persists as through the descendants of Ham, set against the true church which inheres in Shem's lineage.[506] The "two churches" that accord with the serpent's seed and women's seed emerge also through the descendants of Ishmael and Isaac respectively.[507] Again, the theme is repeated through the struggle between Esau and Jacob.[508] Clearly, the "two churches" are not tied to a single bloodline as Esau is a child of Isaac. Instead, the "false church" emerges to "strike the heel" of the promised seed anywhere the true church exists. Luther's ecclesiology is patterned after his *theologia crucis*. The false church will often achieve all the world's glory, riches and accolades while the true church suffers quietly at its hand. Accordingly, Luther identifies the Cainite church with the church of the pope in his day.[509] As a true corpus Christi the true church is glorified not through worldly splendor, power, or prestige. Following the cruciform pattern of Christ, the true church is

---

[506] "The descendants of Ham, namely, Nimrod and the others, had invaded the region that had fallen to Shem, the heir of the promise concerning Christ. Because they were inclined toward despotism, they had a desire not only to drive out the descendants of Shem but also to establish a new government and a new church. Even though there is no written record of what they attempted against the true church, against Noah himself, the ruler of the church, and against his pious posterity, it can nevertheless be surmised by analogy if we carefully consider the actions of our opponents at the present time. For Satan, who incites the ungodly against the true church, is a*l*ways the same." *Lectures on Genesis (1535/38)*, *LW* 2:219.

[507] "This is why we say in the Creed: I believe in the holy church; that is, the church which has the Word by which all things are consecrated (1 Tim. 4:5). But this church puts up with Ishmael, its persecutor, until the words and prayer of Sarah and Isaac begin, that is, until the true church, by its persistent prayer and crying, brings it about that Ishmael is cast out. Yet Ishmael does not believe this until he experiences it in very fact." *Lectures on Genesis (1535/38)*, *LW* 4:34.

[508] "Esau prefers the pottage to his birthright; that is, he is the church in regard to number, but he follows his flesh and blood and seeks gain in godliness. Thus the false church feigns godliness merely in order to enjoy the pleasures and honors of this world. But the true church seeks eternal life through patience and faith. The others are beasts of the belly, and their god is the belly." Ibid., 408.

[509] "This wrath of Cain we also observe in the Cainite church of the pope. What irritates the pope, the cardinals, kings, and princes more than that I, a beggar, give preference over their authority to the authority of God and in the name of the Lord reprove what deserves reproof? Even they themselves acknowledge that there are many things which are in need of a thoroughgoing reformation. But that an inconspicuous human being, and one who stepped out of an inconspicuous nook into public life, should carry this out—this is something utterly unbearable for them. Therefore they oppose us with their authority and attempt to overwhelm us by means of it." *Lectures on Genesis (1535/38)*, *LW* 1:252.

so he is consistent re'i body "

revealed through suffering and the cross. Most everything Luther asserts about the personal body of the believer, who bears "crosses" according to his daily calling, applies to the corporate body of the church as well.

While the false church of the serpent's seed can arise apart from any particular lineage to "strike" at the heel of the true church, those who belong to the lineage of the "false church" are no wise condemned on account of their bloodline. One's birthright matters not before God. Even those who are *no respected persons'* born of Cain could be saved, and Luther imagines some were, by returning in faith to the promise. "Those who deserted [Cain] and joined the true church were saved, although they had to despair of the glory that Christ would be born from their body."[510]

The Eschatalogical Body

While the reality of redemption is to be lived out through Christian vocation here and now, the reality of sin still pervading the flesh is undeniable. There is still a greater hope for the final consummation of our redemption. That Luther derived great comfort from the resurrection is undoubtable. In 1542 his thirteen-year-old daughter Magdalena died. As the coffin was being lowered to the ground Luther is reported to have cried out, "*Est resurrectio carnis!*"[511] This is a redemption that is already ours but is not yet fully possessed.

Luther, again, sees in the conflict between Cain and Abel the consistent character of God persisting from the time of the fall until the day of the resurrection. When Cain is confronted regarding the murder of his brother, Luther discerns in God's concern for Abel an "excellent theological doctrine and comfort." God continues to show concern for Abel even after he has died. *plus the O.T.* "This plainly indicates the resurrection of the dead, inasmuch as God *acknowge* declares Himself to be the God of Abel, who is dead, and inquires about Abel, *God is the God* who is dead."[512]

There is, evidenced by Abel, both an affirmation of the persistence of *of the living* life after death, in the intermediate state with God, and an anticipation of

---

BUT in "Gods' mind" there can only be the 'present' beloved — i.e. Cain cannot kill Abel in Gods' mind...

[510] Ibid., 292.

[511] *WaTr* 5:194; *LW* 54:433: "There is a resurrection of the flesh!" Martin Brecht discusses the funeral in detail in *The Preservation of the Church*, 237-238.

[512] Ibid., 285.

no, evidence that God does not forget, does not self-limit to time.

the greater hope of the resurrection of the body. As already indicated, Luther sees in God's ongoing concern for Abel evidence of the resurrection. That said, on account of the resurrection which he has yet to experience, "Abel, though dead, lives; and in another life he is canonized by God Himself in a better and truer manner than all whom the pope has ever canonized." This life in the intermediate state, while not the fully realized redemption of the body, is still considered "a better life than before." "We live this physical life in sins, and it is subject to death; but that other life is eternal and without any afflictions, physical or spiritual."[513]

While Abel lives according to the promise in his faith, even though he has died, Abel's blood still calls out to God for justice. "The fact is that Abel's blood, which, during his life, was very quiet, now cries out. Now Abel accuses his brother before God as a murderer, although while living he had disregarded all his brother's wrongs." Luther derives comfort from this fact in the light of those who still in his day suffer persecution at the hands of popes and princes. The blood of the martyrs "will not keep silence," In due time, their blood "will compel God to come down from heaven and execute on earth a judgment that will be unbearable for the enemies of the Gospel."[514] A coming judgment, and resurrection of the dead, will occur at which time God's justice will be enacted against the ungodly. This is, for Luther, a great comfort that is likewise a source of great terror for the enemies of the Gospel.

but also God will make all things new... complex

Probably the most thorough examination of death and resurrection in Luther's works is found in a series of seventeen sermons on 1 Corinthians 15 preached in 1532-1533 and published in the form of a commentary in 1534. According to Gerhard Sauter, in these sermons "the Reformer develops his theological understanding of the resurrection in a more comprehensive and multifaceted way than anywhere else."[515] In his *Lectures on Genesis* Luther certainly evokes the doctrine of the resurrection but never fully expounds

---

[513] Ibid.

[514] Ibid., 288.

[515] Gerhard Sauter, "Luther on the Resurrection," *Harvesting Martin Luther's Reflections on Theology, Ethics, and the Church*, Kindle Edition, ed. Timothy J. Wengert (Grand Rapids, MI: Eerdmans, 2004), Kindle Loc., 1060-1287. For another analysis of the body in Luther's sermons on 1 Corinthians 15 see Cortright, *Poor Maggot Sack That I Am*, 229-240.

upon it. In order to fully comprehend Luther's theology of the resurrected body, an examination of his earlier sermons on 1 Corinthians 15 will be necessary to supplement Luther's statements on the topic in his Genesis lectures.

That Christ himself arose from the dead is, for Luther, "the chief article of the Christian doctrine."[516] Following Paul's logic in vv. 12-15, affirming Christ's resurrection and the resurrection of humanity go hand-in-hand. If there is no bodily resurrection, one cannot say that Christ was raised either. If Christ was not raised, Paul says, "then our preaching is in vain and your faith is in vain." Luther reflects, then, on the significance of the resurrection for all preaching and the means of grace. The Christian and his Christ are inexplicably linked together through Holy Baptism.

> What does Baptism avail you if you do not hope for another life?"
> So he remarked earlier: "If the dead do not arise, both our
> proclamation and your faith are futile." For if there is no other
> life, why should anyone preach, or why should anyone go to hear
> someone preach? Such a person would be just as much inclined
> to put God off entirely as they who believe nothing at all do. If
> there is nothing to the resurrection, one does not need Baptism
> either. For no one may be baptized for the purpose of obtaining
> enough to eat and to drink or for the purpose of filling his chests
> and granaries.[517]

ie spiritual benefit

For these purposes, much of Luther's sermons on 1 Corinthains 15 need not be addressed. What is of pivotal importance, though, is Luther's understanding of what the resurrected body will be like. How much continuity is there between the resurrected body and the body we presently possess? Luther addresses this matter primarily in his commentary on Paul's words in verses 35-38:

> But someone will ask, "How are the dead raised? With what kind
> of body do they come?" You foolish person! What you sow does

---

[516] *Commentary on 1 Corinthians 15, LW* 28:94.

[517] Ibid., 146.

not come to life unless it dies. And what you sow is not the body that is to be, but a bare kernel, perhaps of wheat or of some other grain. But God gives it a body as he has chosen, and to each kind of seed its own body.[518] *as at our first life*

Luther affirms that there will be continuity between man's present body and the resurrected body in its created essence, while recognizing that the use of the body will change. "The body retains its nature, but the use of the body does not remain the same."[519] Christians will continue to have a vocation, as vocation is an essential component of creaturely identity, but as various callings have been instituted on account of man's needs in the fallen world, the person's position will be different in the eschaton. That said, what this sort of "vocation" might be in the eschaton is impossible to discern according to our present experience. There will be no needs or wants in the resurrection as "we will possess everything in God, who will be 'everything to everyone.'"[520] Luther recognizes that there will be different degrees of glory in the resurrection. "In short, before God all will be alike in faith and grace and heavenly essence; but there will be a difference in works and their glory. It is like fashioning a hatchet, a nail, a key, or a lock from one and the same iron. All are the identical essence, and yet they serve various uses and functions."[521]

Luther spends considerable time reflecting on Paul's metaphor of the body that is sown, like a seed, in the ground to sprout again into new life. As a seed is something plain and simple, and what sprouts from it is greater, so also the body "will return in a form so honorable and precious that its future honor and glory will surpass the present shame and dishonor many thousand times."[522] Luther takes time to explain Paul's language when he says "It is sown a physical body, it is raised a spiritual body." This, Luther

---

[518] 1 Corinthians 15:35-38 (ESV)

[519] *Commentary on 1 Corinthians 15, LW* 28:171. *does he say why?*

[520] Ibid., 172.

[521] Ibid., 173.

[522] Ibid., 187.

says, seems to be an unusual saying and needs some explanation. By "spiritual body" Paul is not implying that the body is not physical. "When it is called a spiritual body, this does not imply that it no longer has physical life or flesh and blood. No, then it could not be called a true body."[523] Instead, what Paul calls the "physical body" is what could be more easily termed a "natural body" that depends upon the earth for sustenance. This "spiritual body," Luther envisions will not need to eat, sleep or digest but will be "nourished and preserved spiritually by God and has life entirely in Him."[524] Keep in mind the previous discussion on Luther's view of the Holy Spirit and "spirituality." To be "spiritual" does not mean immaterial, but always refers to the Holy Spirit in whom man has life. Consequently, "physical" in Paul's usage here is not "materiality" *per se*, but has to do with the sustenance of life through physical, that is earthly, means. A spiritual life is a bodily life sustained, ultimately in the resurrection of the body, by the body's communion with Christ's body in the Holy Spirit.

> It will be a completely spiritual existence, or life, of the whole person, covering both body and soul. It will issue from the Spirit and will come immediately from or through God, so that we will be illumined by Him and know Him not only with regard to the soul, but our whole body will be pervaded... Thus you must learn to understand the words 'natural' and 'spiritual' correctly and distinguish in accordance with their usage in Scripture. Here the body is not to be distinguished from the soul, as we customarily do when we hear the words spirit or spiritual. No, we must understand this to mean that the body, too, must become spirit or live spiritually. We have already begun to do that through Baptism, by virtue of which we live spiritually with regard to the soul and God also views and regards the body as spiritual. It is only that the body must first depart from this temporal life

---

[523] Ibid., 189.

[524] Ibid.

before it becomes completely new and spiritual and lives solely
of and by the Spirit.[525]

Luther can make this statement with confidence. Recognizing that our
current bodies cohere with the "first Adam," but our resurrected bodies will
be like that of the "second Adam," namely Christ, Luther can discern what
the fullness of resurrected life will be like by considering the resurrected
Christ. While Jesus no longer had bodily needs and wants after the
resurrection, but nonetheless was able to eat, he demonstrated that "He has
a true and genuine body with flesh and blood."[526] The Christian, Luther
affirms, truly has a share in his resurrected reality even now through faith
in the promises the Word of God speaks concerning Baptism. The Christian
can live this reality "now" even while he awaits for this temporal life to pass
away. The Christian lives according to the resurrection by embracing life as
God's creature, fulfilling his daily callings, and seeing hope even in what the
senses perceive only as perishable and transitory. Under the *theologia crucis*
the Christian lives a life defined by resurrection, but veiled under these
present sufferings, *Anfechtungen*, and the cross. The Christian cannot despise
his body in this present life because to do so is to despise the body in the
resurrection as well. The body now and then share the same essence. Gerhard
Sauter summarizes Luther's sermons on 1 Corinthians 15 with regard to the
implications of the resurrection for the present Christian life:

> For Martin Luther the time of human existence is not a period
> of preparation for eternal life, nor is it simply a period of testing,
> however much he has emphasized—and had to emphasize to be
> faithful to Scripture—that the decision concerning life with God
> is made now and not sometime in the future. In our lifetime the
> promise of life with God reaches us. For this very reason "this
> lifetime" is the space in which hope can grow, because it is held
> in the confidence in "life as such," for Jesus Christ, the Crucified,
> Resurrected, and Coming One embraces life. What has been

---

[525] Ibid., 190, 192.

[526] Ibid., 193.

experienced, suffered, done or left undone, in communion with him will perish nevermore.[527]

This means that the Christian truly participates, proleptically, in the reality of the resurrection as he lives and goes about his life in faith. This is a faith, of course, that clings to Christ through the means of grace and is lived out through believer's life according to his daily calling. Living live, then, in communion with Christ these things will never pass away but will shine forth as one's splendor in the eschatological resurrection. *Simply put, when we live in Christ, by*

Something of Luther's perspective on the so-called "intermediate *grace,* state" should be addressed. The "intermediate state," between death and *our life* the final resurrection, is not thoroughly investigated by Luther. While he *is in* does speak of "the sleep of death" he does so mostly in the sense that St. *Christ's* Paul does when speaking of those who have "fallen asleep in Christ" (1 Cor. *and,* 15:18; 1 Thess. 4:14). The question of "soul sleep," versus a conscious *just so, awareness of one's place with the Lord while awaiting the resurrection is not* *awakening* one Luther pursues. According to Sauter, "That which happens to us and in which we cannot participate cannot be measured in terms of human time; it remains hidden from our sight. For this reason Luther speaks about the 'sleep of death' rather than of an 'interim state.'"[528] Still, Luther's comments in *The Genesis Lectures* have been pointed to in defense of a *N: doctrine of "soul sleep," "Thus after death the soul enters its chamber and* *in God's* is at peace; and while it sleeps, it is not aware of its sleep." In truth, however, *mind* Luther's comments immediately before this statement indicate that "there is a difference between the sleep or rest of this life and that of the future life...the soul does not sleep in the same manner. It is awake. It experiences visions and the discourses of the angels and of God. Therefore the sleep in the future life is deeper than it is in this life. Nevertheless, the soul lives before God."[529] In short, it appears that Luther advocates a sleep of sorts for the human soul after death, but he does so only to remain faithful to *that is what is cogent : we live, dying or living, in Christ*

---

[527] Sauter, "Luther on the Resurrection," Kindle Loc., 1287.

[528] Sauter, "Luther on the Resurrection," Kindle loc. 1119

[529] *Lectures on Genesis, LW* 4:313.

Paul's language of the same. He grants a certain awareness in the intermediate state, but also recognizes that as beings who live in space and time, any existence apart from time is impossible to fully comprehend, All at once he says that the soul "sleeps," but also says it is "awake." Luther does not advocate a doctrine of "soul sleep," *per se*.[530]

The Redeemed Body in John Paul II

Having already articulated what John Paul II terms the essential "spousal" meaning of the body, in terms of the resurrection of the body certain clarifications are made. If Jesus' dialogue with the Pharisees on the dissolubility of marriage signaled a return to "the beginning," it is Jesus' dialogue with the Sadducees who incorrectly "say there is no resurrection" (Matt. 22:23) that signals a hope in a "new meaning" of the body for the future. Relying on the law of so-called levirate marriage from Deuteronomy 25:7-10 the Sadducees propose a hypothetical situation that they imagine would complicate the position of those who affirm the resurrection of the body. A woman who had married seven brothers, each one after the previous one died, finally dies herself. "In the resurrection, when they will rise, whose wife will she be? For the seven had married her" (Mark 12:23). Jesus answers them as follows: "Is not this the reason you are wrong, that you know neither the Scriptures nor the power of God? For when they rise from the dead, they take neither wife nor husband, but are like angels in heaven" (Mark 12:24-25).

Christ seems to reveal a new "nuptial" meaning to the resurrected body. John Paul II calls this the "virginal" meaning of being male and female. The human being, in the duality of male and female, does not cease to be male and female in the resurrection. The original, "virginal," meaning of the body is for life in communion of persons. Marriage and procreation give concrete reality to that meaning for "historical man," but in the

[handwritten margin note: not true in Christ these categories do not matter]

---

[530] Other Reformers—particularly those associated with the English reformation—later advocated for "soul sleep" more decidedly. *The Forty-Two Articles* (1553), produced under Thomas Cranmer's guidance, explicitly confessed the doctrine of soul sleep stating that after death all "sleep" until judgment day. See W.F. Wilkinson, ed. *The Articles of the Church of England*, 2nd ed. (London: John W. Parker, 1850), 104. Later, the *Westminster Confession of Faith* (1647) rejected the teaching stating that "The Bodies of men, after death, return to dust, and see corruption: but, their Souls (which neither dye, nor sleep) having an immortal subsistence, immediately return to God who gave them" (32.1).

[handwritten note: forget the Greek, sheds of Hebrew nepheth and scriptural claims of our breath returning to God] 250

resurrection the meaning of the body will correspond to man's being created in the image and likeness of God. There will be continuity with man's experience of his body in the "historical dimension," while it will be a whole new experience at the same time.[531]

That man now possesses a "natural body" that would be sown in the earth through death, and will receive a "spiritual body" (1 Cor. 15:44) in the resurrection is not, for John Paul II, a move from materiality to immateriality. Like Luther, the pope sees the spirit/flesh dichotomy in scripture as an always-material reality in either condition. What the Apostle Paul is getting at through this language is not an escape from corporeality, but a supremacy of "spirituality over sensuality" in the bodily life and resurrection.[532]

According to John Paul II "the resurrection constitutes the definitive accomplishment of the redemption of the body."[533] The Apostle Paul speaks of both the body's redemption (Romans 8:23) and *"the completion of this redemption in the future resurrection"* (1 Cor. 15:42-49). All human creatures

---

[531] "...*the original* and fundamental *meaning of being a body*, as also of being, as a body, male and female—that is, precisely that 'spousal' meaning—*is united to the fact that man is created as a person and is called to a life 'in communione personarum.'* Marriage and procreation do not definitively determine the original and fundamental meaning of being a body nor of being, as a body, male and female. Marriage and procreation only give concrete reality to that meaning in the dimensions of history. The resurrection indicates the closure of the historical dimension. And so it is that the words 'when they rise from the dead, they will take neither wife nor husband' (Mk 12:25) not only express clearly what meaning the human body will not have in the 'future world,' but also allows us to deduce that the 'spousal' meaning of the body in the resurrection to the future life will perfectly correspond both to the fact that man as male-female is a person, created in the 'image and likeness of God,' and to the fact that this image is realized in the communion of persons. That 'spousal' meaning of being a body will, therefore, be realized as *a meaning that is perfectly personal and communitarian at the same time.*

When we speak about the body glorified through the resurrection to new life, what we have in mind is man, male and female, in all the truth of his humanity, who *together with the eschatological experience of the living God* (with the vision 'face to face') *will experience precisely this meaning of his body.* This will be a completely new experience, and yet, at the same time, it will not be alienated in any way from the experience man shared 'from the beginning' nor form that which, in the historical dimension of his existence, constituted in him the source of the tension between the spirit and the body, mainly and precisely with reference to the procreative meaning of the body and of [its] sex. The man of the 'future world' will find in this new experience of his own body *the fulfillment* of what he carried in himself perennially and historically, in some sense, as an inheritance and even more so as a task and objective, as the content of ethos." *TOB,* 399-400.

[532] Ibid., 401.

[533] Ibid., 405.

251

live presently between the "first Adam" and the "second Adam," who is Christ. "The humanity of the 'first Adam,' the 'man of earth,' carries within itself, I would say, a *particular potentiality* (which is capacity and readiness) *for receiving* all *that the 'second Adam' became*, the heavenly Man, namely, Christ: what he became in his resurrection."[534] There is a tension, as in Luther, between the "now" and the "not yet" in terms of the Christian's present condition between the two Adams.

Recognizing that the resurrection is the "definitive accomplishment" of the body's redemption, the question of justification deserves some attention. At times, John Paul II's conception of justification may seem similar to Luther's. He speaks of justification through "faith" frequently, but for John Paul II this faith is a faith formed by and active in love.[535] Faith, for Luther, is not a quality that inheres in man *per se* but is the simple reception of God's gift. Thus, for Luther, "faith alone" saves because salvation is wholly dependent upon the gift which faith receives. Faith, for John Paul II, is seemingly defined more in terms of a quality, or activity, in man. "This 'justification' by faith does not constitute simply a dimension of the divine plan of salvation and of man's sanctification, but according to St. Paul it is *a real power at work in man that reveals and affirms itself in his actions*."[536] As such, "faith" is seen almost as an active force that progressively leads man's redeemed body toward its resurrection consummation. Thus, for Luther the "now" and "not yet" tension is one that persists perpetually in the Christian life. The "old Adam" coheres in man alongside the "new man" equally until the eschaton. For John Paul II, while man lives always between the two Adams, it is not a paradox in tension but more like a continuum through which one progresses by faith active in love.

Some clarification of this point, though, is in order. John Paul II's perspective is nuanced somewhat differently than the *fides formata* that is

---

[534] Ibid., 407.

[535] "...the antithesis between 'body' and 'Spirit,' between life 'according to the flesh' and life 'according to the Spirit,' profoundly permeates the whole Pauline doctrine of justification. With exceptional force of conviction, the Apostle to the Gentiles proclaims that man's justification is achieved in Christ and for Christ. Man reaches *justification in 'faith that works through love'* (Gal. 5:6), and not only by observing individual precepts of the Old Testament law..." Ibid., 338.

[536] Ibid., 333.

rebutted in Article IV of the *Apology of the Augsburg Confession*.[537] Recall from John Paul II's perspective on "original shame" that the core problem of man's sinful condition is that man is "alienated from the Love that was the source of the original gift."[538] If faith consists in the reception of this gift again, the very gift man receives in redemption is love itself through a reconstituted communion with God and his image.

The incarnation of Christ becomes decisively important here. As John Paul II put it, "Through the fact that the Word of God became flesh, the body entered theology...through the main door."[539] Anderson and Granados summarize John Paul II's insights on the redemptive significance of Christ's body:

> Because the body's vulnerability is openness to God, it is not foreign to the Son. Rather the body, being made for communion with the original Giver, is a perfect vehicle for expressing Jesus's identity as the Father's only begotten Son. The Son himself is total openness and receptivity to the Father, and the Son's filial attitude eliminates any possible conflict between his divine identity and his flesh. On the one hand, the incarnate Son's flesh displays his essential communion with the Father. On the other hand, the Incarnation doesn't destroy human bodily nature but perfects it and manifests its full truth. *Indeed, Christ's existence perfects the language of the body, fully revealing its true nature as relationship with the Father, dependence on him, and acceptance of his gift.* Therefore, Christ's fulfillment of the body's language is the highest expression of original solitude. Original solitude, remember, is based on the fact that, from the very first moment of its existence, the body is a sign revealing the Giver as the origin and destiny of life. The Incarnation takes this revelation and raises it to a whole new level; the Son becomes man in order

---

[537] See Kolb, Wengert and Arand, eds. *The Book of Concord: The Confessions of the Evangelical Lutheran Church*, 138.

[538] *TOB*, 239.

[539] Ibid., 221.

to show us in his own body the (paternal) face of the original Giver...Christ's (Sonship) restores the original meaning of the body as a manifestation of God, even as he integrates this manifestation into his eternal filial relation to the Father.[540]

By offering himself as a gift for humanity Jesus Christ reconnects original solitude and original unity. As Adam once accepted Eve as a gift from God, Christ fully accepts and affirms humanity as the Father's gift. This elucidates the significance of Christ's role not only of "Son" but also as "Bridegroom." Through his suffering and the cross, Christ fulfills the nuptial meaning of the body. This is not merely a restoration of what was lost in the fall, but is "the most eloquent 'statement' of these original experiences that the body's language has ever uttered."[541]

Accordingly, in John Paul II's thought, works of love are not only a "fruit of faith," but we are the fruits of Christ's love. It is the Holy Spirit who "transforms us into Christ's image of the Son and Bridegroom."[542] Through the Holy Spirit we become participants in his love and sacrifice and our bodies take on a new character of holiness as the Spirit's temple. "The redemption of the body brings with it the establishment in Christ and for Christ of a new measure of the holiness of the body. Paul appeals precisely to this holiness when he writes in 1 Thessalonians that one should 'keep one's own body with holiness and reverence.'"[543]

Conclusion

This chapter and the preceding ones have considered Luther's thoughts regarding the human body in the light of recent somatologies, particularly, of John Paul II's *Theology of the Body*. Luther's voice in his Lectures on Genesis, consistent with his other works, reveals an essentially positive view of the body. His exclamation in *The Large Catechism*, "I am God's Creature!" well articulates Luther's perspective on the body in only a few words. Belonging to God, there is no doubt that man is a dependent being

---

[540] Anderson and Granados, *Called to Love,* 132.

[541] Ibid., 140.

[542] Ibid., 141.

[543] *TOB,* 351.

who derives his very identity from God's activity. *Coram Deo* man stands, in the body, as a passive agent receiving all things from God's grace. Nonetheless, as God's creature man lives as a creature amongst creatures. *Coram mundo* man lives out his daily life and calling as God's agent, or "mask," exhibiting dominion through love and sacrifice for one's neighbor. All of this happens precisely in and through the body. Called to have dominion over creation implies responsibility to care for and discipline one's own body as well. Through the two kinds of righteousness man is able to comprehend his true human identity as God's creature precisely in relational terms. To be fully human is not about escaping the body, but it implies embracing the body through which man engages relationship in both realms. God initiates his saving activity through the means of grace, appealing to man's five senses, so that the total man would be saved both in body and soul. God is the sole actor in man's redemption. Man, in turn, lives out his creaturely identity with respect to his neighbor in Christ's image.

While it is, admittedly, difficult to carry on any conversation between theologians of various centuries, not to mention one between Luther and a pope, the language John Paul II has introduced in his *Theology of the Body* coheres in part with Luther's perspective on the human being as God's creature. There were, as was noted throughout this discussion, several points of departure between the two. Perhaps most important is the emphasis in John Paul II on the nuptial meaning of the body, as an essential component of being human, whereas for Luther spousal love reflects God's love in creation. For Luther, everything that is essential about being human was already there even before woman was made. While a spousal union might lead man and woman together to embrace their humanity, as it was intended to be by God, that is a far cry from saying that spousal union defines man essentially. By and large, however, the dominant categories and themes pursued by John Paul II typically compliment, rather than contradict, Luther's perspective on the body. This is true, as was demonstrated, particularly in the light of Luther's paradigmatic two kinds of righteousness. Luther's theology puts skin on some of John Paul II's thought. The reality of bodily life, particularly as God engages the human creature through corporeal means and employs the human creature as his very agent of dominion, makes the "hermeneutic of the gift" through which the nuptial body is understood as something very relevant to daily life in creation. For Luther, however, this is not something realized wholly in spousal terms. The "gift" is inherent in the relationship between Creator and creature—righteousness *coram Deo*. Luther's work calls the creature back to creation itself where he may serve his neighbor—righteousness *coram mundo*. The body should be understood in terms of "gift" from the very beginning. We receive freely, apart from any merit of our own. We give the gift through active obedience in gratitude for God's grace given freely to us. Concerning good works, in the *Smalcald Articles*, Luther writes that "the human creature should be called and should be completely righteous and holy—according to both the person and his or her works—by the pure grace and mercy that have been poured and spread over us in Christ."[544]

While it may not be true that Luther ever articulated a comprehensive systematic theology of the body, *per se*, there is plenty to go on from Luther that allows subsequent generations of Christians to construct a theology of the body that is profoundly relevant for Christian living today. In a world where the body, and therefore man's creaturely identity, is constantly under assault a fundamental theology of the body must inform Christian proclamation. The body is inescapable and, as much as some might try, it is a topic that cannot be ignored if one is to take his Christian identity seriously.

---

[544] Kolb, Wengert and Arand, eds. *The Book of Concord: The Confessions of the Evangelical Lutheran Church*, 325.

CHAPTER 6:
CONCLUSION

THE VERY FIRST QUESTION IN THE *HEIDELBERG CATECHISM* begins by affixing God's ownership upon the entire human creature as the only comfort that persists from life through death: "..<u>I am not my own</u>, but belong—<u>body and soul, in life and death—to my faithful Savior</u>, Jesus Christ."[545] Zacharias Ursinus penned these words undoubtedly influenced by the Melanchthonian Lutheran tradition—thus it should be no surprise that these words reflect heavily the language Luther had already employed in his *Small Catechism.*[546]

It behooves the reader to recall the very first words with which John Calvin began his *Institutes of the Christian Religion:* "Nearly all the wisdom we possess, that is to say, true and sound wisdom, consists of two parts: the

---

[545] Heidelberg Catechism, Q1. In Lyle D. Bierma, *The Theology of the Heidelberg Catechism: A Reformation Synthesis (Columbia Series in Reformed Theology).* (Louisville, Westminster John Knox Press, 2013), 13. Bierma compares the German from both Ursinus' *Heidelberg Catechism* and Luther's *Small Catechism* and demonstrates striking parallels between the two.

[546] In the *Small Catechism,* Luther had previously confessed the unity of the total person in the First Article of the Creed, "I believe that God has made me and all creatures; that He has given me my body and soul, eyes, ears, and all my members, my reason and all my senses, <u>and still takes care of them.</u>" Similarly, like Ursinus, Luther confesses one's ownership by God by summarizing the Second Article of the Creed, "I believe that Jesus Christ…is my Lord, who has redeemed me, a lost and condemned person, purchased and won me from all sins, from death, and from the power of the devil…that I may be His own and live under him in His kingdom and serve Him in everlasting righteousness, innocence, and blessedness." Martin Luther, *Luther's Small Catechism* in *The Lutheran Study Bible.* (St. Louis: Concordia Publishing House, 2009) xxxvi-xxxvii.

knowledge of God and of ourselves."[547] It is this author's hope that this book has proven to be valuable on both fronts. While one might suppose that a theology of the body is concerned, primarily, with knowledge about the nature of man, because the body itself is the locus whereby the relationship between God and man is expressed most evidently throughout Scripture—a distinction aided and exemplified by Luther's paradigmatic two kinds of righteousness—a theology of the body is also important in wisdom's pursuit of knowing God. To exorcise the body from one's anthropology will inevitably impact one's theology.

This is precisely why a *theology* of the body is not altogether the same thing as philosophical or even biblical anthropology. Undoubtedly, theologies of the body will engage biblical anthropology. This book has done so, as well. That said, a theology of the body is concerned more with the body's role within the relational dynamic between the human creature and his Creator. By extension, therefore, it is concerned with how the human creature relates bodily to the rest of creation. A theology of the body, properly articulated, will undoubtedly prove helpful for understanding man. But this is a secondary purpose for a theology of the body. What a proper theology of the body must do is express the body's revelatory and relational role with respect to God. A proper theology of the body cannot begin merely by analyzing the constituent parts of man, but must begin and end with God who created and sustains the human being in total—body and soul, in life and death. As such, a theology of the body encompasses all of what Calvin considered the beginnings of wisdom.

What makes Luther particularly helpful—in contrast to the other magisterial reformers—is his own background in dealing with very personal matters related to his own body. He was keenly aware, particularly due to the disciplines he practiced as an Augustinian monk, how the treatment of the body could affect one's spiritual wellbeing. He frequently reflects on his own well-documented health problems in the language of spiritual warfare. Bodily ailments were more, for Luther, than natural illness but were attacks by the devil meant, in his case, to dissuade his work on behalf of the Gospel. Thus, Luther could refer to his body as a poor maggot sack, on one hand,

---

[547] Jean Calvin, *Calvin's Institutes.* Edited by Donald K. McKim. (Westminster John Knox Press, 2001), 1.

while praising the Lord for his body's essential goodness on the other. The Christian life could not be, as with some monastic orders, a mere inward spiritual practice but must take on flesh and bone, aka the Christian's vocation, in service to neighbor. That the medieval church had prioritized the inward and reflective life of the Christian, elevating monastic vows to a place higher than even Christian baptism, was one of Luther's greatest laments. Just as the Lord chooses to deal with the totality of man—body and soul—so also man must live out his Christian faith in totality by getting his hands dirty in the muck and the mire of whatever one's calling leads him to do in service of others. Accordingly, Luther in his *Small Catechism* moves away from the "holy orders" of the monks and creates a rhythm of regular *Jewish* prayer that accords with the pattern of common life in the world—getting up in the morning, preceding and following meals, before going to bed at night, etc.[548] These regular and daily activities, such as working for food, eating meals, attending worship and getting rest, were not merely bodily acts done to survive but they encompassed the heartbeat of the Christian life which takes hold in one's station in the world as the place where he is called to both receive the graces of God and to embody the love of Christ in acts of mercy and service, caring for oneself with the provisions of God and giving of one's abundance and efforts to become an instrument of God's provision for others.

Luther grounded this viewpoint in what he called the two kinds of righteousness—a pattern he saw reflected throughout Scripture beginning in Genesis and articulated explicitly in Paul's letter to the Galatians. While the concept of the covenant did not factor in as prominently in Luther's writings as it did for Zwingli, Calvin and subsequent reformed theologians, the two kinds of righteousness was Luther's way of addressing many of the same themes that later covenantal theologians would also articulate.[549] Just as for covenantal theologians the covenant concept unites every epoch in Scripture in to a single narrative of salvation (contra dispensationalism) for

---

[548] See Arand, *That I May be His Own*, 151-152.

[549] It might have been that Luther avoided the concept of covenant because of how the Franciscans during his day had employed the notion of covenant to bolster their perspective of justification which affirmed that grace only becomes effective after one had done all that he can do to fulfill God's law by his own efforts. See Coughlin, "Law and theology: Reflections on what it means to be human from a Franciscan perspective." *John's L. Rev.* 74 (2000): 609ff.

Luther the two kinds of righteousness also revealed the enduring character of God and the manner of his relationship and salvific purposes for mankind. Just as covenantal theologians affirm that God initiates the covenant relationship with man by his own sovereign will and choice, Luther affirms that righteousness *coram Deo* exists solely by God's call and election of man, apart from anything within man that might make him more or less worthy based on his own performance. Covenantal theologians, likewise, affirm that within the covenantal relationship the human being has certain responsibilities which emerge from the terms of that relationship.

Accordingly, Luther also articulated a "active" or "horizontal" righteousness, *coram mundo,* which flowed out of the relationship God had first initiated with man in the beginning. Luther even took pains to distinguish between what he sometimes called the "active righteousness" of the Christian from works that might seem outwardly similar by unbelievers, which he sometimes called "civil" righteousness. This is why, also, Luther argued that Christians have a vocation, but unbelievers do not. They certainly have a *stand,* in life, and may be used by God in their station but because they do not possess the vertical relationship with God their place in the world is not a calling, or vocation, properly defined.[550] As such, no matter how one behaves in the world outwardly, he cannot be called a Christian—or even properly and fully human—apart from the vertical relationship established by God according to His good pleasure and will. From a Reformed perspective, Luther's two kinds of righteousness is thoroughly covenantal.[551]

---

[550] Gustaf Wingren, *Luther on Vocation*, Translated by Carl C. Rasmussen. (Evansville, IN: Ballast Press, 1999), 1-13.

[551] A qualifier here is certainly in order. Luther is often accused of denying a "third use" of the law which, in Reformed theology is the law's proper use. In the *Smalcald Articles*, for example, Luther affirmed two offices or functions (*officium legis*) of the law. While Melanchthon had developed a third use (*usus legis*) as early as his 1534 *Scholia* on Colossians, Luther seemed to shy away from that terminology even though he agreed with his younger colleague in substance. Luther's concern was that using the same terminology for the first and second use/function of the law as the third was confusing. After all, the one who uses the law in the first two instances is God through the Holy Spirit. With the "third" use, it is man who uses the law in the context of the new obedience. Accordingly, while it is common to suggest that Luther rejected the third use of the law, this is not accurate. He embraced it in substance, as evidenced by his opposition to Agricola and as manifest in his exhortations to good works in his sermons, even if he has reservations about the language. See Timothy J. Wengert, *Law and Gospel: Philip Melancthon's Debate with John Agricola of Eisleben over Poenitentia.* (Grand Rapids, Baker Academic, 1997), 177ff.

From a Lutheran perspective covenantal theology is of near identical kin with the terms of the two kinds of righteousness which forms the backbone of Luther's thought and the Lutheran confessions.[552]

Perhaps no insight is more important in Luther's theology of the body than his emphasis on the unity of the totality of man—*totus homo*. One cannot separate the spirit or soul from the body, locating sin or righteousness in one or the other without it impacting the whole person. As Luther said, "the whole man is a spiritual man insofar as he savors the things that are of God, and the whole man is carnal insofar as he savors the things that are his own."[553] Luther arrives at this insight based on Paul's exhortation to glorify God in the body, as the body is a temple of the Holy Spirit (1 Cor. 6:19-20). Thus, Luther employed the analogy of the Mosaic tabernacle to represent the constituent parts of man. Just as the tabernacle, or the temple, was differentiated between a holy of holies, the holy place, and the outer courts, with the outer courts directing the worshippers to the presence of God at its heart, whatever man holds at the heart of his spirit in faith is also reflected by the body. Thus, man is given a vocation and as a mask of God, *larvae Dei*, man in the body becomes the "outer courts" whereby works of love are directed toward the object of one's faith, the Lord alone. Thus, for Luther, the notion that one could be carnal in the flesh while still spiritual in the soul, would be untenable. To be fully human means that the totality of man has a singular orientation—toward the spiritual or toward the carnal.

John Paul II's theology of the body has been evoked throughout the course of this book as well. The terms and categories expressed by the former pontiff likewise cohere well with the above. Undoubtedly, there are significant and pivotal insights within John Paul II's work that conflict with Luther's perspective—and continue to mark crucial divisions between Roman Catholics and the churches of the Reformation—but the centrality of divine love reflected particularly through the spousal union of man and woman is a welcome insight that reframed in two kinds of righteousness or covenantal terms can be embraced. That is, insofar as man's nuptial

---

[552] See Arand, "Two Kinds of Righteousness as a Framework for Law and Gospel in the Apology."

[553] *Lectures on Galatians (1519), LW* 27:367.

261

relationships are said to illustrate and even participate in God's vision for human beings without going so far as to say that man is essentially nuptial. Mankind is, indeed, nuptial in nature, but this is not his essence. Luther's two kinds of righteousness guards against this error, for it confuses the horizontal relationship between man and woman, with the vertical relationship God establishes with man *coram Deo.* Thus, Luther's paradigm offers a healthy corrective to John Paul II's somatology.

More importantly, however, many of Luther's insights gleaned from all of the above cohere with a theology of the body deciphered from the Old and New Testaments (see Chapter 2). There is, indeed, nothing new under the sun. Many of the concerns of the biblical writers—such as Paul's rebuttal of the Corinthian spiritualizers—reflect persistent attitudes amongst Christians still today. At the same time, however, the modern world has raised questions relevant to the body that the biblical texts do not explicitly address. A systematic appropriation of biblical teaching—reflected by the terms Luther articulates as addressed here—can help Christians today address many of the pivotal questions of our times. Throughout the course of this book some of these discussions have been initiated. Issues related to physical fitness, body image, nutrition and health have all been tentatively addressed. Issues related to human sexuality from the permeance of marriage, to pornography, homosexuality and transgenderism have been considered. *still going to demonstrate that...*

These are addressed in Wisdom literature

The advent of <u>post-humanism,</u> the notion that human beings are effectively transcending their bodies through technology, is likely the next major anthropological challenge Christian theology must address. While some of these issues can be addressed biblically (*i.e.* marriage/divorce, homosexuality, etc.) the ideological landscape and the terms in which these issues confront contemporary Christians are often expressed in terms that the biblical writers never considered. Accordingly, a systematic framework whereby Christians today can address these issues in a manner that moves beyond biblical proof texting is necessary. It is this author's sincere hope that this book has offered a framework whereby contemporary Christians might continue to make an unequivocal confession of faith regarding such contemporary issues of the body in a way that is biblically faithful and thoroughly insightful and relevant to the issues of our day.

BIBLIOGRAPHY

Allen, Diogenes. *Philosophy for Understanding Theology*. Atlanta: John Knox Press, 1985.

Anderson, Carl and Jose Granados. *Called to Love: Approaching John Paul II's Theology of the Body*. New York: The Crown Publishing Group, 2009.

Arand, Charles P. *That I May Be His Own: An Overview of Luther's Catechisms*. Saint Louis: Concordia Academic Press, 2000.

_____."Two Kinds of Righteousness as a Framework for Law and Gospel in the Apology." *Lutheran Quarterly* 15 (2001): 417-439.

_____. "A Two-Dimensional Understanding of the Church for the Twenty-First Century." *Concordia Journal* 33, no 2. (2007): 146-65.

Arand, Charles P., and Joel Biermann. "Why the Two Kinds of Righteousness?" *Concordia Journal* 33, no. 2 (2007): 116-35.

Ashley, Benedict. *Theologies of the Body: Humanist and Christian.* Braintree, MA: The Pope John XXIII Medical-Moral Research and Education Center, 1985.

Augustine, Saint. *The Rule of Saint Augustine.* Translated by Raymond Canning. Kalamazoo, MI: Darton, Longmann and Todd Ltd., 1996.

Bainton, Roland H. *Here I Stand: A Life of Martin Luther.* New York: Abingdon-Cokesbury, 1950.

Barr, James. *The Garden of Eden and the Hope of Immortality*. Minneapolis: Fortress Press, 1993.

Bierma, Lyle D. *The Theology of the Heidelberg Catechism: A Reformation Synthesis (Columbia Series in Reformed Theology)*. Louisville, Westminster John Knox Press, 2013.

Bauckham, Richard. *God and the Crisis of Freedom: Biblical and Contemporary Perspectives*. Louisville: Westminster John Knox Press, 2002.

Bayer, Oswald. "Nature and Institution: Luther's Doctrine of the Three Orders." *Lutheran Quarterly* 12 (1998): 125-159.

Benedict XVI. *God Is Love: Deus Caritas Est*. San Francisco: Ignatius Press, 2008.

Berry, Wendell. *The Art of the Commonplace: Agrarian Essays of Wendell Berry*. Berkley: Counterpoint, 2002.

Brueggeman, Walter. *Book that Breathes New Life (Theology and the Sciences)*. Minneapolis: Fortress Press, 2005.

_____. *Genesis: Interpretation: A Bible Commentary for Teaching and Preaching*. Kindle edition. Louisville: Westminster John Knox Press, 1982.

Bloesch, Donald G. *Freedom for Obedience: Evangelical Ethics in Contemporary Times*. San Francisco: Harper & Row, 1987.

Bloomquist, Karen and John Stumme, eds. *The Promise of Lutheran Ethics*. Minneapolis: Fortress Press, 1998.

Bluhm, Heinz. "Martin Luther and the Idea of Monasticism." *Concordia Theological Monthly* 34, no. 10 (1963): 594–603.

Bonhoeffer, Dietrich. *Creation and Fall*. New York: Touchstone, 1997.

Braaten, Carl E. and Lavonne Braaten. *The Living Temple: A Practical Theology of the Body and the Foods of the Earth*. New York: Harper & Row, 1976.

Brecht, Martin. *Martin Luther: His Road to Reformation, 1483-1521*. Translated by James L. Schaaf. Minneapolis: Fortress Press, 1985.

_____. *Martin Luther: Shaping and Defining the Reformation, 1521-1532*. Translated by James L. Schaaf. Minneapolis: Fortress Press, 1990.

_____. *Martin Luther: The Preservation of the Church, 1532-1546*. Translated by James L. Schaaf. Minneapolis: Fortress Press, 1993.

Brown, Peter. *The Body and Society: Men, Women, and Sexual Renunciation in Early Christianity*. New York: Columbia University Press, 1988.

Bultmann, Christoph, Volker Leppin, and Andreas Lindner, eds. *Luther und das monastische Erbe. Vol. 39 of Spätmittelalter, Humanismus Reformation*. Tübingen, Germany: Mohr Siebeck, 2007.

Bultmann, Rudolf. *Theology of the New Testament, 2 vols*. New York: Charles Scribner's Sons, 1951–55

Bynum, Caroline Walker. *Fragmentation and Redemption: Essays on Gender and the Human Body in Medieval Religion*. New York: Zone Books, 1991.

Calvin, Jean. *Calvin's Institutes*. Edited by Donald K. McKim. Westminster John Knox Press, 2001.

Cary, Phillip. *Augustine's Invention of the Inner-Self*. Oxford: Oxford University Press, 2000.

Chen, Sunny Y. *The Social and Corporate Dimensions of Paul's Anthropological Terms in the Light of Discourse Analysis*. PhD. Diss. MCD University of Divinity, 2014.

Cohen, Shaye JD. *Why Aren't Jewish Women Circumcised?: Gender and Covenant in Judaism*. Univ. of California Press, 2005.

Congar, Yves. *I Believe in the Holy Spirit*. New York: The Crossroad Publishing Company, 2001.

Conzelmann, Hans. *Theology of the New Testament*, trans. John Bowden. New York: Harper & Row, 1969.

Cooper, Adam G. *Life in the Flesh: An Anti-Gnostic Spiritual Philosophy*. Oxford: Oxford University Press, 2008.

Cooper, John H. *Body, Soul, & Life Everlasting: Biblical Anthropology and the Monism-Dualism Debate*. Kindle edition. Grand Rapids: William B. Eerdmans Publishing Co., 1989.

Corcoran, Kevin J. *Rethinking Human Nature: A Christian Materialist Alternative to the Soul*. Grand Rapids, Baker Academic, 2006.

Cortright, Charles L. "Poor Maggot Sack That I Am: The Human Body in the Theology of Martin Luther." PhD. diss., Marquette University, 2011.

Coughlin, John J. "Law and theology: Reflections on what it means to be human from a Franciscan perspective." *John's L. Rev.* 74 (2000): 609ff.

Debus, Allen G. *Man and Nature in the Renaissance.* Cambridge: Cambridge University Press, 1978.

Di Vito, Robert A. "Old Testament anthropology and the construction of personal identity." *The Catholic Biblical Quarterly* 61, no. 2 (1999): 217–238.

Dost, Timothy. *Renaissance Humanism in Support of the Gospel in Luther's Early Correspondence: Taking All Things Captive.* London: Ashgate, 2001.

Elert, Werner. *The Christian Ethos.* Philadelphia: Muhlenberg Press, 1957.

Emme, Dietrich. *Martin Luthers Weg ins Kloster: Eine wissenschaftliche Untersuchung in Aufsätzen.* Regensburg, Germany: Verlag Dietrich Emme, 1991.

Forbes, Andrew, Daniel Henley, and David Henley. *Health and Well Being: A Medieval Guide.* Thailand: Cognoscenti Books, 2013.

Frazer, James George. *The Golden Bough: A Study in Magic and Religion.* Bartleby.com, 2000

Gabor, Ittzes. *The Breath Returns to God Who Gave It: The Doctrine of the Soul's Immortality in Sixteenth-Century German Lutheran Theology.* Ann Arbor, MI: ProQuest LLC, 2008.

Gibbs, Jeffrey. "Five Things You Should Not Say at Funerals." *Concordia Journal* 29, no. 3 (2003): 363–66.

———. "Matthew 1:1–11:1," *Concordia Commentary.* (St. Louis: Concordia Publishing House, 2006

Gilson, Etienne. *The Christian Philosophy of St. Thomas Aquinas.* Notre Dame, IN: University of Notre Dame Press, 1956.

Green, Joel B. *Body, Soul, and Human Life (Studies in Theological Interpretation).* Kindle edition. Grand Rapids, MI: Baker Publishing Group, 2008.

Green, Joel B., Stuart L. Palmer, and Kevin Corcoran, eds. *In Search of the Soul: Four Views of the Mind-Body problem.* InterVarsity Press, 2005.

Hafer, Tom P. *Faith & Fitness: Diet and Exercise for a Better World.* Minneapolis: Augsburg Fortress, 2007.

Hendrix, Scott. "Luther on Marriage" In *Harvesting Martin Luther's Reflections on Theology, Ethics, and the Church*, edited by Timothy J. Wengert, Kindle Location 1817–1985. Grand Rapids: Eerdmans, 2004. Kindle Edition.

Hoy, Michael. "A Theology of the Body: Body, Genes, and Culture. Who's Holding the Leash?" In Christianity and the Human Body: *Proceedings of the ITEST Workshop October, 2000.* Saint Louis: ITEST Faith/Science Press, 2001.

Iserlow, Erwin. "*Sacramenutm Et Exemplum: Ein Augustinisches Thema Lutherischer Theologie.*" In *Reformata Reformanda: Festgabe Fuer Huert Jedin Zum* 17.Juni 1965. Edited by Erwin Iserlog and Konrad Repgen, 247–64. Muenster Westf.: Verlag aschendorff, 1965.

John Paul II. *Man and Woman He Created Them: A Theology of the Body.* Translated by Michael Waldstein. Boston: Pauline Books and Media, 2006.

_____. *Roman Triptych. Meditations.* Translated by Jerzy Peterkiewics. Washington, DC: United States Catholic Conference, 1993.

_____. Memory and Identity: Conversations at the Dawn of a Millennium. New York: Rizzoli, 2005.

Juntunen, Sammeli. "Luther and Metaphysics: What is the Structure of Being according to Luther?" in *Union with Christ: The New Finnish Interpretation of Luther.* Edited by Carl E. Braaten and Robert W. Jenson. Grand Rapids, MI: Eerdmans, 1998.

Keefe, Donald. "Body–Soul: Death–Resurrection." In *Christianity and the Human Body: Proceedings of the ITEST Workshop October, 2000.* Saint Louis: ITEST Faith/Science Press, 2001.

Keener, Craig S. *The IVP Bible Background Commentary: New Testament.* 2nd ed. Downers Grove, IL: IVP Academic, 2014.

_____. *A Commentary on the Gospel of Matthew.* Grand Rapids: Eerdmans, 2010

Kolb, Robert and Charles P. Arand. *The Genius of Luther's Theology: A Wittenberg Way of Thinking for the Contemporary Church.* Grand Rapids, MI: Baker Academic, 2008.

Kolb, Robert, Timothy J. Wengert, and Charles P. Arand, eds. *The Book of Concord: The Confessions of the Evangelical Lutheran Church.* Minneapolis: Fortress Press, 2000.

Kolb, Robert. "God and His Human Creatures in Luther's Sermons on Genesis: The Reformer's Early Use of His Distinction of Two Kinds of Righteousness." *Concordia Journal* 33, no. 2 (2007): 166–84.

_____. "God calling, 'Take care of my people': Luther's concept of vocation in the Augsburg Confession and its Apology." *Concordia Journal* 8 (1982): 4–11.

_____. "Luther on the Two Kinds of Righteousness: Reflections on His Two-Dimensional Definition of Humanity at the Heart of His Theology." *Lutheran Quarterly* 13 (1999): 449–466.

_____. *Martin Luther: Confessor of the Faith.* Oxford: Oxford University Press, 2009.

Kupczak, Jarosla. *Destined for Liberty: The Human Person in the Philosophy of Karol Wojtyla/John Paul II.* Washington, DC: CUA Press, 2000.

Kurzweil, Ray. *The Singularity is Near: When Humans Transcend Biology.* New York: Penguin Group, 2005.

Ladd, George E. *The Pattern of New Testament Truth*. Grand Rapids, MI: Eerdmans, 1968

Lessing, Reed R. "The Good Life: Health, Fitness, and Bodily Welfare." In *The American Mind Meets the Mind of Christ*. Edited by Robert Kolb, 30-41. Saint Louis: Concordia Seminary Press, 2010.

Lexutt, Athina, Volker Mantey, and Volkmar Ortmann, eds. *Reformation und Mönchtum. Vol. 43 of Spätmittelalter, Humanismus Reformation*. Tübingen, Germany: Mohr Siebeck, 2008.

Lohse, Bernhard. *Martin Luther's Theology: Its Historical and Systematic Development*. Minneapolis: Fortress Press, 1999.

Louv, Richard. *Last Child in the Woods: Saving Our Children from Nature-Deficit Disorder*. Chapel Hill, NC: Algonquin Books, 2008.

Lumpp, David A. "Luther's Two Kinds of Righteousness: a Brief Historical Introduction." *Concordia Journal* 23 (1993): 27-38.

Luther, Martin. "Commentary on 1 Corinthians 15." In Commentaries on 1 Corinthians 7, 1 Corinthians 15, Lectures on 1 Timothy, edited by Hilton C. Oswald, 59-213. Vol. 28 of *Luther's Works*. Edited by Jarslov Pelikan. Translated by Edward Sittler. Saint Louis: Concordia, 1973.

_____. "Disputation Against Scholastic Theology, 1517." In Career of the Reformer I. edited by Harold J. Grimm, 3-16. Vol. 31 of *Luther's Works*. Edited by Helmut T. Lehmann. Philadelphia: Fortress Press, 1957.

_____. "Lectures on Genesis" In *Luther's Works*, Vol. 1-8, edited by Lews W. Spitz, Vol. 1-8 of Luther's Works. Edited by Jarslov Pelikan. St. Louis: Concordia, 1960.

_____. "The Disputation Concerning Man." In Luther's Works, Vol. 34: Career of the Reformer IV, edited by Lews W. Spitz, 133-144. Vol. 34 of *Luther's Works*. Edited by Helmut T. Lehmann. Philadelphia: Fortress Press, 1960.

_____. "The Gospel for the Sunday after Christmas, Luke 2." In Sermons II, edited by Hans J. Hillerbrand, 102-148. Vol. 52 of *Luther's Works*. Edited by Helmut T. Lehmann. Saint Louis: Concordia, 1974.

_____. "The Judgment of Martin Luther on Monastic Vows, 1521" In The Christian in Society I, edited by James Atkinson, 243-400. Vol. 44 of *Luther's Works*. Edited by Helmut T. Lehmann. Philadelphia: Fortress Press, 1966.

_____. "Lectures on 1 Timothy" In Commentaries on 1 Corinthians 7, 1 Corinthians 15, Lectures on 1 Timothy, edited by Hilton C. Oswald, 215-384. Vol. 28 of *Luther's Works*. Edited by Jarslov Pelikan. Translated by Edward Sittler. Saint Louis: Concordia, 1973.

_____. "Lectures on Galatians 1535" In Vol 26-27 of *Luther's Works*. Edited by Jarslov Pelikan. Saint Louis: Concordia, 1963.

_____. "Sermon on Soberness and Moderation against Gluttony and Drunkenness" In Sermons I, edited by John W. Doberstein, 289-300. Vol. 51 of *Luther's Works*. Edited by Helmut T. Lehmann. Saint Louis: Concordia, 1959.

_____. "Treatise on Good Works, 1520." In The Christian in Society I, edited by James Atkinson, 15-114. Vol. 44 of *Luther's Works*. Edited by Helmut T. Lehmann. Philadelphia: Fortress Press, 1966.

_____. "The Sermon on the Mount." In The Sermon on the Mount and The Magnificat, edited by Jarslov Pelikan, 295-358. Vol 21 of *Luther's Works*. Edited by Jarslov Pelikan. Saint Louis: Concordia, 1956.

_____. "The Magnificat." In The Sermon on the Mount and The Magnificat, edited by Jarslov Pelikan, 1-294. Vol 21 of *Luther's Works*. Edited by Jarslov Pelikan. Saint Louis: Concordia, 1956.

_____. "Two Kinds of Righteousness 1519." In Career of the Reformer I, edited by Harold J. Grimm, 293-306. Vol. 31 of *Luther's Works*. Edited by Helmut T. Lehmann. Philadelphia: Fortress Press, 1957.

_____. "Against Latomus." In Career of the Reformer II, edited by Harold J. Grimm, 135-264. Vol. 32 of *Luther's Works*. Edited by Helmut T. Lehmann. Philadelphia: Fortress Press, 1958.

Ludwig, Garth D. *Order Restored: A Biblical Interpretation of Health Medicine and Healing.* Saint Louis: Concordia Academic Press, 1999.

Masaki, Makito. "Luther's Two Kinds of Righteousness and His Wartburg Postil (1522): How Luther Exhorted People to Live Christian Lives." PhD. diss., Concordia Seminary, 2008.

Meinhold, Peter. *Die Genesisvorlesung Luthers und Ihre Herausgerber.* Stuttgart: W. Kohlhammer, 1936.

Melanchthon, Philip. "*Loci Communes Theologici*" In Melanchthon and Bucer. Edited by Wilhelm Pauck, 3-154. Philadelphia: The Westminster Press, 1969.

Miles, Margaret R. "The Rope Breaks When it is Tightest: Luther on the Body, Consciousness, and the Word." *Harvard Theological Review* 77, no. 3-4 (1984): 239-258.

Moltmann-Wendel, Elisabeth. *I Am My Body: A Theology of Embodiment.* New York: Continuum, 1994.

Muller, Earl. "Toward a Theology of the Human Body." *In Christianity and the Human Body: Proceedings of the ITEST Workshop October, 2000.* Saint Louis: ITEST Faith/Science Press, 2001.

Murphy, Nancey. *Bodies and Souls, or Spirited Bodies? (Current Issues in Theology).* Kindle edition. New York: Cambridge University Press, 2006.

Nagel, Norman. "Luther's Understanding of Christ in Relation to His Doctrine of the Lord's Supper." PhD. diss., University of Cambridge, 1961.

_____. "*Sacrament Et Exemplum* in Luther's Understanding of Christ." In Luther for an Ecumenical Age: Essays in Commemoration of the 450th Anniversary of the Reformation, edited by Carl S. Meyer, pp. 172-99. Saint Louis: Concordia Publishing House, 1967.

Newberg, Andrew B. *Principles of Neurotheology*. Ashgate Publishing, Ltd., 2010.

_____. "The Neuroscientific Study of Spiritual Practices." *Frontiers in Psychology* 5 (2014): 215.

Newberg, Andrew, and Mark Robert Waldman. *Born to believe: God, Science, and the Origin of Ordinary and Oxtraordinary Beliefs*. Simon and Schuster, 2007.

_____. *How God Changes Your Brain: Breakthrough Findings from a Leading Neuroscientist*. Ballantine Books, 2010.

Oberman, Heiko A. *The Dawn of the Reformation: Essays in Late Medieval and Early Reformation Thought*. Grand Rapids, MI: Eerdmans, 1992.

_____. *The Harvest of Medieval Theology: Gabriel Biel and Late Medieval Nominalism*. Cambridge: Harvard University Press, 1963.

O'Grady, Michael J. and James C. Capretta. 2012. Assessing the Economics of Obesity and Obesity Intervention. Campaign to End Obesity. http://obesitycampaign.org/documents/StudyAssessingtheEconomicsofObesityandObesityIntervention.pdf (accessed March 21, 2012).

Paul VI. 1968. *Humanae Vitae*. http://www.vatican.va/holy_father/paul_vi/encyclicals/documents/hf_p-vi_enc_25071968_humanae-vitae_en.html (accessed February 1, 2013).

Prenter, Regin. *Spiritus Creator*. Translated by John M. Jenson. Eugene, OR: Wipf and Stock Publishers, 1953.

Prokes, Mary Timothy. *Toward a Theology of the Body*. Grand Rapids, MI: Eerdmans, 1996.

Rendtorff, Rolf. "Some Reflections on Creation as a Topic of Old Testament Theology," in Eugene Ulrich, *et al.*, eds., *Priests, Prophets and Scribes. Essays on the Formation and Heritage of Second Temple Judaism in Honour of Joseph Blenkinsopp.* (Sheffield, England: Sheffield Academic Press, 1992): 204-212.

Reynolds, Philip L. *Food and the Body: Some Peculiar Questions in High Medieval Theology*. Boston: Brill, 1999.

Robertson, O. Palmer. *The Christ of the Covenants*. Phillipsburg, NJ: Presbyterian and Reformed Publishing Co., 1980.

Rombs, Ronnie J. *Saint Augustine and the Fall of the Soul*. Washington, D.C.: The Catholic University of America Press, 2006.

Roper, Lyndal. "Martin Luther's Body: The 'Stout Doctor' and His Biographers." *American Historical Review* 115, 2 (April 2010): 351-384.

Sartre, Jean-Paul. *Being and Nothingness*, Translated by Hazel Barnes. New York: Philosophical Library, 1956.

Sasse, Hermann. *This is My Body: Luther's Contention for the Real Presence in the Sacrament of the Altar.* Adelaide: Openbook Publishing, 1975.

Sauter, Gerhard. "Luther on the Resurrection." In *Harvesting Martin Luther's Reflections on Theology, Ethics, and the Church.* Edited by Timothy J. Wengert, Kindle Location 1060-1292. Grand Rapids: Eerdmans, 2004. Kindle Edition.

Schlink, Edmund. *Theology of the Lutheran Confessions.* Translated by Paul F. Koehneke and Herbert J.A. Bouman. Philadelphia: Muhlenberg Press, 1961.

Schmitz, Kenneth L. *At the Center of the Human Drama: The Philosophical Anthropology of Karol Wojtyla/John Paul II.* Washington DC: CUA Press, 1993.

Schnelle, Udo. *Theology of the New Testament,* trans. M. Eugene Boring. Grand Rapids: Baker, 2009.

Scharlemann, Martin H., ed. *What, Then, is Man? A Symposium of Theology, Psychology, and Psychiatry.* Saint Louis: Concordia, 1958.

Schneider, Carolyn. "Theological Meaning in Genetic Research and Evolutionary Theory." In *Christianity and the Human Body: Proceedings of the ITEST Workshop October, 2000.* Saint Louis: ITEST Faith/Science Press, 2001.

Schor, Juliet B. *The Overspent American: Why We Want What We Don't Need.* New York: Harper Perennial, 2009.

Schwanke, Johannes. *Creatio Ex Nihilo: Luthers Lehre Von Der Schopfung Aus Dem Nichts in Der Groben Genesisvorlesung (1535-1545).* Berlin: Walter De Gruyter Inc, 2004.

_____. "Luther on Creation." In *Harvesting Martin Luther's Reflections on Theology, Ethics, and the Church.* Edited by Timothy J. Wengert, Kindle Location, pp. 871-1060. Grand Rapids: Eerdmans, 2004. Kindle Edition.

Schwarz, Hans. *The Human Being: A Theological Anthropolgy.* Grand Rapids: William B. Eerdmans Publishing Co., 2013.

Seeberg, Erich. *Studien zu Luthers Genesisvorlesung.* Gütersloch: Bertelsmann, 1932.

Séguin, Michel. "The Biblical Foundations of the Thought of John Paul II on Human Sexuality." *Communio* 20, no. 2 (1993): 266-289.

Sitzmann, Manfred. *Mönchtum und Reformation: Zur Geschichte monastischer Institutionen in protestantischen Territorien.* Insingen, Germany: Neustadt a. d. Aisch., 1999.

Sider, Ronald J. *Andreas Bodenstein von Karlstadt: The Development of His Thought, 1517-1525.* Boston: Brill, 1997.

Spitz, Lewis W. "Luther's impact on modern views of man." *Concordia Theological Quarterly* 17, no. 1 (1977): 26-43.

Sri, Edward. *Men, Women and the Mystery of Love: Practical Insights from John Paul II's Love and Responsibility.* Cincinnati: Servant Books, 2007.

"Together With All Creatures." A Report of the Commission on Theology and Church Relations of The Lutheran Church—Missouri Synod. St. Louis, April 2010.

"The Benefits of Physical Activity." Harvard School of Public Health. http://www.hsph.harvard.edu/nutritionsource/staying-active-full-story/ (accessed February 6, 2014)

"The Creator's Tapestry." A Report of the Commission on Theology and Church Relations of the Lutheran Church–Missouri Synod. St. Louis, December 2009.

Trigg, Jonathan D. *Baptism in the Theology of Martin Luther.* Boston: Brill, 2001.

von Loewenich, Walter. *Martin Luther: The Man and His Work.* Translated by Lawrence W. Denef. Minneapolis: Augsburg, 1986.

von Rad, Gerhad. "The Theological Problem of the Old Testament Doctrine of Creation, 1936," in *The Problem of the Hexateuch and Other Essays.* Translated by E. W. Trueman Dicken. New York: McGraw-Hill, 1966. 131–143.

Walton, John H. *The Lost World of Adam and Eve: Genesis 2-3 and the Human Origins Debate.* Downers Grove, IL: IVP Academic, 2015.

_____. *The Lost World of Genesis One: Ancient Cosmology and the Origins Debate.* Downers Grove, IL: InterVarsity Press, 2010.

Wendebourg, Dorothea. "Luther on Monasticism." *Lutheran Quarterly* 19, no. 2 (2005): 125–152.

Waltke, Bruce K., *Genesis: A Commentary.* Grand Rapids: Zondervan, 2001

Ward, Graham. "Transcorporeality: The Ontological Scandal." In *The Radical Orthodoxy Reader.* Edited by John Milbank and Simon Oliver, pp. 287–307. New York: Routledge, 2009.

Weinrich, William. "Creation ex Nihilo: The Way of God," *Logia* 4, no. 2. (April, 1995): 37–42.

Wengert, Timothy J. *Law and Gospel: Philip Melancthon's Debate with John Agricola of Eisleben over Poenitentia.* Grand Rapids, Baker Academic, 1997.

Wingren, Gustaf. *Creation and Law.* Translated by Ross Mackenzie. Edinburgh: Oliver and Boyd, 1961.

_____. *Luther on Vocation.* Translated by Carl C. Rasmussen. Evansville, IN: Ballast Press, 1999.

Wojtyla, Karol. *The Jeweler's Shop: A Meditation on the Sacrament of Matrimony Passing on Occasion into Drama.* San Francisco: Ignatius Press, 1992.

_____. *Love and Responsibility.* San Francisco: Ignatius Press, 1993.

Wright, N.T. *Surprised By Hope: Rethinking Heaven, the Resurrection, and the Mission of the Church.* New York: HarperCollins, 2008.

Young, E.J., *In the Beginning: Genesis 1-3 and the Authority of Scripture.* Carlisle, PA: The Banner of Truth Trust, 1976.

ABOUT THE AUTHOR

R. T. Fouts (M.Div., Concordia Seminary; Ph.D., Reformation International Theological Seminary) is a theologian, freelance writer, fitness enthusiast, husband and father living in middle America. He is passionate about bringing Reformation theology to bear on important issues facing the contemporary world. Check out his website at RTFouts.com.

Who we say Christ is?

Bach + Palestries

4B c, - immediately - theol anthropology
creation/salvation - > makes justified person

baptism justified - > in Christ's image -
meaning through vocations
in God created offices.

(personal cross - Sorry you neighbor
in vocation.)

what it is to be human. -
"reteach way"
[christic 2nd person] Godly
Dialog > Within Theol anthropology

in present form > not an aberration

fluid. > passing away...
sex + gender - vocational matters

[no vocation about faith.]

Made in the USA
Middletown, DE
11 August 2019